The Po
American

The Power of the American Presidency

❧ *1789–2000* ❧

Michael A. Genovese
Loyola Marymount University

New York   Oxford
OXFORD UNIVERSITY PRESS
2001

Oxford University Press

Oxford   New York
Athens   Auckland   Bangkok   Bogotá   Buenos Aires   Calcutta
Cape Town   Chennai   Dar es Salaam   Delhi   Florence   Hong Kong   Istanbul
Karachi   Kuala Lumpur   Madrid   Melbourne   Mexico City   Mumbai
Nairobi   Paris   São Paulo   Singapore   Taipei   Tokyo   Toronto   Warsaw

and associated companies in
Berlin   Ibadan

Copyright © 2001 by Oxford University Press, Inc.

Published by Oxford University Press, Inc.,
198 Madison Avenue, New York, New York 10016
http://www.oup-usa.org

Oxford is a registered trademark of Oxford University Press

Library of Congress Cataloging-in-Publication Data
Genovese, Michael A.
   The power of the American presidency : 1789–2000 / Michael A. Genovese.
      p.   cm.
   Includes bibliographical references and index.
   ISBN 0-19-512544-4 (cloth) — ISBN 0-19-512545-2 (pbk.)
      1. Executive power—United States—History.   2. Presidents—United States—History.
   I. Title.
   JK 516.G49 2000
   352.23'0973—dc21   99-040993

9 8 7 6 5 4 3 2 1

Printed in the United States of America
on acid-free paper

To Mango

❧ Contents ❧

Preface

Whenever presidency scholars congregate in groups larger than two and shop-talk drifts to the trials and tribulations of teaching a course on the American presidency, one of, if not the first, complaints heard is "students today are a-historical; they know virtually nothing about any president who came before George Bush!"

It's not completely our students' fault. We live in a society that is a-historical, our popular culture celebrates the here-and-now, and precious little attention is devoted to the past (the "past" is what happened, "history" is what we say happened). "Live for today" is the motto: "what could we possibly learn from the past?" is our question.

What can we learn from the past? Plenty. This is especially true when we examine the American presidency. For rooted in the historical antecedents are lessons in both the limits and possibilities of presidential performance. We can see that while there are differences between the presidencies of George Washington and Bill Clinton, there are also some striking similarities, chords that run throughout American history which suggest that in certain areas of presidential politics, the more things change, the more they stay the same. Clarence Darrow once said, "History repeats itself. That's one of the things wrong with history."

This is the story of the history of presidential power, of the rise and fall, rise, fall, and rise and fall of presidential power. It begins with the first, and arguably greatest president, George Washington, and ends as America faces a new millennium. It is the story of ambitious men, vain men, insecure men, troubled men; some kind, some corrupt; some highly skilled, others quite inept; some who achieved greatness, others who are deemed failures.

This is also the story of an institutional tug-of-war between the presidency and Congress. The Constitution is, in scholar Edward S. Corwin's words, "an invitation to struggle" for control of power. Over the course of U.S. history, strong presidents and demanding times led to strong presidencies; at other times the Congress asserted its constitutional authority and chained in the executive.

When evaluating presidential power, four variables (remember, a variable is something that "varies") are of special concern: The *individual*, the *institution*, the *system*, and the *times*. The president is *one man*, but the presidency is an *institution*, an institution situated in a *system*. That system, a "separation of powers," inhibits presidential power and forces the president to gain consent or agreement when he wishes to act. Presidents have very little independent authority. In almost all areas, presidents must gain cooperation from Congress in order to succeed. At *times* (especially during a crisis) the Congress is more willing to defer to a president's wishes. At other times, the Congress jealously guards its power.

"Presidential power" is a bit of a misnomer. Presidential *influence* or *leadership* is more important.[1] Presidents have *limited* and *shared* powers. They are well positioned to exert influence and leadership, but their power is hemmed in by a variety of forces, most importantly the Congress.

And presidential power is not static. It fluctuates, changes, rises, and declines. Skilled executives in demanding times can have considerable power; less skilled or less ambitious executives who govern in calmer, less troubled times may have very limited power. A president's power is different, at different times, with different presidents.

The executive office is *elastic*, *bendable*, it can expand to meet aggressive and skilled leaders and contract when times call for a return to normalcy. The natural state of the president's power however is rather limited. Special people in special times can expand power but, soon, the natural state of a president's more limited authority contracts the office. To understand the fluctuations in presidential power over time, we must remember that the office is *elastic* and *adaptable*.

The presidency serves multiple purposes for the American system. Not only is the president a head of government, but he also serves as head of state. The president is expected to set the nation's agenda, solve the nation's problems, insure peace and prosperity, even improve the weather (global warming).

Paradoxically, presidents are expected to serve simultaneously as *order affirming* and *order shattering* leaders. Presidents affirm order by appealing to history, tradition, the intent of the framers, supporting the status quo, *and* serving the needs of capital accumulation and economic stability. They shatter order by promoting change, reform, and by adapting the nation to the forces of modernization.

How do they perform these seemingly contradictory tasks? Abraham Lincoln's Gettysburg Address and Second Inaugural Address serve as model examples. Lincoln, in the face of one of the most difficult conflicts in U.S. history, used this crisis as an opportunity to recast, reconceptualize, and reshape the nation's future. He led the nation into the future by reinterpreting its past. Lincoln honored the nation's past (order affirming) by reinventing it (order shattering/order creating). His call to base America's future on a commitment to the principles of the Declaration of Independence was both homage to the past and an animating vision for the future.

In general, the presidency "has been the major instrument by means of which modernizing elites have sought to overcome or remove obstacles to the expansion and revitalization of American capitalism."[2] It is that but much more. The presidency has been, for the most part, the primary agent of modernization on several fronts.

The presidency helps ease the tensions and transition to a new order. The ability of the institution to change and adapt—the presidency's "adaptation capability"—allows it to see the nation through new challenges and changing circumstances. In a functional way, the presidency advances the needs of modernization, adaptation, and change. But not all presidents do this. Many are mere clerks. Few are genuine leaders. Some defend the old or crumbling order long after logic and self-interest dictate; others recognize, embrace, and make room for change.

The presidency seems at times to be all things to all people. To Samuel Huntington, it is a conservative institution in a conservative world. To Arthur M. Schlesinger, Jr., it is a liberal institution in a conservative world. In a peculiar sort of way, they are both right. "The presidency is the locus of modernization."[3] It legitimizes and helps pave the way for change. While the system gravitates toward stasis, the presidency reflects the changing social, economic, and political forces of the times, and also enables the system to accommodate these changes. "Disruption of the status quo is basic to the politics presidents make and, beyond that, to the dynamics of American political development in the largest sense."[4]

In this way, as Skowronek writes, the presidency is an *order shattering, affirming, and creating* institution:

> "The presidency is an *order-shattering* institution in that it prompts each incumbent to take charge of the independent powers of his office and to exercise them in his own right. It is an *order-affirming* institution in that the disruptive effects of the exercise of presidential power must be justified in constitutional terms broadly construed as the protection, preservation, and defense of values emblematic of the body politic. It is an *order-creating* institution in that it prompts each incumbent to use his powers to construct some new political arrangements that can stand the test of legitimacy within the other institutions of government as well as the nation at large."[5]

Or, the presidency is a " . . . battering ram, and the presidents who have succeeded most magnificently in political leadership are those who have been best situated to use it forthrightly as such."[6]

This book is an effort to come to grips with this complex and perplexing office, an office Thomas Jefferson referred to as "a splendid misery." Designed to provide the reader with a brief (and hopefully lively) text that traces the evolution and devolution of presidential power over the course of U.S. history, it is also an effort to give readers a sense of the dynamism of this unique office and the variations in skills and personalities of its occupants.

This book is also an attempt to fill a void in scholarship on the presidency. Designed to be a short, and therefore somewhat cursory, history of the ebb and flow of presidential power over the course of United States history, my goal is to touch on all the presidents, the high and low points, the rise and fall of power, and the forces and factors that shaped the contours of the office. Given the goal of brevity, we must necessarily skate rather quickly over many key points.

Several themes run throughout this work: the rise and fall of presidential power; the continuous struggle between the president and Congress; the variations in style, personality, and dominance of the different presidents; crisis versus normal conditions; the elasticity and adaptability of the office; the expansion over time of U.S. economic and military and presidential power; and finally the academic debate over whether there are two or three different presidencies over time (Traditional, Modern, and Postmodern).

These words seem to characterize the history of the American presidency: ELASTIC, ADAPTABLE, and VARIABLE.

The presidency is elastic in that it is capable of stretching itself and its powers far beyond what the Constitution might suggest. It is just as capable, however, of shrinking to embarrassingly limited proportions of weakness and dependency.

It is adaptable in that no other branch of government has been able to meet new challenges, rising demands, and altered expectations quite as well as the presidency. Congress and the courts change rather slowly, as personnel changes. But the presidency can change literally overnight. In a fast-changing world, this makes the presidency a truly "modern" institution.

The presidency is variable in that it varies dramatically from incumbent to incumbent, issue to issue, season to season. Presidents have substantial authority in foreign affairs, but limited power in the domestic arena. They are granted wide-ranging power in the midst of crisis, but are imprisoned in a straitjacket in normal times.

Thus the presidency is no one thing, but many things; powerful and weak, big and small, a threat to liberty, and a humble servant. It has the potential to be big and powerful, but it might also be small and weak.

Some scholars refer to the presidency as PROTEAN, that is, variable, taking on different forms. There is some truth to this. The Constitution, vague and ambiguous as it sometimes is, allows this; circumstance sometimes demands it; individual presidents sometimes create it. And so, we are confronted with the many-sidedness of the American presidency. It is an office capable of exercising awesome powers, but might also be restricted and enchained. The office is not always used to its full potential—that requires the right timing, the right circumstances, the right skills of a president, the right opportunities—but the potential is there, latent perhaps, but there waiting to be used.

Over time, the presidency has served many needs and interests: chief modernizing agent of the nation, protector of the status quo, defender of liberty, symbol of nationhood, source of unity, leader in war and crisis, national highlighter of issues, moral educator, and much more. The office has been praised and scorned. Some great and good men served, and some small, hateful men did as well. The office remains what it has been for over two centuries: a grand paradox.[7]

This book builds on my own previous works, but I also stand on the shoulders of giants. The works of Edward S. Corwin, Richard Neustadt, Arthur M. Schlesinger, Jr., James M. Burns, Thomas E. Cronin, and others, greatly influenced the development of my thinking about presidential politics. Two presidential scholars in particular played an enormous role in my development: the late William W. Lammers, with whom I studied at the University of Southern California, and Thomas E. Cronin, who befriended and supported me as I entered the professional realm of presidential scholarship. Both Lammers and Cronin represent the best of the scholar/gentleman, and have served as generous and caring role models and mentors (good guys *do* finish first). I am grateful for the confidence you have shown in me and the support you have given over the years.

I owe a great deal to the many people who have helped see me through this project. My research assistants Pauline Batrikian, Astrid Morales, and Mayra Vallin did most of the hard work, trooping to the library, checking details, saving me from myself. Gioia Stevens, my editor at Oxford University Press, was a joy to work with. Typist Monica LaBelle translated my scribbles into the computer. Thank you. Financial support from Loyola Marymount University helped move this project ahead as well.

❧ 1 ❧
"A Republic, if you can keep it"*

> Between the idea
> And the reality
> Between the motion
> And the act
> Falls the Shadow
> —T. S. ELIOT, FROM "THE HOLLOW MEN"

The presidency was invented more than 200 years ago as a relatively small, controlled office with limited powers. Today, the office is larger, more powerful, but still (usually) quite controlled and limited.

In some ways the presidency of today closely resembles the institution of 1789 or 1820. The Constitution remains largely unchanged, and very little is done today by presidents that wasn't done 200 or 150 or 100 years ago by one president or another. And presidents still face an array of constraints, the most important of which is the Congress. Thus, the office of today has clearly traceable roots to the office of Washington and Jefferson.

Yet in other ways, it seems a vastly different office. The presidency of today has more power, greater responsibility, higher demands and expectations; and the U.S. today is the world's military and economic superpower. Recent presidents were more actively and openly involved in the legislative process than their early predecessors, the president's staff has grown tremendously in recent years, management has become a more effective tool of policy. The president of today "heads" an enormous bureaucracy (including a National Security State diminished but by no means dismantled in the post-Cold War era) and faces a television/media age more intrusive, pervasive, and personal than before. The revolution in communications and technology has created a smaller, closer, and more interrelated world (as well as a more dangerous world, with the proliferation of nuclear weapons), and the expansion of democracy—both at home and abroad—has created more voices and more demands on government. Also, today's presidents must actively campaign for the office by going to the people for approval. It has only been in the past 150 years or so that active, public campaigning was deemed appropriate. These changes have taken place without a constitutional transformation of the office. As political scientist David K. Nichols

*Benjamin Franklin.

1

argues, "The increased activity of the President can be attributed to broad changes in the character of government and society, and not to a change in the balance of power between the President and the other branches."[1]

Similar, but different! Some presidency scholars argue that the presidency should be divided into different periods or eras: the *Traditional Presidency* (1787 to 1932), a *Modern Presidency*[2] (1932 to 1980), and a *Postmodern Presidency*[3] (1980 to today). Are these distinctions useful and appropriate, or is there really only one presidency worth examining?

I would argue that while in many ways the presidency of today does closely resemble the presidency of the 1780s, the previously mentioned differences do warrant a different classification scheme. There is, I argue, a Traditional and Modern presidency. Similar, but different.

Yes, the "modern" presidency is different from the Washington or Tyler presidencies. Would anyone say in the 1840s or 1880s that "the president is the most powerful person in the world?" That is said, and believed, and possibly true today, however.

If the presidency is an ever-changing institution, highly flexible, elastic and adaptable, one thing has remained the same over the years: presidents view their job as a thankless task, an all but unwinnable situation, a heavy burden. It remains the most miserable job that is so aggressively sought after. One might well ask: If this is such a thankless job, why do so many work so hard and want it so badly?

"A splendid misery" is how Thomas Jefferson described the job of being president. Others have expressed similar discomfort with the office. George Washington felt like "a culprit going to the place of his execution." Andrew Jackson called it "a situation of dignified slavery." The White House "is a prison" lamented Warren Harding. Harry Truman called the White House "the big white jail." And Bill Clinton referred to the White House as "the crown jewel of the penitentiary system."

A sampling of the sentiments of some of those who have occupied the presidency reveals a pattern of critical thought stunning in its consistency. The first president, George Washington, said "I had rather be in my grave than endure another four years as President." . . . John Quincy Adams said he could "scarcely conceive a more harassing, wearying . . . condition of existence." . . . President Polk complained that "the public have no idea of the constant accumulation of business requiring the President's attention." . . . President Theodore Roosevelt noted that "every day, almost every hour, I have to decide very big as well as very little questions." . . . President Taft said, "one trouble is no sooner over in this office than another arises." . . . Woodrow Wilson stated "the amount of work that a President is supposed to do is preposterous," and concluded "my work can be properly done only if I devote my whole thought and attention to it and think of nothing but the immediate task at hand." . . . President Eisenhower observed that "the duties of the President are essentially endless. No daily schedule of appointments can give a full timetable—or even a faint indication—of the President's responsibilities. Entirely aside from the making of important decisions, the formulation of policy through the National Security Council and the Cabinet, cooperation with the Congress and with the States, there is for the President a continuous burden of study, contemplation and reflection."

"My God," James Garfield once asked, "What is there in this place that a man should ever want to get into it?" John Adams noted that "No man who ever held the office of president would congratulate a friend on obtaining it. He will make one man ungrateful, and a hundred men his enemies, for every office he can bestow" and "If I were to go over my life again, I would be a shoemaker rather than an American statesman." And Jefferson said, "To myself personally, it brings nothing but unceasing drudgery and daily loss of friends." John Quincy Adams said, "The four most miserable years of my life were my four years in the presidency." Martin Van Buren noted "As to the presidency, the two happiest days of my life were those of my entrance upon the office and my surrender of it." James Buchanan told newly elected President Abraham Lincoln "If you are as happy, my dear sir, on entering the White House as I in leaving it and returning home, you are the happiest man in the country." Soon Lincoln understood what Buchanan meant: "From my boyhood up, it was my ambition to be president. Now I am president of one part of this divided country, at least; but look at me! I wish I had never been born!" Herbert Hoover noted "This job is nothing but a twenty-ring circus—with a whole lot of bad actors" and "All the money in the world could not induce me to live over the last nine months. The conditions we have experienced make this office a compound hell."

More than any of the American institutions of government, the presidency can only be comprehended in terms of the office's historical development. This development had peaks and valleys. The ambiguous wording of the Constitution, the gaping silences at points, has allowed the office to shrink and enlarge as times and people pushed and pulled for power.

Brick by brick, an institution was built up over time. Sometimes a brick or two was removed, but overall one can see a building up of the office over time. Not all presidents had the determination, skill, interest, or circumstances to use the full measure of the resources available, but each brick added to the presidential arsenal, made it easier for presidents who followed to cite precedent and thus claim legitimacy for the expansion of power.

The presidency was invented at the Constitutional Convention of 1787. But the roots of the office run deep in history. To understand the adaptive and flexible nature of this office, it is necessary to demonstrate how the institution came into being and the type of leadership the framers expected of this unique office.

From Divine Right of Kings to Servant of the People

The Europe from which the framers of the U.S. Constitution fled was a world of kings and hereditary monarchies. In England, a nascent Parliament was in the process of a long march designed to wrestle power away from the king and give it first to the representative of the landed barons, and later to the representatives of the people.

When the Americas were first colonized, the Age of the Divine Right of Kings was giving way to more limited and representative forms of power. During the Divine Right of Kings, a monarch could *Rule* or *Command*. After all, he claimed an authority based on the will of God. To challenge the king was to challenge God. For a king, this is very firm ground on which to stand. Presidents today might look back enviously at that time as "the good old days."

But as the church and the barons challenged the king's power, a long, slow transformation took place. The Divine Right of Kings (God) was slowly (and often painfully) replaced by the Divine Right of the People (Democracy) through their representatives.[4]

In this new configuration, authority and legitimacy that once came from God now came from something called "the People." This new secular base of authority made it more difficult to gain compliance. Consent replaced Command; Leadership replaced Rule; Influence and Persuasion replaced Orders. Government officials had to *lead*, not merely command. Eventually, rule of the people through elected representatives made the government the servant of the people. "In America," Tom Paine pointed out, "the law is king."

The American Revolution took place in the middle of this transformation. At the time of the colonists' break with Great Britain, antimonarchical sentiment was strong. Jefferson's *Declaration of Independence* was, in addition to being an eloquent expression of democratic and revolutionary faith, a laundry list of charges leveled against the tyrannical king. And propagandist supreme, Tom Paine, stigmatized England's King George III as "The Royal Brute of Britain."

Anti-Executive feelings were so strong that when the postrevolutionary leadership assembled to form a government, their *Articles of Confederation* contained *no executive*! So weak and ineffective were the Articles that Noah Webster said they were "but a name, and our confederation a cobweb." Over time however, the absence of an executive proved unworkable, and slowly and quite grudgingly an acceptance of the inevitability of an executive became more commonly accepted.

But this would be no strong, independent executive. The new nation was reluctant, but willing, to accept the necessity of an executive, but the fear of tyranny continued to lead them in the direction of a very limited and constrained office.

The ideas on which the framers drew in inventing a presidency are diverse and complex. They took a negative example away from their experiences with the king of England. Their fear of the executive imbedded in the framers a determination *not* to let the new American executive squint toward monarchy.

Several European political theorists opened the framers' imaginations to new possibilities for governing. John Locke's *Second Treatise on Gov-*

ernment (1690) and Montesquieu's *The Spirit of the Laws* (1748) were especially influential.

From their understanding of history the framers drew several lessons. In studying the collapse of Greek (Athenian) democracy, the founders deepened their already profound suspicions of democracy. Thus, they were determined to prevent what some framers referred to as mobocracy. A tyranny of the people was just as frightening as a tyranny of the monarchy. From their examination of the Roman Republic and its collapse from the weight of empire, the founders understood how delicate the balance between the Senate and the will of the emperor were. An emperor armed as tribune of the people, bent on imperial pursuits, led to tyranny just as surely as monarchy and mobocracy.

While less understood, the lessons the framers drew from the Native Americans clearly had an impact on the writing of the Constitution. While the framers looked across the Atlantic and saw hereditary monarchies, they looked down the road and could see a sophisticated, democratic, egalitarian government in action: the Iroquois Confederation. This union of six tribes/nations, organized along lines similar to a separation-of-powers system, was the model for Ben Franklin's 1754 Albany Plan of Union, and was much studied by several of the framers.

On July 27, 1787, the drafting committee of the Constitutional Convention met at the Indian Queen Tavern to agree on a draft of the Constitution to submit to the entire convention. The committee's chair, John Rutledge of South Carolina, opened the meeting by reading aloud an English translation of the Iroquois' tale of the founding of the Iroquois Confederacy. Rutledge's purpose was to underscore the importance for the new nation of a concept embedded in the tradition of the Iroquois Confederacy: "We" the people, from whence all power derives.[5] While this concept also has European roots, nowhere in the Old World was it being practiced. The neighbors of the Constitution's framers, however, had for decades been living under a Constitution that brought this concept to life, and one which had an impact on the men who met in Philadelphia in that hot summer of 1787.

The experience with colonial governors further added to the framers' storehouse of knowledge. Those states with weak executives, states dominated by the legislature with a defanged governor, seemed less well run than states like New York, which had a fairly strong, independent governor. Such examples softened the fears of executive tyranny among the founders. Thus, slowly over time, the anti-executive sentiments began to wane, and there developed a growing recognition that while executive tyranny was still to be feared, an enfeebled executive was also a danger to good government.

Under the Articles, the national government was weak and ineffective. In each state, minor revolts of debtors threatened property and order. The most famous of these was the Shay's Rebellion (1787). These mini-revolutions put a fear into the propertied classes. Some longed for the imposed order of a monarchy. "Shall we have a king?" John Jay asked of Washington during the Shay's Rebellion.

This was not the first time Washington had been approached with such a suggestion. A few years earlier, in 1782, army units stationed in Newburgh, New York, threatened to meet and make Washington monarch. But Washington found out about the Newburgh Conspiracy and quickly put an end to it. The impact of these pushes towards monarchy further persuaded the framers of a need for an executive in America.

As the framers met in Philadelphia, most of those present recognized (some quite reluctantly) the need for an independent executive with *some* power. But what? No useful model existed anywhere in the known world. They would have to invent one.

Inventing the Presidency

The American Revolution against Great Britain was in large part a revolution against authority. Historian Bernard Bailyn said the rebellion against Britain made resistance to authority "a doctrine according to godliness."[6] The colonists were for the most part defiant, independent, egalitarian, and individualistic. The symbols and rallying cries were anti-authority in nature and once it became necessary to establish a new government, it was difficult to reestablish the respect for authority so necessary for an effective government.

Reconstructing authority, especially executive authority, was a slow, painful process. By 1787, when the framers met in Philadelphia "for the sole and express purpose of revising the Articles of Confederation . . . [in order to] render the federal constitution adequate to the exigencies of government and the preservation of the Union," there was general agreement that a limited executive was necessary to promote good government. But what kind of executive? One person or several? How should he be selected? For how long a term? With what powers?[7]

No decision at the convention was more difficult to reach than the scope and nature of the executive. They went through proposals, counterproposals, decisions, reconsiderations, postponements, reversals, until finally a presidency was invented.[8]

The confusion reflected what political scientist Harvey C. Mansfield, Jr. referred to as the framers' "ambivalence of executive power."[9] There were widespread and divergent views on the creation of an executive office. Initially, most delegates were considered "congressionalists," hoping to create a government with a strong Congress and a plural executive with very limited power. Delegate George Mason proposed a three-person executive, one chosen from each region of the nation. Delegate Roger Sherman described this plural executive as "no more than an institution for carrying the will of the legislature into effect."

But there were also advocates for a strong, unitary executive. Alexander Hamilton initially wanted to institute a version of the British system of government on American soil, along with a monarch. However, there was little support for such a proposal, and Hamilton quickly backed away.

James Madison, often referred to as the father of the U.S. Constitution, had surprisingly little impact on the invention of the presidency, even going so far as to write in a letter to George Washington shortly before the convention "I have scarcely ventured as yet to form my own opinion either of the manner in which [the executive] ought to be constituted or of the authorities with which it ought to be clothed."

Probably the most influential framer on the invention of the presidency was James Wilson of Pennsylvania. At first, Wilson sought the direct popular election of the president, but eventually lost that battle and instead helped develop what became the Electoral College. He also greatly influenced the choice of a single over a plural executive.

In the end, the framers wanted to strike a balance in executive power. Making the presidency too strong would jeopardize liberty; making the office too weak would jeopardize good government. But just how to achieve balance remained a thorny issue.

Unlike the Congress and the Judiciary, for which there was ample precedent to guide the framers, the presidency was truly new, invented in Philadelphia, different from any executive office that preceded it.

The president would not be a king, he would not be sovereign. He would swear to protect and defend a higher authority: the Constitution.

The framers faced several key questions. First, how many? Should it be a single (unitary) or plural executive? Initial sympathy for a plural executive eventually gave way to a single executive, primarily because that was the best way to assign responsibility (and blame) for the execution of policy. The second question was how to choose the executive. Some proposed popular election, which was rejected because the framers feared the president might become tribune of the people. Others promoted selection by the Congress, but this was rejected on grounds that it might make the president the servant of Congress, and it would undermine the separation of powers. Finally, the framers invented an Electoral College as the best of several unappealing alternatives.

Next, how long? Should the president serve for life? A fixed term? Two years, four years, six years? If for a fixed term, should he be eligible for reelection? After much hemming and hawing they decided on a four-year term with reeligibility as an option. But the president could be removed—impeached—for certain not very clearly delineated offenses.

The toughest question related to how much power the president should be given. In a way, the framers deftly avoided this issue. Since they could not reach a clear consensus on the president's power, they decided to create a bare skeleton of authority. They left many areas vague and ambiguous; they left gaping silences throughout Article II. How could the framers—so afraid of the mob and the monarchy—leave so important an issue so poorly answered? The answer is: George Washington.

Any examination of the invention of the presidency that did not take George Washington into account would be remiss. Each day, as debate after debate took place, the men of Philadelphia could look at the man presiding over the convention, secure in the knowledge that whatever else became of the presidency, George Washington would be its first officeholder. So confident were the framers (and the public as well) of Washington's skills, integrity, and republican sentiments, they felt comfortable leaving the presidency unfinished and incomplete. They would leave it to Washington to fill in the gaps and set the proper precedents.

After the convention, delegate Pierce Butler acknowledged Washington's influence in this excerpt from a letter to Weedon Butler:

> I am free to acknowledge that his powers (the President's) are full great, and greater than I was disposed to make them. Nor, *entre nous*, do I believe they would have been so great had not many of the members cast their eyes towards George Washington as President; and shaped their ideas of the powers to be given to a President by their opinions of his virtue.

Of course, Washington would not always be the president. Thus, while the framers trusted Washington, could they trust all of his successors? Leaving the presidency unfinished opened the door for future problems in the executive. Ben Franklin pointed to this when he noted "The first man, put at the helm, will be a good one. Nobody knows what sort may come afterwards."

Washington, then, is the chief reason why the presidency is so elastic. The office was left half finished with the expectation that Washington would fill in the gaps. In many ways he did. But this also left openings that future presidents were able to exploit on the road to an expanding conception of executive power.

The presidency that emerged from the Philadelphia convention was an office with "very little plainly given, very little clearly withheld . . . the Convention . . . did not define: it deferred."[10] This meant that the presidency would be shaped, defined, and created by those people who occupied the office and the times and demands of different eras. The framers thus invented a very "personal presidency," and much of the history of presidential power stems from the way presidents have understood and attempted to use the office to attain their goals. As Alan Wolfe has written: "The American presidency has been a product of practice, not theory. Concrete struggles between economic and political forces have been responsible for shaping it, not maxims from Montesquieu."[11] The unsettled nature of the presidency was a marked characteristic of this peculiar office and, to some, the genius of the framers. The Constitution that emerged from the Philadelphia convention was less an act of clear design and intent and more a "mosaic of everyone's second choices."[12] The presidency, left unfinished and only partially formed, had yet to be truly invented.

The President of the Constitution

The framers invented a presidency of some strength, but little independent power. They put the president in a position to lead (influence, persuade), but not command (order).

What exactly did the framers create? What structure or skeleton of power and government did the founders of the U.S. system design? The chief mechanisms they established to control as well as to empower the executive are as follows: (1) *Limited Government*, a reaction against the arbitrary, expansive powers of the king or state, and a protection of personal liberty; (2) *Rule of Law*, so that only on the basis of legal or constitutional grounds could the government act; (3) *Separation of Powers*, so that the three branches of government each would have a defined sphere of power; and (4) *Checks and Balances*, so that each branch could limit or control the powers of the other branches of government.

In this structure, what *powers* and *resources* has the president? Limited powers. Constitutionally, the United States faces a paradox: the Constitution both *empowers* and *restrains* government. In fact, the Constitution does not clearly spell out the power of the presidency. Article I is devoted to the Congress, the first and constitutionally the most powerful branch of government. Article II, the executive article, deals with the presidency. The president's power cupboard is—compared to that of the Congress—nearly bare. Section 1 gives the "executive power" to the president but does not reveal whether this is a grant of tangible power or merely a title. Section 2 makes the president commander-in-chief of the armed forces but reserves the power to *declare* war for the Congress. Section 2 also gives the president absolute power to grant reprieves and pardons, power to make treaties (with the advice and consent of the Senate), and the power to nominate ambassadors, judges, and other public ministers (with the advice and consent of the Senate). Section 3 calls for the president to inform the Congress on the state of the Union and to recommend measures to Congress, grants the power to receive ambassadors, and imposes upon the president the duty to see that the laws are faithfully executed. These powers are significant, but in and of themselves they do not suggest a very strong or independent institution, and certainly not a national leadership position.

Presidential Power and the Constitution

Presidential power, when viewed from a constitutional perspective, is both specific and obscure: specific in that some elements of presidential power are clearly spelled out (e.g., the veto power, a pardon power); obscure in that the limits and boundaries of presidential power are either ill-defined or open to vast differences in interpretation (e.g., the president's power in foreign affairs and his power over the military). In an effort to understand presidential power, the Constitution is a starting point, but it provides few definitive answers. The Constitution, as it relates to the powers of the president, raises more questions than it answers.

As historical circumstances have changed, so too has the meaning or interpretation of the Constitution. The scope and meaning of the executive clause (Article II) of the Constitution has changed to meet the needs of the times and the wishes (demands) of strong presidents. The skeleton-like provisions of Article II have left the words open to definition and redefinition by courts and presidents. This skeleton-like wording leaves it up to an aggressive chief executive and a willing Supreme Court to shape the actual parameters of such powers. In effect, history has rewritten the Constitution. For two centuries, we have been debating just what the words of the Constitution mean, and this debate is by no means over. The words are "flexible" enough to mean different things in different situations. Thus one can see the elasticity of options open for both the Supreme Court and the president. On the whole though, a more "expansive" view of presidential power has taken precedence over a more "restrictive" view. The history of the meaning of presidential power through the Constitution has been one of the expansion of power and the enlargement of the meaning of the words of the Constitution.

The presidential office gets power from a variety of sources, both constitutional and extraconstitutional. While the Constitution must be the starting point for any analysis of presidential power, it is by no means the final word on the subject. The loose construction of the words of the Constitution: "the executive power shall be vested in a president . . . take care that the laws be faithfully executed . . . etc.," has been used to view the powers of the president in expansive or elastic terms.

The Constitution gives us an outline of the powers of the president, but not a picture. For the president is much more than the Constitution leads us to believe. As Haight and Johnson write: " . . . the Presidency is above all an integrated institution, all of whose parts interlock with one another. Any description that discusses these parts individually cannot help being partially misleading." Thus, one cannot simply look at the Constitution and define and describe "presidential power." The presidency is more than the sum of its constitutional parts.

Presidential power exists in two forms: *formal* powers, and *informal* powers. To understand presidential power, one must understand how both the formal and informal powers work and interact and how the combination of the two can lead to dominance by a president who, given the proper conditions and abilities, is able to exploit his power sources.

Formal Powers

The formal powers of the president revolve around the constitutional powers to "command." They involve those areas of the Constitution that clearly place powers and responsibilities on the shoulders of the president.

The formal powers of the president are derived essentially from the Constitution. Those powers "derived" from the Constitution extend, however, beyond the strictly legalistic or specifically granted powers that find their source in the literal reading of the words of the constitution. Additionally, presidents have

Enumerated powers (those that the Constitution expressly grants);

Implied powers (those that may be inferred from power expressly granted);

Resulting powers (those that result when several enumerated powers are added together); and

Inherent powers (those powers in the field of external affairs that the Supreme Court has declared do not depend upon constitutional grants but grow out of the existence of the national government).

INFORMAL POWERS

This in part leads us to the informal powers of the president, which find their source in the "political" as opposed to the "constitutional." They are the powers that are either not spelled out in the Constitution, those acquired through politics, or those that are "missing" from the Constitution. Richard Neustadt, in his *Presidential Power* discussed the informal power of the president to "persuade." Neustadt and others feel that the power to persuade is the most important of all the presidential powers.

These informal powers of the president rely upon his ability to engage in the personal part of politics. All presidents have and can use their formal powers, but the informal powers require skill at persuasion, personal manipulation, and mobilization. These skills may be difficult to cultivate but, in the long run, changing the minds of people may be more powerful than ordering someone into compliance. In the informal powers of the president, some can see the breaking point between those presidents characterized as "great" or aggressive, and those who rate less favorably in the eyes of historians. The great presidents have been able and willing to exploit the informal powers at the disposal of a president.

Thus, the president has two types of power: *formal*, the ability to command, and *informal*, the ability to persuade. The president's formal powers are limited and (often) shared. The president's informal powers are a function of skill, situation, and the political times. While the formal power of the president remains fairly constant over time, the president's informal powers are quite variable, dependent on the skill of each individual president. This is not to suggest that the president's formal powers are static—over time, presidential power has increased significantly—but the pace of change has been such that it was well over a hundred years before the presidency assumed primacy in the U.S. political system.

The constitutional structure of the government *disperses* or *fragments* power: with no recognized, authoritative vital center, power is fluid and floating, and no one branch can very easily or freely act without the consent (formal or tacit) of another branch. Power was designed to counteract power; ambition to check ambition. This structure was developed by men whose memories of tyranny and the arbitrary exercise of power by the king of England were fresh in their minds. It was a structure designed to force a *consensus* before the government could act. The structure of government created by the framers did not create *a* leadership institution, but several— three separate, semi-autonomous institutions that shared power. As James Pfiffner notes, "The Framers designed a system of shared powers within a system that is purposefully biased against change." The forces of the status quo were given multiple veto opportunities; the forces of change were forced to go into battle nearly unarmed.

Because there are so many potential veto points, the American system generally alternates between stasis and crisis, paralysis and spasm. On occasion, the branches are able to cooperate and work together to promote change, but it is especially difficult for the president and Congress—deliberately disconnected by the framers—to forge a union. The resulting paralysis has many parents, but the separation of powers is clearly the most determinative.

In the 1780s, monarchy was the European norm. The inventors of the presidency had very few role models upon which to base their executive. When invented over 200 years ago, the presidency was a unique, and in many ways a peculiar, institution. Chosen by an unorthodox invention, the Electoral College, the office had limited powers in a checks-and-balances system with ambiguous constitutional authority, sharing most powers with a strong and in some ways dominant Congress.

Ratification: Is the President a King?

The invention of the presidency in Philadelphia was but one step in the creation process. The system of government still had to be ratified by the states. And one of the chief bones of contention was the presidency—could the president become a king?

Two opposing camps formed: the federalists, who supported the ratification, and the anti-federalists, most of whom sought a more democratic and decentralized government. It was the anti-federalists who were most suspicious of presidential power.

Hamilton, Madison, and John Jay began writing broadsides in support of the new Constitution (*The Federalist Papers*), noting the limits on presidential power. The anti-federalists raised concerns about the presidency "squinting towards monarchy." Edmund Randolph of Virginia said the presidency could be "the foetus of monarchy," George Mason saw the presidency as an "elective monarchy;" and Patrick Henry thought the new presidency "squints toward monarchy."

Thomas Jefferson, American minister in Paris, was uneasy about some aspects of the new Constitution. "Reason and experience," he wrote to John

Adams in November of 1787, "prove to us that a chief magistrate, so continuable, is an officer for life. When one or two generations shall have proved that this is an office for life, it becomes on every succession worthy of intrigue, of bribery, of force, and even of foreign interference. It will be of great consequence to France and England to have America governed by a Galloman or Angloman. Once in office, and possessing the military force of the union, without either the aid or the check of a council, he would not easily be dethroned, even if the people could be induced to withdraw their votes from him. I wish that at the end of the 4 years they had made him for ever ineligible a second time. . . . "

Alexander Hamilton, chief advocate of energy in the executive, countered the anti-federalist view by arguing "a feeble execution is but another phrase for a bad execution; and a government ill executed, whatever it may be in theory, must be, in practice, a bad government." And "energy" was both a crucial "character in the definition of good government" and the defining attribute of the executive itself.

Hamilton's direct challenge to the anti-federalist charges, *The Federalist*, No. 69, a comparison between the newly created president and the king of England, is worth quoting at length:

> The President of the United States would be an officer elected by the people for *four* years; the King of Great Britain is a perpetual and *hereditary* prince. The one would be amenable to personal punishment and disgrace [through impeachment]; the person of the other is . . . inviolable. The one would have a *qualified* negative upon the acts of the legislative body; the other has an *absolute* negative. The one would have a right to command the military and naval forces of the nation; the other, in addition to this right, possesses that of *declaring* war [a right reserved to Congress in the Constitution], and of *raising* and *regulating* fleets and armies [likewise, a responsibility of Congress] by his own authority. The one would have a concurrent power [with the Senate] in the formation of treaties; the other is the *sole possessor* of the power of making treaties. The one would have a like concurrent authority in appointing to office; the other is the sole author of all appointments. The one can confer no privileges whatsoever; the other can make denizens of aliens, noblemen of commoners; can erect corporations with all the rights incident to corporate bodies. The one can prescribe no rules concerning the commerce of currency of the nation; the other is in several respects the arbiter of commerce. . . . The one has no particle of spiritual jurisdiction; the other is supreme head and governor of the national church! What answer shall we give to those who would persuade us that things so unlike resemble each other? The same that ought to be given to those who tell us that a government, the sole power of which would be in the hands of the elective and periodical servants of the people, is an aristocracy, a monarchy, and a despotism.

In the end, the federalist arguments won out, and the Constitution won ratification. But the suspicions raised by the anti-federalists did not disappear. They would help shape the debate on presidential power for decades to come.

The Evolution of Presidential Power

If the Constitution invented the outline of the presidency, and George Washington operationalized their incomplete creation, history and experience more fully formed this elastic institution. Over time, the presidency evolved from "chief clerk" to "chief executive" to national leader. The presidency is less an outgrowth of the constitutional design and more a reflection of ambitious men, demanding times, exploited opportunities, and changing international circumstances.

Was the growth of presidential power inevitable? Theodore Lowi and Benjamin Ginsberg see the development of the presidency in this way: "A tug of war between formal constitutional provisions favoring a chief clerk president and a theory of necessity favoring a chief executive president has persisted for two centuries. . . . But it was not until Franklin Roosevelt that the tug of war seems to have been won for the chief executive presidency, because after FDR . . . every president was strong whether he was committed to the strong presidency or not."[13]

Opportunity and necessity: two words that best describe why, over time, the power of the presidency has expanded. The original design created opportunities for ambitious men, especially in times of necessity, to increase presidential power. The presidency—elastic, adaptable, chameleon-like—has been able to transform itself to meet what the times needed, what ambitious officeholders grabbed, what the people wanted, and what world events and American power dictated.

In many ways, the rise of presidential power is a surprise. From an anti-executive bias (Revolution) to no executive (Articles) to a limited executive (the Constitution) to today, the presidency has not been one thing, but many. And presidential power has not been static, but dynamic (see Table 1.1).

TABLE 1.1 Executive Fluctuations in America

Time	Description	Condition
1760–70	Anti-executive	versus Crown
1770–87	No Executive	Articles of Confederation
1787–1820	Limited Executive	Constitution
1820–30	Democratic Executive	Jacksonian Era
1830–60	Reaction	Congressional Government
1860–70	Executive Emergencies	Lincoln/Civil War
1870–88	Reaction	Congressional Government
1888–1920	America Enters the World	McKinley to Wilson
1920–32	Reaction	Congressional Government
1932–45	Heroic Presidency	FDR, New Deal and WWII
1945–70	National Security State	Cold War Presidency
1970–88	Anti-presidency	Imperial Presidency
1988–?	Divided and Divisive	Post Cold War Presidency

Understanding Presidential Greatness

While there is no commonly accepted standard for what constitutes great-ness, presidents tend to be judged on the basis of (a) the scope of the prob-lems they faced; (b) their efforts in dealing with these problems; (c) the vi-sion they had for the nation; (d) what they were able to accomplish; and (e) the long-term impacts of their actions. Also, experts are very hard on pres-idents whose administrations were rife with corruption.

Those presidents considered "great" have several things in common: they governed in *demanding times*; succeeded at *expanding the powers* of the office; demonstrated a high degree of *skill* in the uses of power; and had a *high purpose.*

Great presidents were concerned with getting and using power. Some who grabbed too much power endangered the republic. There is a fine line between being conscious of your power stakes and doing anything to get power. That is why the framers separated and shared government power.

Those generally considered the "great" presidents are Lincoln, Washing-ton, and FDR. The "near greats" include Jefferson, Jackson, Wilson, Teddy Roosevelt, Truman, and Polk. The "failures" are Pierce, Buchanan, Andrew Johnson, Grant, Harding, Hoover, and Nixon.[14] While there are some dis-agreements between ratings in different polls, most credible polls are sur-prisingly consistent in their rankings of the best and worst presidents.[15]

The great presidents generally had an expansive view of the office. They enlarged the presidency. They saw the president as a leader not a clerk; they sought to expand the presidency. They rode waves of social change and promoted the people's interests. They usually had unified party gov-ernment behind them (divided governments tend not to produce great or powerful presidents). The great ones were sensitive about power and not afraid to use it (no wallflowers here). They usually had a vision for a better nation, were able to articulate that vision and give direction, and they could move the machinery of government while achieving that vision. They served in tough times (often wars or crises) and helped the nation overcome hard-ship. Great presidents were skilled politicians. They often had an electoral mandate. They often added new weapons to the president's arsenal (as voice of the people, crisis manager, director of the economy, legislative chief). They changed the office and sometimes the nation. They were inclusive and democratic. They appealed to our better angels.

Aeschylus reminds us that "Great spirits meet calamity greatly," and so it is with presidents. Those presidents who faced, and conquered, calami-ties earned reputations for greatness. But to be seen as great, opportunities for greatness had to be available. Teddy Roosevelt occasionally complained that he governed in times that were too boring to allow him to reach for greatness. So, too, were Bill Clinton's ambitions frustrated by presiding over peace and prosperity. When things are going well, the window of political opportunity is not open for very much political opportunity. Good times do not make for great presidents.

My own rating, which is very similar to most of the mainstream ratings, is seen in Table 1.2.

Conclusion

The presidency is a complex, multidimensional, contradictory, paradoxical *office*. It is embedded in a *system*—the separation of powers—that limits and frustrates the use of power. The office has been occupied by *individuals* from a wide range of backgrounds, possessing varied skills, motives, and ambitions. They served under drastically different conditions and *circumstances*. It should not then surprise us that the history of the presidency reflects the rise and fall, ebb and flow, of power.

The presidency has been shaped by the varied individuals, operating within a dynamic system under changing circumstances. Some presidents have been strong, others weak. Some eras demand change, others defy it. The presidency has been shaped by industrialization, by the Cold War, by American superpower status, by economic booms and busts, by wars and demands for racial change, by increasing democratization, and by the demands of capitalism.

Presidents helped shape some of these changes, were victims of others, and innocent bystanders of still others. Great social movements, technological changes, newly emergent groups, and a host of other forces created opportunities and restraints on leadership. The story of the rise and fall of presidential power is a complex and perplexing one. It is a story of elasticity and adaptability; of leadership and clerkship; of strong and weak officeholders; of change and stasis. (See Table 1.3).

TABLE 1.2 Presidential Rating

Great Presidents:	(1) Lincoln	Below Average:	(23) Taft
	(2) F. D. Roosevelt		(24) Van Buren
	(3) Washington		(25) Reagan
	(4) Jefferson		(26) Hayes
Near Greats:	(5) Jackson		(27) Arthur
	(6) Wilson		(28) Hoover
	(7) T. Roosevelt		(29) B. Harrison
	(8) Polk		(30) Taylor
	(9) Truman		(31) Tyler
Above Average:	(10) J. Adams		(32) Fillmore
	(11) Madison		(33) Coolidge
	(12) Eisenhower		(34) Pierce
	(13) Kennedy	Failures:	(35) A. Johnson
	(14) Monroe		(36) Buchanan
	(15) McKinley		(37) Nixon
	(16) L. B. Johnson		(38) Grant
Average:	(17) Cleveland		(39) Harding
	(18) J. Q. Adams	Not Rated:	Garfield
	(19) Carter		W. H. Harrison
	(20) Ford		
	(21) Clinton		
	(22) Bush		

TABLE 1.3 Synopsis of Presidential Administrations

President	Party	Political Changes	Cultural and Technological Changes	Achievements	Rating
George Washington 1789–1797 President Number 1	N/A	First presidential election (1789) Bill of Rights (1791) Jay Treaty (1794) Creation of two political parties (1790s)	1st Census: U.S. population just under 4 million, including approximately 700,000 slaves and 60,000 free blacks (1790) Cotton Gin (1793) Washington, D.C. established as nation's capital (1790) U.S. Navy (1794) 1st U.S. Opera (1796) 1st Paddle-wheel steamboat (1797)	Set valuable and lasting precedents; "invented," in practice, much of the presidency; nation-building	#3 Great
John Adams 1797–1801 Number 2	Federalist	Alien and Sedition Acts (1798) Undeclared naval war with France (1798–1800)	Washington becomes U.S. Capital (1800) Library of Congress established (1800)	Avoided major war with France	#9 Above Average
Thomas Jefferson 1801–1809 Number 3	Democratic-Republican	War with Tripoli (1801–1805) Louisiana Purchase (1803) Marbury v. Madison (1803) Lewis & Clark Expedition (1804) Congress bans African slave trade (1808)	Fulton's Steamboat (1807) Gas street lighting introduced (1806) Webster publishes 1st U.S. dictionary (1806) "America the Beautiful" (1808)	Greatly expanded size of U.S. (Louisiana Purchase); peaceful transition from one party rule to another; exerted party leadership	#4 Great
James Madison 1809–1817 Number 4	Democratic-Republican	War of 1812 Treaty of Ghent (1814)	U.S. population over 7 million (1810) "Uncle Sam" invented (1812) "Star Spangled Banner" (1814)	Led nation into unnecessary war	#14 Above Average

TABLE 1.3 (*continued*)

President	Party	Political Changes	Cultural and Technological Changes	Achievements	Rating
James Monroe 1817–1825 Number 5	Democratic-Republican	McCulloch v. Maryland (1819) Missouri Compromise (1820) Monroe Doctrine (1823)	1st Passenger railway Washington Irving publishes "Rip Van Winkle" and "Legend of Sleepy Hollow (1820); Clement Moore writes "Twas the Night Before Christmas" (1822) U.S. flag design established (1818)	Attained Florida from Spain; Created Monroe Doctrine; Signed Missouri Compromise	#15 Above Average
John Quincy Adams 1825–1829 Number 4	Democratic-Republican	Democratic Party formed (1828)	Erie Canal opens (1825) 50th Anniversary of Declaration of Independence (1826) Cooper's "Last of the Mohicans" published (1826) Photographic camera (1826) 1st U.S. ballet (1827) "Freedom's Journal," 1st Negro newspaper (1827)		#16 Above Average
Andrew Jackson 1829–1837 Number 7	Democrat	Nat Turner Rebellion (1831) Whig Party formed (1834) Battle over National Bank (1830–1832) Battle of the Alamo (1836)	U.S. Census places population at 13 million (1830) Colt revolver (1835) 1st Anti-slavery Society (1834) U.S. is debt free for first time in history (1836)	Expanded presidential power and linked president to public opinion	#7 Near Great

President	Party	Legislation/Treaties	Events & Culture	Notable	Ranking
Martin Van Buren 1837–1841 Number 8	Democrat	Independent Treasury Act (1840)	Morse telegraph (1837) Women given legal control over property (1839) Bicycle invented (1839) First university degrees for women (1841)	Nation entered economic depression	#20 Average
William Henry Harrison 1841 Number 9	Whig			Was president for only one month	Not Rated
John Tyler 1841–1845 Number 10	Whig		Typewriter (1843)	Established precedent that upon death of a president, the vice president becomes president	#29 Below Average
James K. Polk 1845–1849 Number 11	Democrat	Oregon Treaty (1846) Mexican War (1846–48) "Manifest Destiny" (1845)	Poe's "The Raven" (1845) Sewing machine (1846) Smithsonian Institution (1846) Women's rights Convention (1848) California Gold Rush (1848)	"Forced" a war with Mexico	#12 Above Average
Zachary Taylor 1849–1850 Number 12	Whig	Compromise of 1850	U.S. Census places population at 23 million (1850)		#27 Below Average
Millard Fillmore 1850–1853 Number 13	Whig		New York Times begins publishing (1851) Melville's "Moby Dick" (1851) Elevator (1852) Stowe's "Uncle Tom's Cabin" (1852) Hawthorne's "The Scarlet Letter" (1852)	Opened trade with Japan; Great Compromise of 1850	#30 Below Average

TABLE 1.3 (*continued*)

President	Party	Political Changes	Cultural and Technological Changes	Achievements	Rating
Franklin Pierce 1853–1857 Number 14	Democrat	Kansas-Nebraska Act (1854) Republican Party formed (1854)	Thoreau's "Walden" (1854) "Whitman's Leaves of Grass" (1855) "Jingle Bells" (1857)	Gadsden Purchase	#32 Below Average
James Buchanan 1857–1861 Number 15	Democrat	Dred Scott v. Sanford (1857) John Brown's Raid (1859) South Carolina secedes from Union (1860) Confederate States formed (1861)	Trans-Atlantic telegraph (1858) Darwin's theory of evolution (1859) J. S. Mill's "Essay on Liberty" (1859) Pony express (1860)	Could not halt the movement to Civil War	#34 Failure
Abraham Lincoln 1861–1865 Number 16	Republican	Civil War (1861–65) Emancipation Proclamation (1863) Assassinated (1865)	"Battle Hymn of the Republic" (1862) Gettysburg Address (1863)	Held nation together through Civil War; freed slaves	#1 Great
Andrew Johnson 1865–1869 Number 17	Republican	Tenure in Office Act (1865) 13th Amendment abolishes slavery (1865) Civil Rights Act (1866) Reconstruction Act (1867) Johnson impeached but escapes conviction by one vote (1868) 14th Amendment (1868)	Ku Klux Klan formed (1866) Women's Rights Convention (NYC) (1866) Winchester rifle (1866) Alcott's "Little Women" (1866) Alaska Purchase (1866) Horatio Alger's "Ragged Dick" (1866) Dynamite (1867) Transcontinental railroad (1869)	Battled with Congress (unsuccessfully) over Reconstruction	#33 Failure

President	Party	Political/Social Events	Cultural/Technological Events	Notes	Rating
Ulysses S. Grant 1869–1877 Number 18	Republican	Wyoming, first state to allow women to vote (1869); 15th Amendment (1870); First Blacks in Congress (1870); Civil Rights Act (1874)	Electric chair (1870); U.S.Census places population at nearly 40 million (1870); "Whistler's Mother" (1871); Battle of Little Big Horn (1876); Telephone (1876); Twain's "Tom Sawyer" (1876)	Scandal plagued administration	#36 Failure
Rutherford B. Hayes 1877–1881 Number 19	Republican	Reconstruction ends (1877); Bland-Allison Act (1877)	Knights of Labor formed (1878); Phonograph (1878); Electric light (1879); Salvation Army begins (1880); U.S. Census places population at over 50 million (1880)	Ended Reconstruction; Civil Service reform efforts	#22 Average
James Garfield 1881 Number 20	Republican			Killed early in term	Not Rated
Chester A. Arthur 1881–1885 Number 21	Republican	Pendleton Act (1883)	Red Cross begins (1881); Statue of Liberty (1883); Washington Monument begun (1884); Twain's "Huckleberry Finn" (1885)	Civil Service reform; modernized Navy	#23 Average
Grover Cleveland 1885–1889 Number 22	Democrat	AFL organized (1887)	Geronimo surrenders (1886); Silent motion pictures (1889)	Reform of government	#See Cleveland Second Term
Benjamin Harrison 1889–1893 Number 23	Democrat	Sherman Anti-Trust Act (1890); Wounded Knee massacre (1890); Populist Party formed (1892)	Basketball invented (1891); Pledge of Allegiance (1892); Gas powered and electric automobile (1893)	Strong foreign policy; enlarged navy	#26 Average

TABLE 1.3 (*continued*)

President	Party	Political Changes	Cultural and Technological Changes	Achievements	Rating
Grover Cleveland 1893–1897 Number 24	Democrat	Plessy v. Ferguson (1896)	"America the Beautiful" (1893) Kipling's "Jungle Book" (1894) X-ray (1895) Crane's "Red Badge of Courage" (1895) First modern Olympics (1897)		#23 Average
William McKinley 1897–1901 Number 25	Republican	Spanish-American War (1898) Hawaii annexed (1898) Assassinated (1901)	Aspirin (1899) U.S. Census places population at nearly 76 million (1900) Radio (1901) Stock market collapse (1901)	Pushed into war with Spain; beginning of U.S. "empire"; U.S. becomes a "world power"; acquired Philippines, Hawaii, Guam, and Puerto Rico as U.S. possessions	#18 Average
Theodore Roosevelt 1901–1909 Number 26	Republican	Trust-busting (1902) Panama Canal (1904) Immigration Act (1907)	Wright brothers' flight (1903) First World Series (1903) London's "Call of the Wild" (1903) 1st Direct blood transfusion (1905) Upton Sinclair's "The Jungle" (1906) Theodore Roosevelt wins Nobel Peace Prize (1906)	Activist president; used "bully pulpit"; expanded presidential power; trust busters; national parks; Panama Canal	#5 Near Great
William Taft 1909–1913 Number 27	Republican	1st Minimum wage law (1912)	Model T car (1909) Peary reaches North Pole (1909)	Conservation of national resources;	#19 Average

President	Party	Legislation	Events	Description	Rating
Number 27		Federal Income Tax (16th Amendment) (1913)	NAACP established (1910) Boy Scouts and Camp Girls established (1910) U.S. Census places population at 92 million (1910) Pulitzer Prize established (1911)	post office reform; trust buster	
Woodrow Wilson 1913–1921 Number 28	Democrat	Federal Reserve Act (1913) World War I (1914–1918) Prohibition (18th Amendment) (1919) Women attain right to vote (19th Amendment) (1920)	Panama Canal opens (1914) Einstein's "Theory of Relativity" (1915) Chaplin's "The Tramp" (1915) 1st Rose Bowl game (1916) "Red Scare" raids (1920) Submachine gun (1920)	Reformed banking laws; anti-trust laws; war leadership; promoted League of Nations and "14 Points"; enlarged presidential power	#6 Near Great
Warren Harding 1921–1923 Number 29	Republican	Naval Arms Limitation Pact (1921)	Insulin (1922) Television (1923) Gershwin's "Rhapsody in Blue" (1923)	Weak president; scandal-plagued administration	#37 Failure
Calvin Coolidge 1923–1929 Number 30	Republican	Scopes Trial (1925) Kellog-Briand Pact (1928)	Sound films (1923) 1st Presidential radio broadcast (1923) Fitzgerald's "The Great Gatsby" (1925) Frozen food (1925) Scopes "Monkey Trial" (1925) Lindbergh crosses Atlantic in airplane (1927) Stalin gains control of Soviet Union (1928) Penicillin (1929) Mickey Mouse (1929)	Weak president	#31 Below Average

TABLE 1.3 (*continued*)

President	Party	Political Changes	Cultural and Technological Changes	Achievements	Rating
Herbert Hoover 1929–1933 Number 31	Republican	Stock Market crash and Great Depression (1929)	Museum of Modern Art (1929) 1st Computer (1930) Empire State Building (1931) Huxley's "Brave New World" (1932) 1st Woman elected to U.S. Senate (1932)	Unfairly blamed for Depression, helpless in its wake	#21 Average
Franklin D. Roosevelt 1933–1945 Number 32	Democrat	New Deal (1933) Social Security (1935) Court Packing Plan (1937) World War II (1939–1945) Lend-lease (1941) Pearl Harbor bombing (1941) Nazis begin systematic extermination of Jews (1942) Relocation of Japanese-Americans (1942)	1st Woman appointed to Cabinet (1933) Radar (1935) 1st Xerox machine (1938) "Gone With The Wind" (1939) Helicopter (1939) Steinbeck's "Grapes of Wrath" (1939) "God Bless America" (1939) Manhattan Project (1942) "Casablanca" (1942)	Activist president; expanded presidential power; saw nation through two crises	#2 Great
Harry S Truman 1945–1953 Number 33	Democrat	Atomic bomb dropped on Japan (1945) World War II ends (1945) Truman Doctrine (1947) Cold War (1947) National Security Act (1947) Marshall Plan (1947) West Berlin airlift (1948) NATO (1949) "Containment" of Soviet Union (1949) Korean War (1950)	Atomic bomb (1945) 1st electronic digital computer (1946) Jackie Robinson, 1st Negro major league baseball player (1947) Supreme Court bans prayer in public schools (1948) Orwell's "1984" (1949) Red Scare/McCarthyism (1950)	Developed U.S. response to Soviet Union; U.S. becomes leader of Free World; National Security State created	#8 Near Great

President	Party	Events		Comment	Ranking
Dwight D. Eisenhower 1953–1961 Number 34	Republican	War in Korea ends (1953) Civil Rights Act (1957) Troops sent to desegregate Little Rock schools (1957) U-2 shot down (1960)	U.S. Census places population at 150 million (1950) Salinger's "The Catcher in the Rye" (1951) Video camera (1951) 1st jet service (1952) Hemingway's "The Old Man and the Sea" (1952) H-bomb (1952) 1st Nuclear power plant (1957) Freedom Rights (1961) Berlin Wall (1961)	Returned nation to relative calm after tumultuous years of depression, World War II, and nascent Cold War	#11 Above Average
John F. Kennedy 1961–1963 Number 35	Democrat	Bay of Pigs (1961) Peace Corps (1961) Cuban missile crisis (1962) Nuclear Test Ban Treaty (1963) Assassinated (1963)	1st American in space (1961) Martin Luther King, Jr. leads Civil Rights Movement (1963) Heller's "Catch-22" (1961) John Glenn orbits Earth (1962)	Peace Corps; Cuban missile crisis	#13 Above Average
Lyndon B. Johnson 1963–1969 Number 36	Democrat	Race riots (1960s) Civil Rights Act (1964) Great Society (1964) Voting Rights Act (1965) Medicare (1966) Thurgood Marshall, 1st Black in Supreme Court (1967) Martin Luther King, Jr. assassinated (1968) Robert Kennedy assassinated (1968)	Martin Luther King, Jr. receives Nobel Peace Prize (1964) 1st successful heart transplant (1967) Anti-war protests (1966 . . . .)	Major achievements in domestic arena overshadowed by Vietnam	#10 Above Average

TABLE 1.3 (*continued*)

President	Party	Political Changes	Cultural and Technological Changes	Achievements	Rating
Richard M. Nixon 1969–1974 Number 37	Republican	Environmental Protection Agency established (1970) Voting age lowered to 18 (26th Amendment) (1972) Detente (1972) Nixon visits China (1972) Watergate (1972) SALT I (1972) Vietnamization (1973) Vice President Agnew resigns (1973) Roe v. Wade (1973)	1st Man on the Moon (1969) Kent State massacre (1970) U.S. Census places population at over 203 million (1970) OPEC crisis (1973)	Ended war in Vietnam; improved relations with Soviet Union and China; Watergate scandal, named unindicted co-conspirator, resigned in disgrace	#35 Failure
Gerald Ford 1974–1977 Number 38	Republican	Resigns from office (1974) Ford pardons Nixon (1974) Vietnam War formally ends (1975)		Helped heal wounds of Vietnam and Watergate; 1st non-elected president	#24 Average
Jimmy Carter 1977–1981 Number 39	Democrat	U.S. opens formal relations with China (1978) Camp David Accords (1978) U.S.-Iran hostage crisis (1979) SALT II (1979) Panama Canal Treaty (1978)	U.S. boycotts Moscow Olympics (1980) U.S. Census places population at 226 million (1980)	Focused on human rights	#25 Average

Ronald Reagan 1981–1989 Number 40	Republican	Iran frees U.S. hostages (1981) Assassination attempt (1981) Sandra Day O'Connor, 1st Woman on Supreme Court (1981) Equal Rights Amendment fails (1982) 241 Marines killed in Beirut bombing (1983) Granada invasion (1983) U.S. mines harbors in Nicaragua (1984) Reagan turns executive power over to Vice President Bush during operation (1985) Iran-Contra scandal (1986) INF Treaty (1987)	AIDS identified (1981) National debt passes one trillion dollars	Restored confidence in U.S.; allowed budget deficit to skyrocket; scandal-plagued administration	#28 Below Average
George Bush 1989–1993 Number 41	Republican	Soviet empire implodes (1989) U.S. invades Panama (1989) Berlin Wall falls (1989) Persian Gulf War (1991)	Exxon Valdez oil crisis (1989) Los Angeles race riots (1992)	Gulf War	# Not Rated
Bill Clinton 1993–2001 Number 42	Democrat	Brady Bill NAFTA Family Medical Leave Act Welfare reform Impeachment hearing	World Trade Center bombing (1993)	Dramatically reduced budget deficit; scandals during administration	# Not Rated

᭐2᭐
The Foundational Presidency
George Washington to John Quincy Adams

The presidency of today is the end result of more than 200 years of development. In fits and starts, resembling a roller coaster ride, the presidency has grown and shrunk; presidential power has expanded and contracted. If the presidency has been the product of these fluctuations, the overall trend has been towards growth—unsteady and uneven—but growth nonetheless.

Some presidents enlarged the office; others diminished it. Some left new tools for their successors to use; others left their successors in seemingly impossible situations.

Of all the framers' inventions, the presidency was left least formed. Thus while the office may have been invented by the framers, it was created and brought to life by Washington and his successors. The presidency cannot be understood merely through an examination of the Constitution. It can only be understood when we examine its historical development.

The office that emerged from the Philadelphia convention was incomplete and unformed. Thus, Washington, the first president, ventured into largely uncharted territory. Everything was new. There was some, but precious little, constitutional guidance. Washington would have to invent as he went along. The presidency is an office made in practice as much as one drafted in Philadelphia.

This chapter examines the foundational stage in the development of the presidency. Beginning with Washington, who more than anyone created the presidency by being president, we look at the idea of a constitutional office in practice, and trace the early evolution of the presidency as it became legitimized.

During the foundational stage, the new nation was comprised of 13 states nestled along the eastern seaboard. The U.S. was not a world power, it was barely a nation. By the end of this era, thanks to Jefferson's Louisiana Purchase, the country doubled in size and established itself as an independent nation, and the nascent presidency was born.

George Washington
1789–1797

At 6'3", George Washington[1] was a towering figure. But beyond his imposing physical presence, Washington was the towering figure of his era

George Washington

because of his accomplishments, his character, and the high esteem in which he was held by his contemporaries. Washington was seen as a man of honor, a man of virtue. He was the man who could have been king but chose to be president. That alone endeared him to his countrymen.

In some ways, George Washington is a living icon, more myth than man; a monument, statuesque and seemingly impenetrable; a classical hero in a modern world. He viewed the American experiment in republican government as promising, but fragile. He knew his role in establishing a presidency was of enormous significance. Hoping to establish dignified republican norms and standards, he tried to lead and teach by example that which was required of the new government.

Washington was an enormously complex, even contradictory, man. He was a truly self-created person. Over the years, Washington worked hard at inventing himself, becoming the person of honor and integrity he strove so hard to become. He could be vain, ambitious, and status seeking. He was driven to succeed. Much of his life was an effort to control and direct these ambitions towards noble and selfless goals. This was no easy task. He needed public acclaim, and yet he was personally remote, aloof, even cold. He was, in this sense, a very unlikely hero. He was consumed with success, yet when he could have been king, he refused. Harnessing such ambitions in the service of republican goals made Washington different.

Near the end of the revolution, King George III, Washington's adversary, asked the painter Trumbull, who had just returned to England after a trip to America, what he thought Washington would do after the war. "Go back to his farm," answered Trumbull. To which George III replied, "If he does that, he will be the greatest man in the world."[2] And that is just what Washington did!

Several years later, George III again praised Washington's humility, saying that his voluntary withdrawal from power "placed him in a light the most distinguished of any man living," and referred to him as "the greatest character of his age."[3]

What was it about Washington's character that so impressed his contemporaries? Washington had what in Latin is referred to as "gravitas"—a dignified seriousness; he was a man of substance, of virtue, of honor. He had a dignity and presence that reminded people of the noble Roman, Cincinnatus, who left the plough to save Rome from the barbarian hordes, and then, having saved Rome, returned to his plough. Washington derived honor from selfless service. As Commander of the Army for eight years, he repeatedly rejected offers of dictatorial powers. When independence was won, he voluntarily laid down his command to return to the life of a private citizen.

His huge ego was employed in the service of his community. But his ego and ambition—dangerous attributes in most men—were under strict self-control. Washington's ambition drove him to succeed, and his skills allowed him to achieve much; his self-discipline let him give up power and glory. This is what made him truly great. He wanted power, but did not overtly seek it. He was driven by ambition, but controlled and subjugated that personal ambition to a higher goal. He was an authentic hero; a man to be admired.

Abigail Adams gave the following description of Washington, as "polite with dignity, affable without familiarity, distant without haughtiness, grave without austerity, modest, wise, and good." And 15 years after Washington's death, Thomas Jefferson described Washington:

> His mind was great and powerful, without being of the very first order; his penetration strong ... and, as far as he saw, no judgment was ever sounder. It was slow in operation, being little aided by invention or imagination, but

sure in its conclusion. . . . Perhaps the strongest feature in his character was prudence, never acting until every circumstance, every consideration was maturely weighed . . . but once decided, going through with his purpose, whatever obstacles opposed. His integrity was most pure, his justice the most inflexible I have ever known. . . . He was, indeed, in every sense of the words, a wise, a good and a great man.

At the time of his inauguration, the United States was still a fledgling nation. Most Americans worked the land, felt more loyalty to their state than their country, and possessed a rugged pioneer spirit. There were, at this time, only three commercial banks in the entire nation. The western territories were controlled by European powers. The nation's largest cities, Philadelphia (population 42,000), New York (31,000), and Baltimore (13,000) were tiny by European standards.

Shortly before traveling to New York to be sworn in, Washington wrote to a friend:

My movements to the chair of Government will be accompanied by feelings not unlike those of a culprit who is going to the place of his execution; so unwilling am I, in the evening of a life nearly consumed in public cares, to quit a peaceful Abode for and Ocean of difficulties, without that competency of political skill—abilities & inclination which is necessary to manage the helm.

In his diary, he wrote:

I bade adieu to Mount Vernon, to private life, and to domestic felicity; and with a mind oppressed by more anxious and painful sensations than I have words to express, set out to New York . . . with the best dispositions to render service to my country in obedience to its call, but with less hope of answering its expectations.

George Washington took the oath of office on April 30, 1789. The first of many precedents he set was to add at the end of the oath of office: "so help me God." His inauguration on April 30, 1789, was described by the *Connecticut Courant* (May 4, 1789) as follows:

[NEW YORK, April 25.] Thursday last, between 2 and 3 o'clock p.m. the Most Illustrious PRESIDENT of the UNITED STATES arrived in this city. . . .

It is impossible to do justice in an attempt to describe the Scene exhibited on his Excellency's approach to the city. Innumerable multitudes thronged the shores, the wharves and the shipping—waiting with pleasing anticipation his arrival. His Catholic Majesty's Sloop of War, the *Calviston*—the ship *North Carolina*, (Mr. Dohrman's) and other vessels, were dressed, manned, and highly decorated. His Excellency's Barge was accompanied by Several other Barges, in one of which were the Hon. The Board of Treasury—the Minister of Foreign Affairs—and the Secretary of

War—besides a long train of vessels and boats from New-Jersey and New-York. As he passed The *Calviston* they fired a salute of 13 guns—The Ship *North Carolina*, and the *Battery*, also welcomed his approach with the same number. . . .

The Procession moved through Queen Street to the House prepared for the reception of the President—from whence he was conducted, without form, to the Governor's where his Excellency dined.

This great occasion arrested the publick attention beyond all powers of description—the hand of industry was suspended—and the various pleasures of the capital were concentered to a single enjoyment—All ranks and professions expressed their feelings, in loud acclamations, and with rapture hailed the arrival of the FATHER OF HIS COUNTRY. . . .

The Scene on Thursday last was sublimely great—beyond any descriptive powers of the pen to do justice to—How universal—and how laudable the curiosity—How *sincere*—and, how *expressive* the sentiments of respect and veneration!—All Ranks appeared to feel the force of an expression, that was reiterated among the crowd . . . "WELL, HE DESERVES IT ALL!"

The spontaneous essations of gratitude to the illustrious WASHINGTON, exhibited by all ranks of people, in a thousand various indications of the sublime principle, are the highest reward that virtue enjoys, next to a conscious approbation which always precedes such undissembled testimonials of publick affection.

Many persons who were in the crowd, on Thursday, were heard to say, that they should now die contented—nothing being wanted to complete their happiness, previous to this auspicious period, but the sight of the Saviour of his Country. Some persons, advanced in years, who hardly expected to see the illustrious President of the States, till they should meet him in Heaven, were in the concourse on Thursday, and could hardly restrain their impatience at being in a measure deprived of the high gratification, by the eagerness of the multitudes of children and young people, who probably might long enjoy the blessings.

When George Washington took the oath of office as first president of the new United States in 1789, people had great confidence and trust in him. There were, however, grave doubts about the legitimacy and role of this new office, called a "presidency."

The Constitution, far from settling the question of presidential power, left more questions than answers. The Constitution was vague and ambiguous, barely charting a skeletal organization for the new office. There was confusion over the political role and character of this presidency. Article II, "the executive power shall be vested in a President," settled little. What powers? What limits? What relation to Congress, to the Courts? What connection to the people?

Washington had no deep political or partisan agenda. His goal was to define the office, place it on secure footing, give it some independence, and establish the legitimacy of the new republican government. As president he attempted to be a national unifier, bringing the two bitter rivals, Hamilton and Jefferson, together in his cabinet, hoping to forestall, if not stamp out, the emerging partisan division between these two powerful adversaries and the ideas that animated their public hostility.

Aware of the importance of every step, act, decision, and non-decision, Washington told James Madison: "As the first of everything, in our situation will serve to establish a precedent, it is devoutly wished on my part, that these precedents may be fixed on true principles."

"I walk," he noted, "on untrodden ground. There is scarcely any part of my conduct that may not hereafter be drawn into precedent." He further noted, "Many things which appear of little importance in themselves and at the beginning may have great and durable consequences from their having been established at the commencement of a new general government."

Here was a man creating an institution as he went along. The Constitution of 1787 was painted only in very broad strokes. It was left to Washington (and his successors) to fill in the details. This left considerable leeway for Washington to invent an office. He was not handed a blank page on which to draw, but the openness of the Constitution left room for individuals and events to complete the job the framers started.

During Washington's time a controversy brewed over what the president should be called. Should he have a regal title? Some in the Senate proposed "His Elective Majesty" or "His Elective Highness," or "His Mightiness." John Adams, Washington's vice president, proposed the wordy "His Most Benign Highness" and "His Highness, President of the United States and Protector of Their Liberties." This suggestion brought sneers from Senators who shouted "His Rotundity" and "His Superfluous Excellency" at Adams.

In the end, the House of Representatives decided the issue, simply calling Washington "President of the United States" (although privately, Washington preferred being called "the general").

One American writer noted that "England's greatest contribution to the world is the works of Shakespeare; America's greatest contribution is the character of George Washington." Daniel Webster observed "America has furnished to the world the character of Washington, and if our American institution had done nothing else, that alone would have entitled them to the respect of mankind." The great English prime minister William E. Gladstone placed Washington on the world's highest pedestal "supplied by history for public characters of extraordinary nobility and purity."[4]

Of course, Washington was not without his critics. Democrat Tom Paine felt Washington had betrayed the cause of the revolution, adding " . . . and as to you, sir, treacherous in private friendship . . . and a hypocrite in public life, the world will be puzzled to decide whether you are an apostate or an impostor, whether you have abandoned good principles, or whether you ever had any?" But such harsh words were clearly minority sentiment. More common were words such as those expressed in 1783 by Ezra Stiles, the president of Yale:

O Washington! How do I love thy name! How have I often adored and blessed thy God, for creating and forming thee the great ornament of human kind! . . . Our very enemies stop the madness of their fire in full volley, stop the illiberality of their slander at thy name, as if rebuked from Heaven with a "Touch not mine Anointed, and do my Hero no harm!" Thy fame is of sweeter perfume than Arabian spices in the gardens of Persia. . . . Listening angels shall catch the odor, waft it to heaven, and perfume the universe![5]

Every act had meaning, and Washington was able to establish a number of important, and some lasting precedents. One of his key contributions was in wrestling some executive independence from Congress in several important areas. He established a precedent of hiring and firing (the latter a serious bone of contention) a cabinet and key executive officers.

Washington also fought for a modicum of independent control over foreign affairs and treaty making. Some ongoing negotiations with Native-American tribes put executive-congressional relations to the test early in his administration. The Constitution called for the president to seek the advice and consent of the Senate in making treaties, but what form should this advice take? Washington asked James Madison how to proceed. "Would an oral or written communication be best? If the first, what mode is to be adopted to affect it?" On August 22, 1789, the president asked the Senate for consultation regarding a proposed treaty. Vice President John Adams read a message to the Senate from President Washington, which concerned several points about the treaty, hoping to get the Senate's *advice* and *consent*. A confused Senate, surprised and unprepared to meet Washington's request, couldn't figure out how to respond. Washington grew progressively angrier, declaring "This defeats every purpose of my coming here." So off-put was Washington that he resolved never to seek Senate consultation again.

In truth, most of the fault rested with the president. Had he informed the Senate prior to dropping the treaty on their laps, they might have been better prepared to engage in serious consultation. But this event marked the last time Washington attempted to use the Senate in an advisory capacity. Such consultation that subsequently took place was in private, and thereafter the Senate was not seriously involved in the advise part of Advise and Consent.

In 1791, Washington, influenced by his Treasury Secretary Alexander Hamilton, agreed to support the creation of a Bank of the United States, modeled on the Bank of England. Jefferson quickly challenged the Bank, asking: "Is it constitutional?" Most of the president's cabinet had their doubts. But Hamilton, arguing that the president, like Congress, had *implied powers* which, while not specified, were derived from the Constitution and necessary for the exercise of executive power, won Washington over, and the president signed the Bank into law. Establishing or legitimizing the view that the president had certain "implied powers" set a precedent that further expanded presidential power.

Washington also, though minimally, helped establish what later was to be called "executive privilege." After a failed military expedition by General Arthur St. Clair, the House of Representatives insisted that the War Department produce documents relating to the expedition. Initially reluctant to turn over the documents, Washington discussed the issue in cabinet and eventually not only consented to produce the documents, but also sent his secretaries of war and treasury to testify in person before the Congress.

It was under Washington that the *veto* was first used. The question was: when can a president exercise the veto? Can he veto legislation with which he disagrees, or can he only veto legislation he believes to be unconstitutional? Initially, Washington was reluctant to use his veto power, but Jefferson, warning the president that if unused, the veto power might atrophy, persuaded Washington to veto a bill on grounds that it violated the Constitution. During his eight years in office, he vetoed only two bills. In the first veto, on April 5, 1792, Washington sent the following letter to the House of Representatives;

I have maturely considered the act passed by the two Houses entitled "An act for an apportionment of Representatives among the several States according to the first enumeration," and I return it to your House, wherein it originated, with the following objections:

First, The Constitution has prescribed that Representatives shall be apportioned among the several States according to their respective numbers, and there is no one proportion or divisor which, applied to the respective numbers of the States, will yield the number and allotment of representatives proposed by the bill.

Second, The Constitution has also provided that the number of representatives shall not exceed 1 for every 30,000, which restriction is by the context and by fair and obvious construction to be applied to the separate and respective members of the States; and the bill has allotted to eight of the States more than 1 for every 30,000.

What powers did a president possess to stop a domestic rebellion? In a small way this question arose during what was called the Whiskey Rebellion, of 1794. Militant opposition to a national excise tax on whiskey production grew increasingly violent. In western Pennsylvania there was especially strong defiance.

Washington's initial response was to issue a warning, demanding that the rebels "disperse and retire peaceably to their respective abodes," warning "all persons whomsoever against aiding, abetting, or comforting the perpetuators of the . . . treasonable acts." Washington also called upon the governors of several states to supply a militia force to squelch the rebellion. The troops marched into western Pennsylvania with an impressive show of force. In the face of this army, the rebels dispersed. Two of the rebels were convicted of treason but Washington, confirming yet another presidential power, pardoned both men. In his response to the Whiskey Rebellion, Washington asserted the supremacy of the federal over state governments, and demonstrated that the new government could, and would, enforce the law.

While the Constitution said that major presidential appointments to the executive branch required the "advise and consent" of the Senate, it said nothing of the removal power. Ultimately, this was a question of who controlled the bureaucracy—the president or Congress. In a 29–22 vote, the House decided to give the president removal power. But that would not be the end of the controversy. Far from being settled, the removal power would come back to haunt presidents and congresses in the future.

Another key event in Washington's presidency revolved around foreign affairs. In 1789, the French Revolution began. But over time, it went from great promise to tragedy. Two weeks after Washington's second inauguration, King Louis XVI was beheaded, and soon Great Britain was at war with France. American sympathies were divided. Jefferson and his followers supported France; Hamilton and his followers supported Britain. The political and personal cleavages that had been emerging in America threatened to crack into open warfare.

Hoping to avoid further trouble, in 1793 Washington issued a Proclamation of Neutrality. But Britain ignored the proclamation and began seizing American ships. Washington, still hoping to avoid a conflict, appointed John Jay to negotiate a treaty with Britain. When the terms of the treaty were announced, the Jeffersonians complained that the U.S. had caved in to almost all of Britain's demands. But Washington signed the treaty.

Did the president have the authority to issue a proclamation of U.S. policy? Could the president declare neutrality? A heated debate between Hamilton and Madison took place in the public press. Hamilton, writing under the pseudonym "Pacificus," argued (as always) for an expansive view of presidential power. Madison, writing as "Helvidius," argued that this was an unconstitutional extension of presidential power, a usurpation of congressional authority.

In the end, Hamilton's position won out as Washington *did* declare neutrality—and made it stick. This set an important precedent, allowing the president to set policy in foreign affairs, and it led to a more expansive view of the president's implied powers under the Constitution.

As Washington's second term drew to an end, several disturbing developments made him even more anxious to return to Mount Vernon and the slower pace of private life. First was the schism that developed between Hamilton and Jefferson that led to the development of political parties. The second factor was the development of a partisan press. Hamilton had his *Federal Gazette of the United States*. In response to this, Jefferson and his followers started the *National Gazette*. Washington was criticized in the press as a "supercilious tyrant," and of him it was written "If ever a nation was debauched by a man, the American Nation has been debauched by Washington."

Washington's decision not to seek a third term set a two-term tradition not broken until FDR's presidency. Washington's willingness to step down from power was another mark of his greatness. In his farewell address, he warned "against the baneful effects of the spirit of party," but even as these sentiments circulated, the nascent party split between the Hamiltonian Federalists and Jeffersonian Democratic-Republicans was brewing. Washington had failed in one of his key goals: establishing a system of (partyless) national unity. The fractious spirit of party, perhaps inevitable, took hold even before Washington left office.

George Washington was no great democrat. In fact, he feared the potential excesses of democracy. He was a republican who

> . . . harbored none of the modern reformer's illusions about human perfectibility. Nor did he ever confuse republicanism with pure democracy. Even indirect democracy assumed a virtuous citizenry as the bulwark of popular liberties. Washington had said as much in his first inaugural address, insisting that "there is no truth more thoroughly established than that there exists . . . an indissoluble union between virtue and happiness; between duty and advantage." His was a highly practical idealism, more Roman than Greek in its antecedents, with little of Rousseau's unquestioning celebration of natural man and much of Tidewater Virginia's noblesse oblige.[6]

What was Washington's contribution to this new government and this new presidency? While James Madison is rightfully called the Father of the U.S. Constitution, no one contributed more to the operation of the new government than George Washington. It was Washington, the indispensable man, who put the new constitutional framework on solid footing and served when the Bill of Rights was adopted. It was Washington who invented the presidency.[7]

He was a great man and a great president. In an age when the skilled *uses of power* marked greatness, Washington proved a great man because he willingly relinquished power. In July of 1799, Governor Jonathan Trumbull of Connecticut pleaded with Washington to serve a third term as president. Only Washington, Trumbull wrote, could save the nation from a "French President" (Thomas Jefferson). But Washington refused, claiming that new political conditions in the nation made his presidency unnecessary. It was a new era of more democratic and more party-oriented politics. "Personal influence" no longer mattered as much. Party, not character, determined how people voted. Even if he ran, Washington wrote, he was "thoroughly convinced I should not draw a single vote from the anti-federalist side."[8] King George III said of Washington's retirement from the presidency that it "placed him in a light the most distinguished of any man living," adding that Washington was "the greatest character of the age."

Washington was the source and symbol of national unity at a time when the result of this experiment in republican government was very much in doubt. He domesticated power and facilitated the development of a republican culture to go along with the republican institutions.

Talleyrand, Napoleon's foreign minister, delivered the following tribute to Washington after the great president's death, describing him as "the man who . . . first dared believe that he could inspire degenerate nations with the courage to rise to the level of republican virtue."[9]

Washington was a great doer and a great teacher of the style and substance of republican government. What he did was of immeasurable importance. But what he *did not do* may have been even more significant. He did not take sides in the continental wars that swept Europe as a result of France's revolutionary experiment, buying precious time for the United States to evolve a sense of nationhood. He did not organize a king's party, nor regard himself as a democratically chosen monarch. Most important of all, by voluntarily relinquishing office at the end of two terms, Washington forced a world more accustomed to Caesar than Cincinnatus to revise its definition of greatness. "George Washington was one of the few in the whole history of the world who was not carried away by power," said Robert Frost without a hint of poetic license. Poignant confirmation of this came from none other than Napoleon Bonaparte, who, on his deathbed at St. Helena, far removed from military pomp and glory, sighed, "They wanted me to be another Washington."

John Adams
1797–1801

Short (5′6″), stocky, balding, habitually in poor health, this New England Puritan had a reserved, distant, and aloof personality. While greatly ambitious and in need of personal recognition, John Adams[10] was nonetheless uncomfortable in public situations, of a suspicious nature bordering on paranoia, and prone to depression. Following the dignified and statuesque Washington, Adams seemed almost a comic figure, pompous, vain, and yearning for a stature that nature denied him.

Biographer Gilbert Chinaid called Adams "honest, stubborn, and somewhat narrow," but a fierce patriot who contributed much to the making of America. Peter Shaw saw in Adams a man of contradictions, at war with himself. His passion for fame led to a pomposity which in the end deflated him. He was, in some respects, his own worst enemy.

His private writings revealed a pettiness and resentment, a vanity and smallness unbecoming a person of his stature. He could be rude and grumpy, stubborn and strong willed, cold and narrow-minded, conceited and overly ambitious. In a letter to James Madison, Jefferson wrote of Adams: "He is vain, irritable, and a bad calculator of the force and probable effect of the motives which govern men." Benjamin Franklin said Adams was "always an honest man, often a wise one, but sometimes, and in some things, absolutely out of his senses." In private, George Washington ridiculed Adams (his vice president) for his "ostentatious imitations and mimicry of Royalty."[11]

Accused of being too sympathetic to monarchy, Adams once proposed the pompous title "His Highness the President of the United States of Amer-

John Adams

ica and Protector of the Rights of the Same." Besides being a mouthful, this suggestion aroused ridicule among his contemporaries.

Adams was known to preside over the Senate dressed in a powdered wig, and he often appeared at ceremonial functions with a sword strapped at his waist. Such things made him the object of abuse and derision, earning him the sobriquet "His Rotundity." He even went so far as to predict that eventually the United States would fully embrace the British system.

As was the custom of the times, Adams did not actively campaign for the presidency. Such public-office seeking was frowned upon as unseemly.

It was a time when the landed gentry still dominated the public arena, and the democratization of politics had yet to take place.

George Washington was, to say the least, a tough act to follow. Succeeding an icon is an unenviable task. It was, Adams himself noted, "a novelty" in political affairs, this "sight of the sun setting full-orbit, and another rising (though less splendid)"[12]

Adams's inauguration marked the first of what would be many peaceful and orderly transfers of power. As he entered office, the United States was a mere child, eight years old. The United States population was under 5 million; two-thirds of whom lived within 100 miles of the Atlantic coast.

Adams's presidency was not a happy one.[13] Marked by the beginning of a bitter partisan split between the Federalists (Adams, Alexander Hamilton), versus the Jeffersonians, this split signified the beginning of party politics in the new nation.[14]

Adams believed himself to be limited in the art and craft of politics because he was "unpractised in intrigues of power." Nowhere is this statement more evident than in one of his first presidential decisions. Hoping (in vain it turns out) to establish continuity with the Washingtonian past, Adams asked all of Washington's department heads to remain in his cabinet. This was a grave mistake, as these men proved unloyal to Adams and often looked to Hamilton for guidance. He later described this decision as his greatest mistake, which he believed resulted in the destruction of his presidency.

The cabinet, led by the ambitious and resentful Alexander Hamilton, was often in conflict with the president, who was supposed to control the administration. Adams's political foe, Thomas Jefferson, noted the internal disputes within Adams's Cabinet, remarking that the "Hamiltonians who surround him (Adams), are only a little less hostile to him than to me."[15]

From the moment he entered office, Adams was confronted with a serious crisis: a possible war with France. Still smarting from Washington's neutrality proclamation, the leaders of France pressured the United States to join them in the ongoing war against Great Britain. France, in an effort to press the issue, refused to recognize U.S. diplomats and threatened to hang any American sailor captured on British ships.

Adams called a special session of Congress, and boldly declared he would not permit the United States to be intimidated by these French threats. He called upon Congress to pass legislation to prepare for the nation's defense. Would the dogs of war be unchained?

In early 1798, Adams received word that the French were interested in a deal. Agents of the French government, referred to simply as X, Y, and Z, secretly demanded the payment of bribes before the American envoy could see the foreign minister, Talleyrand. Furious about this demand, Adams at first favored war. But the United States was not prepared for war. Adams went to Congress with a request that American merchant ships be armed. But the Congress resisted. Adams then made the XYZ dispatches public and proclaimed "Millions for defense, but not one cent for tribute."

As preparation for war moved ahead, Adams called General Washington back into the active service of his country. Washington reluctantly agreed.

During this war scare, the Federalists who controlled Congress passed the *Alien and Sedition Acts*, granting extraordinary powers to the government. These acts, clear and direct violations of the Bill of Rights, were used by Adams to shut down opposition-controlled newspapers and to threaten political opponents.

In early 1799 Adams, still hoping to avoid a war for which the United States was ill-prepared, launched another diplomatic overture to France. This caused angry dissent in his own Federalist party. When several Federalist senators warned Adams they would not support him in this, the president threatened to resign and turn the presidency over to Thomas Jefferson. Nothing put greater fear in the hearts of Federalists than the thought of "that radical" Jefferson in the White House (it wasn't called the "White House" then). Adams's peace overtures to France proved successful, and war was averted.

But this incident left scars. Hamilton vowed to wrestle power away from Adams, and in late 1799 and early 1800, the president discovered that Hamilton had been secretly trying to control the cabinet. Enraged, Adams forced his entire cabinet to resign.

In the aftermath of these internecine battles, and with Hamilton writing scathing broadsides against Adams, the Federalists lost the election of 1800 to their dreaded adversary Thomas Jefferson.

For all his limitations and difficulties, Adams ranks in the Above Average category of American presidents. While not an adroit politician (Adams refused to actively lead Congress), and in spite of possessing a quirky personality and somewhat limited view of the office, Adams nonetheless helped establish the presidency and its foreign affairs powers. The first president to live in the still unfinished White House (as it is now called), and much influenced by a strong and outspoken wife (Abigail Adams was derisively referred to as "Mrs. President"), Adams saw America through threatening and turbulent times. He avoided what would certainly have been a costly and probably unwinnable war, and brought the country through the early and potentially explosive era of party formation and conflict.

During Adams's time, the government became firmly established in what Jefferson called "that Indian swamp in the wilderness," Washington, D.C. Jefferson was not alone in his criticism of the nation's capital city. In 1862, novelist Anthony Trollope said, "I . . . found the capital still under the empire of King Mud . . . Were I to say that it was intended to be typical of the condition of the government, I might be considered cynical."

Adams lived to the age of 90. He died on July 4, 1826, the same day as his rival and later friend, Thomas Jefferson. Adams's last words were "Thomas Jefferson still survives." Jefferson, unbeknownst to Adams, had died earlier that day.

Thomas Jefferson
1801–1809

Thomas Jefferson[16] is America's great renaissance man; perhaps the greatest American of all. Inventor, statesman, philosopher, diplomat, lawyer, scientist, humanist, art collector, musician, farmer, founder of the University of Virginia, politician, writer, revolutionary, architect, botanist, and so very much more. A man of insatiable curiosity and unlimited talent, Jefferson, author of the Declaration of Independence and third president of the United States, was one of the most important figures in American history, and one of the most important presidents.

Thomas Jefferson

Tall (6'2") with sandy red hair, hazel eyes, and a weak speaking voice, Jefferson was both loathed and loved. The *Connecticut Courant* (a Federalist newspaper) warned voters prior to the election of 1800, "Murder, robbery, rape, adultury, and incest will all be openly taught and practiced, the air will be rent with the cries of the distressed, the soil will be soaked with blood, and the nation black with crimes." (And you thought today's media was biased!) But years later, President Kennedy, speaking to a gathering of Nobel Prize winners at the White House, said "I think this is the most extraordinary collection of talent of human knowledge that has ever been gathered together at the White House, with the possible exception of when Thomas Jefferson dined alone."

Jefferson's inauguration was something of a precedent setter; at midday on March 4, 1801, Jefferson walked from his boardinghouse to the capitol. There, Federalist and newly appointed Chief Justice John Marshall administered the oath of office to the 57-year-old Jefferson. A peaceful transfer of power, not just from one leader to another, but from one political party to another, took place. Recognizing the partisan divisions that split the nation, Jefferson attempted to strike a chord of harmony in his inaugural address, noting "We are all republicans, we are all federalists." He further noted that

> I know, indeed, that some honest men fear that a republican government can not be strong, that this Government is not strong enough; but would the honest patriot, in the full tide of successful experiment, abandon a government which has so far kept us free and firm on the theoretic and visionary fear that this Government, the world's best hope, may by possibility want energy to preserve itself? I trust not . . . Sometimes it is said that the man can not be trusted with the government of himself. Can he, then, be trusted with the government of others? Or have we found angels in forms of kings to govern him? Let history answer this question.

Margaret Bayard Smith, wife of the editor of the *National Intelligence*, a pro-Jeffersonian paper, described the inauguration in this way: "The changes of administration, which in every government and in every age have most generally been epochs of confusion, villainy and bloodshed, in this happy country take place without any species of distraction, or disorder."[17]

Jefferson wanted to de-pomp the presidency and bring it back to more democratic manners. He did away with bowing, replacing this regal custom with the more democratic handshake. Republican simplicity replaced monarchical pomp. Jefferson abolished the weekly levee, ended formal state dinners, and abandoned Washington's custom of making personal addresses to Congress (this may have been due as much to Jefferson's weak speaking voice as to his republican tendencies). This practice continued until 1913 and the Wilson presidency.

Jefferson utilized the cabinet as a powerful instrument of presidential leadership. His cabinet was loyal, experienced, and committed to pushing the Jeffersonian agenda in Congress.

Jefferson also exerted increased influence over the Congress. Employing the president's power as *party leader*, Jefferson, while respecting the constitutional prerogatives of Congress, nonetheless used a variety of means to press his goals in the legislature. He lobbied key party leaders, drafted bills for his supporters to introduce, authorized key party members to act as his spokesmen in Congress, informally lobbied legislators at social gatherings in the White House, and had cabinet members work closely with the legislature. All this allowed Jefferson to exert a great deal of influence over the Congress.

Jefferson used, with great effect, dinners with legislators as an effective tool of leadership. He would invite ten or so congressmen over to dinner at the White House two or three times per week when Congress was in session. As Jefferson explained his motives:

> I cultivate personal intercourse with the members of the legislature that we may know one another and have opportunities of little explanations of circumstances, which, not understood, might produce jealousies and suspicions injurious to the public interest, which is best promoted by harmony and mutual confidence among its functionaries. I depend much on the members for local information necessary in local matters, as well as for the means of getting at public sentiment.[18]

Jefferson never cast a veto in his two terms as president, and he viewed the veto power quite narrowly, believing it was reserved only for bills deemed of questionable constitutionality (in fact, in the 40 years from 1789 to 1829, a span covering six administrations, only ten vetoes were cast). Given his skilled and activist leadership of Congress, the president was never forced to put his views to the test.

Such activist intervention surprised Jefferson's Federalist critics, who thought the new president's goal was to limit governmental and presidential power. But undoing the Federalist policies required the use of executive leadership; power was needed to vanquish power, and "the more the President exercised power with righteous purpose, the less scrupulous he became towards abjurations of Republican theory."[19]

Jefferson's use of the political party was an innovation in presidential leadership. It was an exercise of extraconstitutional power, but one necessary to make the Constitution operate effectively. This allowed Jefferson to build a strong presidency, responsive to the majority will of the people, as expressed through the political party.

Jefferson's success in Congress was matched by equally impressive failures in his dealings with the judiciary. While the Congress was controlled by Jefferson's Republicans (what today is the Democrat party), the courts were in Federalist hands. In fact, the Supreme Court issued a direct challenge to the President in *Marbury v. Madison*, the famous "midnight judges" case, in which the Court established the doctrine of "judicial review." Prior to that time, it was not settled who the final arbiter of the Constitution would be. Logic and some indications from the framers pointed to the judiciary, but presidents too claimed some authority in determining what the true meaning of the Constitution was. In the long run, the *Marbury* case all but settled the issue in favor of the judiciary.

In *Federalist No. 78*, Alexander Hamilton referred to the judiciary as the "least dangerous branch" of government. Calling it "beyond comparison, the weakest of the three departments of power . . . ," Hamilton went on to reassure the citizenry that the judiciary was not to be feared, for it had too little power to be of any real threat to liberty. But the enfeebled judiciary of Hamilton's writings was not to be, for with the emergence of judicial review and the Marshall Courts decision in *Marbury vs. Madison*,[20] the judiciary moved into the main arena of politics.

John Adams, the outgoing president and a Federalist, made a number of eleventh-hour judicial appointments just prior to leaving office, nominating—of course—Federalists. One of the men commissioned as Justice of the Peace was William Marbury. Ironically, however, the commission was never delivered, in spite of the fact that it was signed by the then President Adams and affixed with the seal of the United States.[21] The new Secretary of State, James Madison, withheld the commission on orders from President Jefferson.

Marbury filed suit in the Supreme Court, seeking a writ of mandamus to require Madison to deliver the commission. Marshall, who was directly involved in the original dispute that produced the case refused to disqualify himself from participation in the Court's action. The Court was then faced with a dilemma. Should it rule directly against the President and thus face the possibility that Jefferson might refuse to comply with the Court's dictate? Such an action might have established the judiciary as the weak sister of the federal government and permanently established the independence of the President and the Congress from the Court's decision. The Marshall Court found a "solution."

After first expounding both the right of the Court to decide on such a matter and the duty of the President to obey such judicial dictates, the Court then did a partial about face and handed the Jeffersonians a backhanded victory. Having established the power of the Court to judicial review, Marshall announced that in the case of Marbury, the Court should not have original jurisdiction as the Judiciary Act of 1789 had granted it, and thus the court could offer no remedy for Marbury. Marshall granted Jefferson the victory in this battle, but won the war by making it clear that the courts had the right to determine the constitutionality of acts by both Congress and the President. It was a judicial stroke of genius, one which paved the way for judicial strength for future courts. As constitutional scholar Charles Warren commented:

> . . . In comprehensive and forceful terms, which for over 100 years have never been successfully controverted, [Marshall] proceeded to lay down the great principles of the supremacy of the Constitution over statute law, and of the duty and power of the Judiciary to act as the arbiter in case of any conflict between the two.[22]

Chief Justice Marshall wrote in his opinion in the Marbury case:

> It is emphatically the province and duty of the Judicial department to say what the law is. Those who apply the law to particular cases, must of necessity expound and interpret that rule. If two laws conflict with each other, the courts must decide on the operation of each.
>
> So if a law be in opposition to the constitution; if both the law and the constitution apply to a particular case, so that the court must decide that case conformably to the law, disregarding the constitution; or conformably to the constitution, disregarding the law; the court must determine which of these conflicting rules governs each case. This is of the very essence of judicial duty.
>
> If, then, the courts are to regard the constitution, and the constitution is superior to any ordinary act of the legislature, the constitution, and not such ordinary act, must govern the case to which they both apply . . .

But this position was not without its detractors. Jefferson, of course, opposed this view, saying that it was explicitly undemocratic. As he wrote in a letter to Thomas Ritchie:

> The judiciary of the United States is the subtle corps of sappers and miners constantly working underground to undermine the foundations of our confederated fabric. They are construing our constitution from a coordination of a general and special government to a general and supreme one alone . . . An opinion is huddled up in conclave, perhaps by a majority of one, delivered as if unanimous, and with the silent acquiescence of lazy or timid associates, by a crafty judge (Marshall) who sophisticates the law to his mind, by the turn of his own reasoning . . . independence of the will of the nation is a solecism, at least in a republican government.[23]

Who determines constitutionality? Who has the final word? The judiciary exclusively? After all, the president swears an oath to "preserve, protect, and defend" the Constitution, and to "take care that the laws be faithfully executed." What happens when the president disagrees with the interpretation of the Court? In practical terms, the Court rarely gets the final, or last, word.[24] It is a dynamic process, with Congress reshaping and the president reinterpreting judicial decisions over time. As Ruth Bader Ginsburg noted shortly before she was appointed to the Supreme Court, judges "play an interdependent part in our democracy. They do not alone shape legal doctrine . . . they participate in a dialogue with other organs of government, and with the people as well."[25]

Even before the Marbury decision, Jefferson declared the Alien and Sedition Acts a constitutional "nullity" and pardoned those prosecuted under it.[26] Arguing that judicial supremacy would transform the Constitution into "a mere thing of wax" that the courts "may twist and shape into any form they please," Jefferson publicly questioned the Court's support of these acts.[27]

The conflict between Jefferson and Marshall was a classic confrontation. It was the clash between great men and great ideas. Jefferson felt the supreme goal of the American Revolution and its aftermath was to foster democracy. Consequently, he did not accept the proposition that the Court, a small group of nonelected government officials, should interfere with the will of the majority as expressed in the laws passed by the Congress. It was, to Jefferson, an interference with the workings of democracy to give the Court the right to overturn congressional acts.[28]

Marshall, an equally strong and determined individual, believed that the supreme role of the government was to protect the Constitution. Without the Constitution, without the guarantees provided by the document, the American system of rights and liberties would be in jeopardy. To Marshall, it was the Constitution which deserved our highest respect and reverence. The Court, by narrowly deciding the case before it, granted Jefferson the immediate, short-term victory, in favor of the ultimate victory: the establishment of judicial review.

Judicial review was firmly established in the Marbury case. This gave political credence to an idea that was discussed, but never ultimately resolved, by the founding fathers. Certainly someone had to be the final arbiter of the Constitution; but the founders never specifically granted that power to any one branch. While most scholars agree that the founders "intended" that the judiciary possess this power,[29] nowhere in the Constitution did they mention judicial review. In effect, the Marbury case ended speculation as to the role the Court would and could play in constitutional interpretation.

If George Washington talked of asserting executive privilege, it was Jefferson who first asserted it. Subpoenaed to testify at the treason trial of Aaron Burr, Jefferson flatly refused to appear. He did, however, release selected documents. This bold assertion established a precedent that partially insulates the executive branch from some intrusions by the legislative and judicial branches.

One of the first dilemmas faced by Jefferson was what to do about pirates operating against American ships in the Mediterranean. The president ordered a squadron of American fighting ships to sail to the region. "But," Jefferson cautioned, "as this might lead to war, I wished to have the approbation of the new administration."[30] At issue was the question of how much authority the president had to initiate potential military action. Jefferson's cabinet agreed that the squadron should be sent to the region to protect American shipping, but they were unsure whether the president alone had the authority to order such an activity. In the end, Jefferson recognized that the Constitution gave Congress the power to declare war, but said that the squadron could engage in defensive actions (a fine line perhaps, but a line nonetheless). Jefferson defined defensive quite broadly, however. This somewhat restrictive view of a president's foreign affairs authority, while powerful in constitutional argument, would, over time, be eroded by events.

One of the greatest challenges to Jefferson's somewhat minimalist view of government came in the Louisiana Purchase controversy. An opportunity presented itself for the United States to double its size for a very small cost. France was willing to sell the Louisiana territory to the U.S. The negotiations were delicate, and Jefferson needed to seize the moment. But nowhere did the Constitution authorize the acquisition of territory by the president or the federal government. What to do?

Jefferson believed that the purchase required a constitutional amendment, and he went so far as to draft a constitutional amendment to give the government power to purchase the Louisiana territory. "The constitution has made no provision for our holding foreign territory," he admitted. Jefferson's argument, made to Senator John Breckinridge of Kentucky, noted that

> The Executive in seizing the fugitive occurrence which so much advances the good of their country, have done an act beyond the Constitution. The Legislature in casting behind them metaphysical subtleties, and risking themselves like faithful servants, must ratify to pay for it, and throw themselves on their country for doing for them unauthorized what we know they would have done for themselves had they been in a situation to do it. It is the case of a guardian, investing the money of his ward in purchasing an important adjacent territory; and saying to him when of age, I did this for your good. I pretend to no right to bind you: you may disavow me, and I must get out of the scrape as I can: I thought it my duty to risk myself for you.[31]

But grand opportunity outweighed constitutional questions, and Jefferson soon changed his tune. Fearing that delay would jeopardize the deal, Jefferson concluded that "the less that is said about my constitutional difficulty, the better; and that it will be desirable for Congress to do what is necessary in silence."[32]

For $15 million (a mere three cents per acre), Jefferson acquired the Louisiana territory from France. But constitutional questions weighed heavily on Jefferson's mind. In a letter to W. C. Clairborne (February 3, 1807) the president wrote: "On great occasions every good officer must be ready to risk himself in going beyond the strict line of the law, when the public preservation requires it; his motive will be a justification."[33]

Several years later (September 20, 1810), in a letter to J. B. Clovin, Jefferson revisited this issue, writing

> A strict observance of the written laws is doubtless one of the high duties of a good citizen, but it is not the highest. The laws of necessity, of self-preservation, of saving our country when in danger, are of a higher obligation . . . To lose our country by a scrupulous adherence to written law, would be to lose the law itself, with life, liberty, property and all those who are enjoying them with us; thus absurdly sacrificing the end to the means.[34]

Jefferson sponsored the Lewis and Clark expedition, an overland exploration of the newly acquired territory. It helped open up the new territory to Americans, and soon, expansion westward would become both a blessing and a curse.

Near the end of his life Jefferson wrote to his dear friend John Adams:

> When all our faculties have left, or are leaving us, one by one, sight, hearing, memory, every avenue of pleasing sensation is closed, . . . when the friends of our youth are all gone and a generation is risen around us whom we know not, is death an evil?

Thomas Jefferson added immeasurably to the growth of the presidency and to the growth of the nation. He was the first president as *party leader*, he led Congress with great skill, he used his *cabinet* very effectively, and began to develop a more direct link between the president and the people. While articulating a more minimalist view of government than his Federalist predecessors, once in office Jefferson fully used, and even expanded, the power of the presidency to achieve his goals. Scholars place Jefferson in the Great or Near Great category. It is a rating richly deserved.

James Madison
1809–1817

At 5′5″, and weighing only 100 pounds, James Madison[35] was the U.S. president with the smallest stature. Known as the Father of the U.S. Constitution, Madison was the last of the framers to serve as President. Madison appeared slightly rigid, and historian Richard Morris argued that he "lacked human warmth."[36] But he was also a man of principle and honor.

During Madison's presidency, power shifted from the presidency to the Congress. One of the chief reasons for this was the development of the congressional nominating caucus which, for a time, chose the party nominees for president and thus made presidents, at least to a degree, servants of the legislature. Also, the rise of the House Speaker (Henry Clay) as a major force in government further shifted power to the Congress.

Madison, like Jefferson, had a republican and limited view of executive power. Unlike Jefferson, Madison was reluctant to abandon this view when necessity warranted.

The seminal event of Madison's presidency was the ill-advised War of 1812. Upon taking office, Madison's most pressing issue was how to keep the United States out of war. France and Britain were still engaged in the Napoleonic wars, and both nations, but most especially Britain, seized American ships at sea and impressed American sailors into service on British war ships. Pressure for war was strong, and Madison finally gave in to congressional pressure and somewhat reluctantly asked for a declaration of war (the first president to do so). In this, Madison followed rather than led. Had

James Madison

he more forcefully exerted presidential leadership, war might have been averted.

The war was badly managed by Madison. The most humiliating moment came when, in August 1814, British troops attacked Washington, D.C., and burned the Capitol building and the White House. Madison was forced the flee the Capitol and witnessed the burning of the White House from the Virginia Hills. His wife, Dolley Madison, remained just long enough to save some priceless objects, among them Gilbert Stuart's portrait of George

Washington. Here is Mrs. Madison's account of the invasion from a letter to her sister:

Tuesday, August 23, 1814

Dear Sister:

My husband left me yesterday to join General Winder. He enquired anxiously whether I had the courage or firmness to remain in the President's House until his return, on the morrow, or succeeding day, and on my assurance that I had no fear but for him and the success of our army, he left me, beseeching me to take care of myself and of the Cabinet papers, public and private.

I have since received two dispatches from him, written with a pencil; the last is alarming, because he desires that I should be ready at a moment's warning, to enter my carriage and leave the city; that the enemy seemed stronger than had been reported, and that it might happen that they would reach the city with intention to destroy it . . . I am accordingly ready; I have pressed as many Cabinet papers into trunks as to fill one carriage; our private property must be sacrificed, as it is impossible to procure wagons for its transportation. I am determined not to go myself, until I see Mr. Madison safe, and he can accompany me—as I hear of much hostility toward him . . . Disaffection stalks around us. My friends and acquaintances are all gone, even Colonel C. with his hundred men, who were stationed as a guard in this enclosure. . . . French John (a faithful domestic) with his usual activity and resolution offers to spike the cannon at the gate, and lay a train of powder which would blow up the British, should they enter the house . . .

Wednesday morning, twelve o'clock—
Since sunrise, I have been turning my spyglass in every direction and watching with unwearied anxiety, hoping to discover the approach of my dear husband and his friends; but, alas, I can descry only groups of military wandering in all directions, as if there was a lack of arms, or of spirits, to fight for their own firesides.

Three o'clock.
Will you believe it, my sister, we have had a battle, or a skirmish, near Bladensburg, and I am still here within sound of the cannon! Mr. Madison comes not; may God protect him! Two messengers, covered with dust, come to bid me fly; but I wait for him. . . . At this late hour a wagon has been procured; I have filled it with the plate and most valuable portable articles belonging to the house; whether it will reach its destination, the Bank of Maryland, or fall into the hands of British soldiery, events must determine. Our kind friend, Mr. Carroll, has come to hasten my departure, and is in a very bad humor with me because I insist on waiting until the large picture of General Washington is secured; and it requires to be unscrewed from the wall. This process was found too tedious for these perilous moments; I have ordered the frame to be broken and the canvas taken out; it is done, and the precious portrait placed in the hands of two gentlemen of

New York for safe-keeping. And now, dear sister, I must leave this house or the retreating army will make me a prisoner in it, by filling up the road I am directed to take. When I shall again write to you, or where I shall be tomorrow, I cannot tell!

The war ended inconclusively. Madison's performance as commander-in-chief, while personally courageous, was strategically flawed. Even one of Madison's more sympathetic biographers found the president's leadership lacking: "The hour had come but the man was wanting. Not a scholar in governments ancient and modern, not an unimpassioned writer of careful messages, but a robust leader to rally the people and unite them to fight was what the time needed, and what it did not find in Madison."[37]

Madison served at a time when congressional power rose and presidential power waned. Perhaps he could have done more to exert leadership, but his opportunity was limited. He accepted congressional power and, believing he was faithfully following the architecture of the Constitution he had so much influence in writing, allowed the power of the presidency to diminish in favor of congressional authority.

James Monroe
1817–1825

The last of the "Virginia Dynasty" (four of the first five presidents were from Virginia), James Monroe,[38] a rugged 6-footer with gray-blue eyes and stooped shoulders, was more caretaker than leader. Chosen for the nomination by the congressional "King Caucus," Monroe presided over relative peace and prosperity, what a Boston newspaper proclaimed as an "era of good feelings."

Although personally forceful, Monroe could also be stiff and formal. John Adams ungraciously called him "dull, heavy, and stupid." Others saw him as honest and straightforward.

Henry Clay was still the very powerful Speaker of the House, and Congress continued to dominate the political arena. Monroe was unable to control his party and thus, it, and the Congress at times, controlled him. Monroe also had a limited view of the executive's role in the political system. Having said all this, it, may come as something of a surprise that Monroe was a fairly successful president with several significant accomplishments.

Monroe saw himself as head of the nation, not of a political party. Being "above politics" had its consequences. The Federalist party all but disappeared in the aftermath of the War of 1812, and new conflicts—those taking place *within* the Republican party—animated politics. Internal strife and rivalries, jockeying for inside position in the selection of presidents, sectional disputes, all caused powerful cleavages.

If all were of one party, at least on the surface, partisan party leadership became all but impossible. Monroe, who had a somewhat ambitious

James Monroe

program, found it difficult to promote that program while remaining true to his republican principles. Stripped of the opportunity for party leadership and hemmed in by self-imposed philosophical constraints, Monroe groped for a viable leadership style. His meager efforts to influence Congress met with stiff opposition from Speaker Clay, who denounced Monroe:

> The Constitutional order of legislation supposed that every bill originating in one house shall there be deliberately investigated, without influence from any other branch of the legislature, and then remitted to the other House for a free and unbiased consideration. Having passed both Houses, it is to be laid before the President—signed if approved, if disapproved to

be returned, with his objections to the originating House. In this manner, entire freedom of thought and action is secured, and the President finally sees the proposition in the most matured form which Congress can give to it. The practical effect, to say no more, of forestalling the legislative opinion, and telling us what we may or may not do, will be to deprive the President himself of the opportunity of considering a proposition so matured and us the benefit of his reasoning, applied specifically to such a proposition; for the Constitution further enjoins upon him to state his objections upon returning the bill.[39]

The tide of power had shifted to the Congress, and they jealously guarded their institutional position. While King Caucus was in decline, the power of congressional committees was on the rise. In this so-called era of good feeling, Monroe tried to become a nonpartisan chief of state, but Congress wanted no part in it. After Monroe won a second term as president, Speaker Clay concluded "Mr. Monroe has just been re-elected with apparent unanimity, but he has not the slightest influence on Congress. His career is closed. There was nothing further to be expected by him or from him."[40] Some era of good feeling!

In spite of these restrictions, Monroe left his mark on America. During his presidency, five new states were added to the union, a series of wars with Native-American nations took place, the United States won control of Florida from Spain, and the Missouri Compromise was reached.

The Missouri Compromise was an attempt to strike a peaceful balance between the slave and free states. The issue of slavery was reaching a boiling point. Monroe's solution was resettlement of blacks back to Africa. It wasn't much of a solution. The split over slavery led to secessionist calls by some southern states. The "compromise" was that for every slave state added to the union, a free state had to be added. Thus, Missouri came in as a slave state, Maine as a free state. It also set up a boundary in the Louisiana Territory, north of which was free, south was slave. This compromise merely postponed confrontation. Thomas Jefferson wrote of the compromise: "This momentous question, like a fire-bell in the night, awakened and filled me with terror. I considered it at once as the knell of the Union. It is hushed, indeed, for the moment. But this is a reprieve only, not a final sentence."[41]

It was in foreign affairs that Monroe is best remembered. After the collapse of the Spanish empire, several European powers attempted to make political headway in the Americas. In response to fears that France, Russia, or Britain might set up colonies in the hemisphere, President Monroe included the following policy pronouncement in his 1823 State of the Union message:

> The occasion has been judged proper for asserting, as a principle in which the rights and interests of the United States are involved, that the American continents, by the free and independent condition which they have assumed and maintain, are henceforth not to be considered as subjects for future colonization by any European powers.

He added:

> . . . We owe, it therefore, to candor and to the amicable relations existing between the United States and those powers to declare that we should consider any attempt on their part to extend their system to any portion of this hemisphere as dangerous to our peace and safety. With the existing colonies or dependencies of any European power we have not interfered and shall not interfere. But with the Governments who have declared their independence and maintained it, and whose independent we have, on great consideration and on just principles, acknowledged, we could not view any interposition for the purpose of oppressing them, or controlling in any other manner their destiny, by any European power in any other light than as the manifestation of an unfriendly disposition toward the United States.

In so announcing, Monroe reinforced a president's power to take the initiative and make policy in foreign affairs. This Monroe Doctrine was not confirmed by Congress, nor did Monroe have to enforce it during his presidency, but it became one of the pillars of U.S. foreign policy. In an age of relative executive weakness, the president could still pull his weight in the making of foreign policy.

Early in Monroe's presidency, Supreme Court Justice Joseph Story noted that "the Executive has no longer a commanding influence. The House of Representatives has absorbed all the popular feeling and all the effective power of the country."[42] Overstated perhaps, but close to the point.

In spite of governing in an era of congressional ascendancy, Monroe did manage to strengthen the power of the presidency in foreign affairs and postponed sectional disputes that were soon to change the era of good feelings to the era of bad feelings and secessionist revolts.

John Quincy Adams
1825–1829

Often dour and disagreeable, enigmatic, prone to bouts of depression, the 5'7", balding John Quincy Adams[43] was the first president to be photographed and also the first elected without receiving a plurality of either the popular or electoral college votes. He was the son of President John Adams. John Quincy Adams was a distinguished diplomat and a mediocre president. "I am a man of reserved, cold, austere, and forbidding manners," Adams said of himself. James Buchanan said of Adams, "His disposition is as perverse and mulish as that of his father." William Henry Harrison said of Adams: "It is said he is a disgusting man to do business with. Coarse, dirty, and clownish in his address and stiff and abstracted in his opinions, which are drawn from books exclusively."

John Quincy Adams

The election of 1824 was one of the most bitter and hostile in history. The results of the general election were inconclusive:

Jackson	99 electoral votes	153,544 popular votes
Adams	84 electoral votes	108,740 popular votes
Crawford	41 electoral votes	46,618 popular votes
Clay	37 electoral votes	47,136 popular votes

Thus, the election was thrown into the House of Representatives. Andrew Jackson led the race but was 32 electoral votes short of victory. Clay, who came in fourth, was dropped from the race, and he could turn his votes over to Jackson or Adams and, in effect, determine the outcome.

On January 9, 1825, Clay met with Adams. The details of their conversation are not known, but shortly thereafter, Clay's support went to Adams, prompting Jackson to complain of a "corrupt bargain." Clay was later appointed by Adams as secretary of state.

As a result of the questionable nature of his election, Adams took office severely wounded. In his inaugural address he noted he was "less possessed of [public] confidence in advance than any of my predecessors." Undeterred, Adams decided to work to strengthen the presidency, and was the first president to attempt to lead Congress openly. In his first annual message to Congress he called for expansive internal improvements and a variety of other new programs. Adams's predecessors harbored doubts about the constitutionality of such spending measures, but Adams rejected this narrow view. In this way, Adams was the first president "to demonstrate the real scope of creative possibilities of the constitutional provision to 'recommend to their [Congress's] consideration such measures as he shall judge necessary and expedient.'"

"His four years in the White House were a misery for him . . . For the remaining twenty years of his life, he reflected on his presidency with distaste, convinced that he had been the victim of evildoers. His administration was a hapless failure and best forgotten, save for the personal anguish it cost him."[44]

The Adams years were a time of harsh political strife but also of great economic expansion and growth. By the end of his presidency, King Caucus, the method whereby congressional caucuses selected presidential candidates, was being replaced by political party conventions. Adams was not a strong president, but his bold reform proposals did open the door for future presidents to promote more openly their legislative programs.

The great experiment in government attempted by the framers worked. A constitutional republic, a risky venture in the late eighteenth century, began to take shape. George Washington, great man and great president, brought the nascent office of the presidency to life. He gave it dignity, some independence, and significant authority. Not all who followed him succeeded. But the office was firmly established, and the occasional strong president, such as Jefferson, came along to add to the power and prestige of the office. At the end of this era, the idea of a presidency became a tangible reality. No small feat in an age of reason full of skeptics.

~3~

Democratization to Decline/
Crisis to Enlargement:
Andrew Jackson to Abraham Lincoln

After the assertion of congressional power in the post-Jeffersonian years, the pendulum swung back toward the presidency in the era of Andrew Jackson and the rise of Democratic politics. Congress reasserted itself after Jackson but, as President Polk demonstrated, presidents could still force the action and control events. After Polk, sectional divisions dominated politics until the Civil War and the rise of Abraham Lincoln as president and war leader.

Andrew Jackson
1829–1837

One of the most interesting and influential presidents in United States history, Andrew Jackson,[1] "Old Hickory," was a cantankerous, dueling, determined, iron-willed, ill-tempered fighter for "the people." John Quincy Adams called Jackson "a barbarian who cannot write a sentence of grammar and can hardly spell his own name." At 6'1", 140 pounds, with bushy, iron-gray hair brushed high above his forehead and clear dark eyes, Jackson was tough and wiry, self-educated, a brawling street-fighter, a man whose opponents called a him savage and a barbarian. In frail health, in part due to the bullets lodged in his body as a result of duels, Jackson was a dynamic, charismatic figure who "democratized" the presidency and won the support of the people, enhanced the power of the office, and caused no end of trouble for his political adversaries. The first political "outsider" to serve as president, he changed the presidency and changed the nation.

The Jacksonian era was a turning point in the history of the presidency. His tenure marked the end of the patrician politics of the founding era. Jackson came into office proclaiming the sanctity of the common man. "The majority is to govern," he stated in 1829, in his first annual message to Congress. During this period, male suffrage expanded (from 1824 to 1828, the number of males eligible to vote increased from 359,000 to 1,155,400), democratization challenged republican traditions, and the presidency became

Andrew Jackson

the tribune of the people, in what carried the potential for a plebiscitary form of political leadership.

Jackson's direct appeals to the people ("people," at the time, referred to white males) for political support marked the beginning of efforts to develop what is called an "electoral mandate"—an election that empowers a president to lead with the support of the people. Earlier presidents made no such claims. Elections were not "power-generating events," they were merely a way to select an office holder. But Jackson transformed elections into mandates. If the president could create the impression that he spoke for and was empowered by "the people", he might have added clout—a mandate—to govern.

At the time of Jackson's election, eleven new states had been added to the union, and the number of white males who were eligible to vote had reached nearly universal proportions, as property requirements for voting were eliminated in nearly all the states. It was the age of Jacksonian Democracy.

"The president," Jackson said, "is the direct representative of the American people." While today such a view seems quite mundane, in the 1820s it was somewhat radical. The framers did not want the president to speak for, or even to, "the people". Such a link risked demagoguery. The framers hoped to give the president protection from the will of the people so he could better exercise sound, independent judgment; likewise they wanted to protect the people from the president so that the president could not influence public passions and impose his will on Congress.

Jackson fundamentally reordered the relationship of the president to the people, laying the groundwork for populist leadership as a way to overcome the roadblocks inherent in the separation of powers. In dismissing the Whig notion that the president was merely to execute the will of the people as filtered through the Congress, Jackson insisted that it was the president who was the direct representative of the people and as such spoke for the people. The Congress should thus follow the will of the people as expressed through the president. Such a notion transformed the president from clerk to leader.

Jackson opened another door for an ambitious president. By "going public," Jackson expanded the presidential arsenal by linking the president to the people. While few of his immediate successors would fully utilize this opportunity for power, it nonetheless established a new and potentially significant source of influence for future presidents.

Jackson expanded presidential power far beyond his predecessors; leading critics referred to him as "King Andrew" and warned of "executive despotism." Scholar Edward S. Corwin wrote that the presidency under Jackson was "thrust forward as one of three equal departments of government, and to each and every of its powers was imparted new scope, new vitality."[2]

Jackson expanded the "spoils" system, wherein those who get elected can distribute the spoils (rewards) of government. "To the victor go the spoils" was the order of the day, and Jackson used this system to reward his friends. Jackson also expanded the use of the presidential veto to gain power over the legislature and set the national agenda on his terms.

He also underutilized his cabinet and formed an informal set of trusted friends and advisers, a "Kitchen Cabinet," as it was called (because they often met in the White House kitchen). Jackson was often at odds with his regular cabinet, most of whom ended up resigning or being replaced in the first term.

Jackson also expanded the president's removal power when, after firing his treasury secretary without approval of Congress, the president established—over the objections of an irate Senate—that a president hires with Senate consent, but fires on his own. The Senate balked, but Jackson maintained they had no business intruding into the business of the executive branch.

The ambitious congressional rivals Webster, Clay, and Calhoun postponed their rivalry to join together in efforts to combat the growing power of Jackson. The *New York American* could not believe that "in this land of liberty, *all* the powers of our national government would be usurped by a single man, possessing no one qualification for any single trust, and who, like a maniac, or a driveller, should make it his daily pastime to tear our constitutional charter into rags and tatters, and trample the rights of the people under his feet?" "OUR LIBERTIES ARE IN DANGER," warned the New York Whig convention of 1834. "At this moment, if by your votes you concede the powers that are claimed, your *president* has become your MONARCH."[3]

The source of Jackson's power was his link to the people. Jackson celebrated the common man. This, of course, greatly threatened the entrenched elites. "Majority rule, egalitarianism, and power to the people were themes consistently reiterated by President Jackson in his official proclamations and messages to Congress. Pro-Jackson newspapers echoed the president's perspective, while the Democratic party, officially formed by Jackson, served as the president's personal tool for converting democratic rhetoric to public policy."[4] William N. Chambers noted: "At the core of Jackson's importance for the American tradition are four great themes or issues: egalitarianism, democracy, and—as instruments—strong presidential leadership and political party action."[5] Corwin added, "Jackson was a more dominant party leader than Jefferson."

"Democracy" began to replace "Republicanism" in the American iconography. Now, "the people," not the Constitution, not the representatives of the people, but the people ruled (through the president)!

The framers harbored some fears of mass-based democracy and attempted to insulate the president from the pull of popular passions, while at the same time creating a distance between an ambitious president and a potentially powerful ally in the people. The framers feared that the people would animate presidential leadership and that a president might enlist the power of the people in his crusades. Jackson turned the framers' system on its head. Rather than go to the people's representatives, Jackson went directly to the people. He envisioned a presidency in union with the will of the people, serving the majority, not checking it. The president was to be tribune of and for the people. Jackson established a popular base of power from which to lead. The Congress, Jackson felt, should follow the will of the people as expressed through the leadership of the president.

Jackson's battles with Congress reached a head over the controversy dealing with the recharter of the Bank of the United States. Jackson opposed recharter of what he saw as a bank serving the elites, not the people. Congress voted to recharter the Bank against Jackson's objections. He vetoed the legislation.

Prior to that time, presidents felt they could veto only legislation they deemed unconstitutional. Jackson transformed the veto power into a policy tool. The president could, Jackson asserted, veto legislation merely because he disagreed with the contents on policy grounds. Jackson vetoed more bills (12) than all his predecessors combined, and he often exercised the veto on purely policy terms. This broadening of the veto power opened new doors in presidential bargaining with Congress. From this point on, Congress had to take into consideration the political preferences of the president.[6]

Senator Henry Clay expressed grave concerns over the rise of the populist presidency and the use of popular appeals in the Bank dispute:

> Sir, I am surprised and alarmed at the new source of executive power which is found in the result of a presidential election. I had supposed that the Constitution and the laws were the sole source of executive authority . . . that the issue of a presidential election was merely to place the Chief Magistrate in the post assigned to him. But it seems that if, prior to an election certain opinions, no matter how ambiguously put forth by a candidate, are known to the people, those loose opinions, in virtue of the election, incorporate themselves with the Constitution, and afterwards are to be regarded and expounded as parts of the instrument.[7]

Clay sponsored a resolution in the Senate censuring Jackson. It read:

> Resolved. That the President, in the late Executive proceedings in relation to the public revenue, has assumed upon himself authority and power not conferred by the Constitution and laws, but in derogation of both.

The censure vote passed, the first of its kind in U.S. history.

During Jackson's presidency issues of slavery and states' rights continued to plague the nation. South Carolina, objecting to a new tariff law, declared the new law "null, void, and no law, nor binding." Jackson's response to this effort at nullification was firm:

> I consider, then, the power to annul a law of the United States, assumed by one state, incompatible with the existence of the Union, contradicted expressly by the letter of the Constitution, unauthorized by its spirit, inconsistent with every principle on which it was founded, and destructive of the great object for which it was formed.

Jackson then sent U.S. troops to the region. Senator Henry Clay came up with a compromise, and the tensions waned, but not before Jackson's vice president, John C. Calhoun, resigned his office to return to South Carolina, run for the Senate, and lead the opposition to Jackson. In the aftermath of this nullification crisis, President Jackson prophetically warned, "The next pretext will be the negro, or slavery question."

Andrew Jackson dramatically changed the presidency. Attaching the presidency to the people created a new and potentially powerful (as well as potentially dangerous) tool of presidential leadership. The framers thought of the House of Representatives as the most democratic branch of government. Jackson saw the presidency as closest to the people. But there was an irony in Jackson's new power, well noted by the great French observer Alexis de Tocqueville: "General Jackson's power is constantly increasing, but that of the president grows less. The federal government is strong in his hands; it will pass to his successor enfeebled."[8]

To be truly powerful, this new presidency had to be linked to the popular will. Presidential power now rested with the people, as well as the Constitution, and presidents needed to animate popular sentiments, something not easily done. Was the president to *lead* or *follow* the people? Could the president consistently lead the people? And if not, would the populist presidency become truly enfeebled?

Jackson's presidency was "no mere revival of the office; it was a remaking of it."[9] But could Jackson's successors fill his shoes?

Martin van Buren
1837–1841

Andrew Jackson's hand-picked successor, the 5'6" Martin Van Buren,[10] dubbed "the little Magician" because of his political adroitness, was no Jackson. Tocqueville was right: Jackson's successors would be enfeebled. And surprisingly, Van Buren was weak in an area for which his skills were legend: as a politician.

President Van Buren's critics could be devastating. John Quincy Adams wrote: "There are many features in the character of Mr. Van Buren strongly resembling that of Mr. Madison—his calmness, his gentleness of manner, his discretion, his easy and conciliatory temper. But Madison had none of his obsequiousness, his sycophancy, his profound dissimulation and duplicity." Folk hero and Tennessee Congressman Davy Crockett said:

Van Buren is as opposite to General Jackson as dung is to diamond. . . . [He] travels about the country and through the cities in an English coach; has English servants, dressed in uniform—I think they call it livery . . . ; no longer mixes with the sons of little tavern-keepers; forgets all his old companions and friends in the humbler walks of life . . . ; eats in a room by himself; and is so stiff in his gait, and prim in his dress, that he is what the English call a dandy. When he enters the Senate-chamber in the morning he struts and swaggers like a crow in a gutter. He is laced up in corsets, such as women in town wear, and, if possible, tighter than the best of them. It would be difficult to say, from his personal appearance, whether he was a man or woman, but for his large red and gray whiskers.

Martin Van Buren

Two weeks after his inauguration, an economic panic hit the U.S. economy: the Panic of '37. Cautious and unsure of himself, Van Buren's response to the panic was modest. As the depression worsened, Van Buren exercised caution, not leadership. Van Buren's lukewarm response to the crisis led critics to dub him "Martin Van Ruin."

Van Buren governed during tough times. That he failed to respond adequately to the demands of the times marked a failure both in his conception of what the office and times required, as well as a failure of will.

In the aftermath of Jackson's expanded presidency, Congress reasserted its prerogatives and the presidency once again began to shrink.

This dynamic and elastic institution, stretched by Jackson, now contracted in the face of an assertive Congress. While Van Buren helped shape the politics of the two-party system in the U.S., he was unable to put it to full presidential use, and Congress, not the president, rose to the forefront.

William Henry Harrison
1841

The less said about the presidency of William Henry Harrison[11] the better. In fact there isn't much to say about Harrison's presidency. At 68, he was

William H. Harrison

the oldest president ever elected (an honor he would hold until Ronald Reagan). He delivered his 8,578-word inaugural address in a driving rainstorm, caught cold, and died a month later. He was the first president to die in office, and served the shortest term in history. Andrew Jackson derisively called Harrison "our present imbecile chief," and John Quincy Adams spoke of Harrison's "active but shallow mind."

Harrison was a Whig (smaller government) president who believed Congress should set the national agenda. He declared in his inaugural address:

> . . . it is preposterous to suppose that a thought could for a moment have been entertained that the President, placed at the capital, in the center of the country, could better understand the wants and wishes of the people than their own immediate representatives, who spend a part of every year among them, living with them, often laboring with them, and bound to them by the triple tie of interest, duty and affection.

Harrison did leave his footprints on one aspect of the presidency. His activist campaign of 1840, using placards, hats, effigies, campaign songs, banners, stump speeches, parades, and other electoral paraphernalia, was the beginning of modern public campaigning. In this sense, the Jacksonian revolution had truly transformed the presidency. Even Whig candidates had to appeal to the people for authority and power.

John Tyler
1841–1845

John Tyler[12] was the nation's first "President by act of God." When William Henry Harrison died one month after his inauguration, the 6-foot-tall, blue-eyed John Tyler, his vice president, became president. Or did he? At that time, it was unclear whether a vice president who replaces a president became Acting President or President.

In the House of Representatives, John McKeon of Pennsylvania introduced a resolution giving Tyler the title "Acting President." The resolution did not carry.

Tyler acted swiftly, claiming both the office and title of President. While critics dubbed Tyler "His Accidency," the new president was determined to exercise fully his new powers, much to the dismay and disappointment of his fellow Whigs.

But asserting and actually grabbing power are two different things. Tyler faced an early test of strength with "his" cabinet (Harrison holdovers, all). Daniel Webster, the secretary of state, tried to put Tyler in his place, announcing at the first cabinet meeting

> "Mr. President," he said at the first Cabinet meeting, "I suppose you intend to carry on the ideas and customs of your predecessor, and that this

John Tyler

administration inaugurated by President Harrison will continue in the same line of policy under which it has begun. It was our custom in the cabinet of the deceased President, that the President should preside over us. Our custom and proceeding was that all measures whatever, however, relating to the administration were brought before the cabinet, and their settlement was decided by a majority—each member, *and the President, having one vote*."

After a short pause, Tyler responded:

> "I beg your pardon, gentlemen. I am sure I am very glad to have in my
> cabinet such able statesmen as you have proved yourselves to be, and I
> shall be pleased to avail myself of your counsel and advice, but I can never
> consent to being dictated to as to what I shall or shall not do. I, as Presi-
> dent, will be responsible for my administration. I hope to have your co-op-
> eration in carrying out its measures; so long as you see fit to do this, I shall
> be glad to have you with me—when you think otherwise, your resignations
> will be accepted."[13]

Cabinet resignations followed shortly. Tyler was a believer in states'
rights, and as he vetoed bill after bill of the Whig legislative agenda, he
alienated his Whig cohorts and his cabinet. On September 11, 1841, every
member of his cabinet, except Webster, sent Tyler their resignations.
Four years later Tyler's veto of a minor revenue bill was overturned by
Congress—the first override in history. (Tyler was also the first president to face an impeachment resolution, which failed to get the necessary votes.) Tyler became, in Henry Clay's words, "a President without a
party."

In domestic affairs, Tyler's vetoes led to gridlock, as the Whig Tyler repudiated nearly every plank of the Whig program. Tyler wanted to run for
reelection, but was, not surprisingly, repudiated—by the Whigs.

As an example of Tyler's stubbornness and difficulties with Congress,
the case of Caleb Cushing is illustrative. Tyler nominated Cushing for secretary of the treasury. When the Senate refused to confirm Cushing, the
president immediately renominated him. Hours later, after the Senate once
again rejected Cushing, Tyler sent Cushing's nomination to the Senate for
a third time. For the third time in one day, the Senate refused to confirm a
president's cabinet appointment.

In between vetoing legislation, Tyler had time to father fifteen children
(the last, Pearl, was born when Tyler was seventy), by far the most pro-
ductive president in history in this area.

James Polk
1845–1849

After the Whig difficulties with Whig president John Tyler, the Democrats
were able to elect the first "dark horse" in history. James Polk[14] wasn't considered a candidate when the Democratic convention began; in fact, his
name did not even appear on the first seven ballots. But after a stalemate
between Martin Van Buren and Lewis Cass, the convention turned to a compromise candidate the 5'8", white-haired James Polk.

Referred to as "Young Hickory" because he was a protégé of Andrew
Jackson, Polk was a strong, assertive president, who expanded the office

James K. Polk

and used war to expand America. While he accomplished much, he had his critics. John Quincy Adams said of Polk:

> He has no wit, no literature, no point of argument, no gracefulness of delivery, no elegance of language, no philosophy, no pathos, no felicitous impromptus; nothing that can constitute an orator, but confidence, fluency, and labor.

In his inaugural address, Polk enunciated an expansive view of the presidency:

> Although . . . the Chief Magistrate must almost of necessity be chosen by a party and stand pledged to its principles and measures, yet in his official action he should not be the President of a part only, but of the whole people of the United States. While he . . . faithfully carries out in the executive department of the Government the principles and policy of those who have chosen him, he should not be unmindful that our fellow-citizens who have differed with him in opinion are entitled to the full and free exercise of their opinions and judgments, and that the rights of all are entitled to respect and regard.

Historian Page Smith called Polk "a petty, conniving, irascible, small-spirited man," and historian Bernard De Voto said that "Polk's mind was rigid, narrow, obstinate, far from first-rate."

Like his mentor Andrew Jackson, Polk saw the presidency as an office of force and leadership. In his first two years in office, his fellow Democrats controlled both houses of Congress, and Polk used this opportunity to chart a bold course in domestic policy, referred to as the "New Democracy." With Polk in the lead, Congress passed tariff reductions and established an independent treasury system. But it was in foreign affairs that Polk really left his mark.

It was a time of "Manifest Destiny," a phrase coined by John L. O'Sullivan, editor of the *United States Magazine and Democratic Review*. It reflected the spirit of expansionism, territorial and otherwise. The movement westward was in full swing, and the age recognized few limits. Was Manifest Destiny merely a rationale for aggressive acquisition, belligerent and militaristic, or was it the realization of a providentially blessed grand design? Whatever it was, Polk exploited the nationalistic mood and led the nation to significant territorial expansion.

Polk's expansionist agenda advocated annexation of Texas and expanding the Oregon border. Getting the Texas territory required some sleight of hand. After being rejected in an effort to purchase the Texas territory from Mexico, Polk ordered General Zachary Taylor to lead an expedition into Texas. In April 1846, U.S. and Mexican troops clashed, setting off a war in which the U.S. acquired Texas, New Mexico, and California. By brute force, Polk acquired a tremendously valuable chunk of land. Next to Jefferson's purchase of the Louisiana Territory, this was the most important acquisition of land in U.S. history. Abraham Lincoln, a congressman at the time, spoke of Polk and the Mexican War, calling the president "a bewildered, confounded, and miserably perplexed man."

But acquisition of new territory raised thorny issues of sectional balance and slavery. A storm was brewing. From this point until the Civil War, slavery and sectional rivalries would dominate American politics.

Polk was a powerful, assertive president who expanded the Jacksonian model of presidential power. Under his leadership, the president began openly to coordinate the development of the federal budget. He chose to serve only one term, but it was a time of great change and expansion.

Zachary Taylor
1849–1850

Zachary Taylor,[15] 5′9″, with blue eyes, the last true Whig president, and the first president elected with no previous political experience, served two years as president. "Old Rough and Ready," an outsider with no clear agenda, he was a relatively ineffective president. He had a narrow view of presidential leadership and chose not to lead the nation. Of Taylor, Polk

Zachary Taylor

said, "General Taylor is, I have no doubt, a well-meaning old man. He is, however, uneducated, exceedingly ignorant of public affairs, and I should judge, of very ordinary capacity."

Taylor's election was the last gasp of a dying Whig party. Given Taylor's Whig view of a limited presidency, he neglected the possible role of legislative leader and even eschewed patronage as beneath him.

Taylor's self-imposed limitations prevented him from attempting the exercise of strong presidential leadership.

"The Executive . . . has authority to recommend (not to dictate) measures to Congress. Having performed that duty, the Executive department of the Government cannot rightfully control the decision of Congress on any subject of legislation . . . the . . . veto will never be exercised by me except . . . as an extreme measure, to be resorted to only in extraordinary cases . . ."

The issue of slavery dominated Taylor's short time as president. The threat of disunion haunted the politics of the day. Taylor, a southerner, was appalled by talk of secession, but felt helpless in the face of fast-moving events. On July 4, 1850, Taylor developed gastroenteritis and died five days later.

Millard Fillmore
1850–1853

After Zachary Taylor's death, Millard Fillmore[16] assumed the presidency. At 5'9", with blue eyes and thin gray hair, Fillmore was nonetheless an imposing figure. He took office as a crisis was looming over slavery. But as Harry Truman said of Fillmore, "At a time we needed a strong man, what we got was a man that swayed with the slightest breeze."

Fillmore accepted the resignations of all department heads and appointed his own cabinet. This bold assertion of control, however, did not extend to the domain of public policy. Fillmore's whiggish tendencies were self-limiting in an age when the hot issue of slavery needed political leadership.

Millard Fillmore was president during the "Great Guano Wars." Guano, bird droppings, was a much sought after fertilizer. American business clashed with the Peruvian government over this odoriferous issue. He who controlled foul excrement controlled a great deal of currency. Fillmore's government successfully negotiated a treaty with Peru granting American business the profitable rights to extract the guano from islands off Peru.[17]

Shortly after taking office, Fillmore signed the Compromise of 1850. Under the Compromise, California was admitted into the union as a free state, the borders of Texas were defined, the territories of New Mexico and Utah were established, and slavery was abolished in the District of Columbia.

Millard Fillmore

The Compromise also contained the controversial Fugitive Slave Law, which required that northerners help return escaped slaves to their southern owners. The Compromise of 1850 may have postponed the Civil War, but it did little to end the strife caused by slavery.

In 1852, the Whigs refused to nominate Fillmore for another term as president. He ended up joining the nativist Know-Nothing party. As the 1856 presidential nominee of the Know-Nothings, Fillmore won only the state of Maryland. He was offered an honorary degree from Oxford University, but declined, stating, "I had not the advantage of a classical education, and no man should, in my judgment, accept a degree he cannot read."

Franklin Pierce
1853–1857

As the conflict over slavery escalated, the new president, the 5′10″, handsome Franklin Pierce,[18] declared in his inaugural address, "I believe that

Franklin Pierce

involuntary servitude, as it exists in different States of this Confederacy, is recognized by the Constitution. I believe that it stands like any other admitted right, and that the States where it exists are entitled to efficient remedies to enforce the constitutional provisions." But such sentiments, while comforting to the southern states, did little to calm the approaching storm.

Pierce, who had penetrating dark eyes and a drinking habit that led adversaries to call him "a hero of many a well-fought bottle," was a believer in limited government and was perceived as a "Doughface," a northerner who supported the south. Theodore Roosevelt called Pierce "a small politician, of low capacity and mean surroundings, proud to act as the servile tool of men worse than himself but also stronger and abler." Harry Truman referred to Pierce as "another one that was a complete fizzle Pierce didn't know what was going on, and even if he had, he wouldn't of known what to do about it." And Herbert Agar wrote that of "all presidents . . . none was more insignificant that Mr. Pierce."[19]

When Franklin Pierce's long-time friend Nathaniel Hawthorne, author of *The Scarlet Letter*, heard of Pierce's election, he wrote to his friend: "Frank, I pity you—indeed I do, from the bottom of my heart." Pierce was probably the last president who might have been able to prevent the Civil War. His inability to resolve what may have been an unsolvable situation contributed to the coming Civil War. During his presidency, a new political alignment was emerging. The Whigs were collapsing and a new Republican faction was forming. This instability, mixed with deep sectional divisions, made Pierce's efforts at party control of the legislature difficult.

In 1853, the U.S. acquired land, now southern Arizona and New Mexico, from Mexico for $10 million in the Gadsden Purchase. This purchase made possible a direct rail link across Texas and the newly acquired territories all the way to California. Pierce also attempted, but failed, to acquire Cuba for the U.S.

Of course, slavery remained the most important and most divisive issue of the era. The controversial Kansas-Nebraska Act of 1854 repealed the Missouri Compromise of 1820 and allowed settlers in Kansas and Nebraska to decide the question of slavery for themselves. Senator Douglas played the lead role in passage of the Kansas-Nebraska Act, as it was an era when senators were more "event-making" than presidents. In general, the North opposed the bill, but Pierce supported it, hoping to diffuse the tension over the slavery controversy. But it was too little, too late, as slavery polarized the nation and took it to the brink of Civil War.

Pierce was a weak president in a time that cried out for leadership. As he left office, the nation closed in on the tragedy of Civil War.

James Buchanan
1857–1861

The presidency of James Buchanan[20] was dominated, even overwhelmed, by tensions between the North and South over the issue of slavery. While

James Buchanan

Buchanan thought slavery was a moral evil, he also recognized a constitutional right of southern states to allow slavery to exist. He tried to steer a middle course between the pro- and anti-slavery forces. He failed.

The nation's only bachelor president, Buchanan, 6-feet tall and droopy-eyed, proved a weak and ineffective president, who failed to head off southern secession. Ulysses S. Grant, in a letter to a friend, referred to Buchanan as "our present granny executive."

Although Buchanan was a strong Unionist, his limited conception of presidential power prevented him from taking steps to stem the breakup.

Once secession began, Buchanan sat paralyzed, believing the federal government had no authority to coerce the southern states to remain a part of the Union. He sat idly by when action was needed.

Buchanan was a strict constitutional constructionist. He believed the president was authorized to take only the action clearly permitted by the Constitution. This limited view of the office limited Buchanan's efforts to end domestic strife and allowed events to accelerate beyond hope. In his final message to Congress, Buchanan said of the president: "After all, he is no more than the chief executive officer of the Government. His province is not to make but to execute the laws."

Two days after Buchanan took office, the U.S. Supreme Court announced its decision in the *Dred Scott* case. Finding slavery to be lawful under the Constitution, it ruled that blacks whose ancestors had arrived in America as slaves did not qualify as U.S. or state citizens and did not have a citizen's right to sue in federal courts. Also, an enslaved black who escaped to a free state or territory must be returned as property to his or her owner. It further held that Congress had no right to ban slavery in a territory and that the Missouri Compromise of 1820 was unconstitutional. The Dred Scott case, rather than resolving the slavery question, added fuel to the already hot flames.

To make matters worse, in August of 1857, a severe economic downturn hit the banking industry, leading to the Panic of 1857. This plunged the nation into a depression and further heightened the already explosive tensions.

But it was the secession threat that most worried Buchanan. While he believed secession was unconstitutional, he also believed the federal government's hands were tied—that it was unconstitutional for the federal government to use force against a secessionist state. Buchanan's unwillingness to be flexible and move beyond this very limited (and given the times, dangerous) view further emboldened southern secessionists. In his last message to Congress, delivered on December 3, 1860, Buchanan meekly noted "Apart from the execution of the laws, so far as this may be practical, the Executive has no authority to decide what shall be the relations between the Federal Government and South Carolina . . ."

On December 20, 1860, South Carolina officially seceded from the Union. Two weeks later, President Buchanan sent a special message to Congress pleading that it was not too late for a compromise. Within weeks, six more southern states withdrew from the Union. It was either disunion or war.

Buchanan operated in difficult times, but he was weak and ineffective. His vacillation and timidity in the face of impending crisis reflected not only his own shortcomings (as great as they were) but the collapse of presidential leadership generally in the pre-Civil War period.

In his final speech to Congress he said, "I at least meant well for my country." But well meaning or not, Buchanan left his successor a seemingly unsolvable crisis. "If you are as happy, Mr. Lincoln, on entering this house as I am in leaving it and returning home," Buchanan told Abe Lincoln, "you are the happiest man in this country."

Abraham Lincoln
1861–1865

Arguably the greatest president in history, Abraham Lincoln[21] transformed the presidency and the nation. No president more fully assumed the pow-

Abraham Lincoln

ers of the office than Lincoln. He entered the White House when several southern stat.... already seceded and war seemed an inevitability. "We must not be enemies," said Lincoln, but added that "the Union of these States is perpetual." But it was too late. He couldn't have it both ways.

Lincoln came to power on the eve of the great Civil War. His accomplishments—seeing the nation through the Civil War, serving as a war president, freeing the slaves, exercising extraordinary emergency power with skill and grace, preserving the Union, and re-creating the American sense of nationhood—serve as tribute to his greatness. A nation on the verge of self-destruction was re-created as a fuller, more democratic, and more just country.[22]

Lincoln was a complex, even contradictory man, whom historian Richard Hofstadter called "thoroughly and completely the politician." Lincoln was capable of eloquence and humor, but also melancholy and deep depression. Tall, a lanky 6'4", and the first president to have a beard, Lincoln looked anything but a president. Yet his external gawkiness masked a dignity and honor of truly remarkable proportions. A man of unquenchable ambition yet deep principle, he commanded a savage war while speaking to our "better angels."

Longfellow saw Lincoln as "a colossus holding up his burning heart in his hand to light up the sea of life." But *Harper's Weekly* referred to Lincoln as "Filthy Story-Teller, Despot, Liar, Thief, Braggart, Buffoon, Usurper, Monster, Ignoramus Abe, Old Scoundrel, Perjurer, Robber, Swindler, Tyrant, Field-Butcher, Land-Pirate" and the *New York Herald* called Lincoln "cowardly, mean, and vicious," adding that the president was "incompetent, ignorant, and desperate."

Walt Whitman described Lincoln:

> . . . his unusual and uncouth height, dress of complete black, stovepipe hat pushed back on the head, dark-brown complexion, seamed and wrinkled yet canny-looking face, his black, bushy head of hair, disproportionately long neck, and hands held behind as he stood observing the people. . . . Four mighty and primal hands will be needed to the complete limning of this man's portrait—the eyes and brains and finger-touch of Plutarch and Aeschylus and Michael Angelo, assisted by Rabelais.[23]

A visitor to the White House from Ohio also described the president:

> Mr. Lincoln was the homeliest man I ever saw. His body seemed to me a huge skeleton in clothes. Tall as he was, his hands and feet looked out of proportion, so long and clumsy were they. Every movement was awkward in the extreme. . . . He had a face that defied artistic skill to soften or idealize. There follows a reference to the oft-mentioned contrast of the face in repose and in animation: It brightened, like a lit lantern, when animated. His dull eyes would fairly sparkle with fun, or express as kindly a look as I ever saw, when moved by some matter of human interest.[24]

Lincoln was a president as teacher. He knew the value of stories and humor as tools of education. Lincoln's stories added depth, meaning, and context to his more important points and messages. His stories brought him closer to his audience and added to his ability to persuade and inspire. So too with his humor. Lincoln often interspersed wit into his speeches and conversations, and to good effect. When asked how he liked being president, Lincoln responded:

> Well, you have heard the story, haven't you, about the man as he was ridden out of town on a rail, tarred and feathered? Somebody asked him how he liked it, and his reply was if it was not for the honor of the thing, he would much rather walk.

A foreign diplomat came upon Lincoln while he was polishing his shoes. "What, Mr. President," he cried, "you black your own boots?" "Yes," said Lincoln, "whose do you black?"

Nearly every day, visitors would go to the White House to see the president. While it sounds amazing in an age of heightened security and risks of terrorist attacks, Lincoln—even during the Civil War—saw nearly every visitor, petitioner, or office-seeker who sought an audience. These "public-opinion baths" helped Lincoln stay in touch with the people.

As Lincoln prepared for what Emerson called "the hurricane in which he was called to the helm," the new president knew war was all but inevitable. He did, however, hold out one last olive branch. At the end of his inaugural address he spoke directly to the southern states:

> In your hands, my dissatisfied fellow-countrymen, and not in mine, is the momentous issue of civil war. The Government will not assail you. You can have no conflict without being yourselves the aggressors. I am loath to close. We are not enemies but friends. We must not be enemies. Though passion may have strained, it must not break our bonds of affection. The mystic chords of memory, stretching from every battlefield and patriot grave to every living heart and hearthstone all over this broad land, will yet swell the chorus of the Union, when again touched, as surely they will be, by the better angels of our nature.

But events had already eclipsed Lincoln's hopes. There would be war.

The Civil War began during a Congressional recess. Lincoln did not, as one might expect, call the newly elected Congress into session; nor did he wait for Congress to authorize action—he acted. The president asked, "Must a government of necessity, be too strong for the liberties of its own people, or too weak to maintain its own existence?" Lincoln exercised extraordinary and extraconstitutional emergency power. Lincoln used emergency powers with relative restraint; he used these powers not to subvert democracy, but to save it.

Rejecting normal constitutional limitations, the president believed it his primary duty to save the Union. This higher goal justified his emergency actions. In a letter to Samuel Chase, Lincoln wrote: "These rebels are violating the Constitution to destroy the Union; I will violate the Constitution, if necessary, to save the Union; and I suspect, Chase, that our Constitution is going to have a rough time of it before we get done with this row."[25]

In an effort to meet the challenge of Civil War, Lincoln took a series of dramatic and constitutionally questionable steps in absence of a declaration of war or congressional authorization: he called for new troops, declared a blockade of southern ports, commenced military action, suspended habeas corpus. Later, in 1862, he would unilaterally order the emancipation of slaves. This Emancipation Proclamation, which Charles A. Beard called "the most stupendous act of sequestration in the history of Anglo-Saxon jurisprudence" was ordered without the consent of Congress.

Lincoln justified his actions on the basis of a "doctrine of necessity":

> [My] oath to preserve the Constitution to the best of my ability imposed upon me the duty of preserving, by every indispensable means, that government. . . . Was it possible to lose the nation and yet preserve the Constitution? By general law, life and limb must be protected, yet often a limb must be amputated to save a life; but a life is never wisely given to save a limb. I felt that measures otherwise unconstitutional might become lawful by becoming indispensable to the preservation of the Constitution through the preservation of the nation. Right or wrong, I assumed this ground, and now avow it. I could not feel that, to the best of my ability, I had even tried to preserve the Constitution, if, to save slavery or any minor matter, I should permit the wreck of government, country, and Constitution all together.

The Civil War forced Lincoln to change the very relationship of the presidency to the constitutional order. The unprecedented emergency of the Civil War, Lincoln believed, allowed him to assume powers no previous president claimed. He would not allow the Union to dissolve and the nation crumble. The president had taken an oath to make sure the laws are faithfully executed. The southern rebellion was preventing that. And so, Lincoln asked: "Are all of the laws *but one* to go unexecuted, and the Government itself go to pieces lest that one be violated?"[26]

Some critics charged Lincoln with setting up a dictatorship. Lincoln felt he had no other choice. Lincoln's use of prerogative power during the Civil War was daunting. So broadly did Lincoln interpret his emergency power that some scholars describe it as a "constitutional dictatorship."[27] Lincoln admitted that some of his actions were not "strictly legal," but they were necessary. Thus, Lincoln greatly expanded the scope of presidential power.

As the war proceeded slowly and painfully toward Union victory, Lincoln used the opportunity to redefine American nationhood. He did so in a variety of ways, but nowhere is his vision more clearly articulated than in his Gettysburg Address, and Second Inaugural Address.

On the battlefield at Gettysburg, Lincoln sanctified the sacrifice made by the troops who fell, but he also distilled the true meaning of the war into a very few words. The blood of the dead and the sacred honor of the past merge to create "a new birth of freedom." The address fused the sacred with the secular, with images of sacrifice and redemption. These brave men died for an abstract but powerful idea: "the proposition that all men are created equal," and that "government of the people, by the people, for the people, shall not perish from the earth."

In a mere 272 words, Lincoln transformed the purpose of the nation. The address, printed in its entirety, reads:

> Four score and seven years ago our fathers brought forth on this continent, a new nation, conceived in Liberty, and dedicated to the proposition that all men are created equal.
>
> Now we are engaged in a great civil war, testing whether that nation or any nation so conceived and so dedicated, can long endure. We are met on a great battle-field of that war. We have come to dedicate a portion of that field, as a final resting place for those who here gave their lives that the nation might live. It is altogether fitting and proper that we should do this.
>
> But, in a larger sense, we can not dedicate—we can not consecrate—we can not hallow—this ground. The brave men, living and dead, who struggled here, have consecrated it, far above our poor power to add or detract. The world will little note, nor long remember what we say here, but it can never forget what they did here. It is for us the living, rather, to be dedicated here to the unfinished work which they who fought here have thus far so nobly advanced. It is rather for us to be here dedicated to the great task remaining before us—that from these honored dead we take increased devotion to that cause for which they gave the last full measure of devotion—that we here highly resolve that these dead shall not have died in vain—that this nation, under God, shall have a new birth of freedom—and that government of the people, by the people, for the people, shall not perish from the earth.

Lincoln gave meaning to the events of Civil War by linking the past (founding of the U.S. and the Declaration of Independence), with the present (tragedy of war, loss, and sacrifice), and to the future (the survivors were to create "a new birth of freedom.") It was a shift from negative liberty to positive liberty, a dramatic transformation of the American ethos. Lincoln elevated the Declaration of Independence over the Constitution as a primary American icon. As historian Garry Wills noted, "Lincoln not only put the Declaration in a new light as a matter of founding *law*, but put its central proposition, equality, in a newly favored position as a principle of the Constitution."[28]

In Lincoln's second inaugural address he revisited some of the themes presented at Gettysburg, but his tone was more religious. The war was divine punishment for the sin of slavery.

> The Almighty has His own purposes. "Woe unto the world because of offences! For it must needs be that offences come; but woe to that man by whom the offence cometh!" If we shall suppose that American Slavery is

one of those offences which, in the providence of God, must needs come, but which, having continued through His appointed time, He now wills to remove, and that He gives to both North and South, this terrible war, as the woe due to those by whom the offence came, shall we discern therein any departure from those divine attributes which the believers in a Living God always ascribe to Him? Fondly do we hope—fervently do we pray—that this mighty scourge of war may speedily pass away. Yet, if God wills that it continue, until all the wealth piled by the bond-man's two hundred and fifty years of unrequited toil shall be sunk, and until every drop of blood drawn with the lash, shall be paid by another drawn with the sword, as was said three thousand years ago, so still it must be said "the judgments of the Lord, are true and righteous altogether."

With malice toward none; with charity for all; with firmness in the right, as God gives us to see the right, let us strive on to finish the work we are in; to bind up the nation's wounds; to care for him who shall have borne the battle, and for his widow, and his orphan—to do all which may achieve and cherish a just, and a lasting peace, among ourselves, and with all nations.

As political scientist Bruce Miroff writes of the second inaugural address:

With the war all but won, with his reelection secured and his place in history already taking form, Lincoln was ready to ask more of the American people than he had ever done before. The second inaugural address called for a painful self-examination, so that the American people could come to terms with their historic failings. Lincoln himself had undergone this self-examination and had accepted the "humiliation" it necessitated. Remaining close to the people as a democratic leader, he asked them to share his experience and to face the deepest truths about themselves. The democratic leader would not speak to the people from on high or proclaim the superiority of his own political burdens; he would educate the people about a legacy of guilt and a possibility of redemption that leader and followers shared. In the second inaugural address, Lincoln left a remarkable example of what democratic leadership in America might attempt to be.[29]

The cumulative effect of these two dramatic speeches underscored the shift that was taking place. As historian James McPherson has written:

The United States went to war in 1861 to preserve the *Union*; it emerged from war in 1865 having created a *nation*. Before 1861 the two words "United States" were generally used as a plural noun: "the United States *are* a republic." After 1865 the United States became a singular noun. The loose union of states became a nation. Lincoln's wartime speeches marked this transition.[30]

While Lincoln was a devoted and masterful politician, during most of his presidency he was largely unpopular and often unsuccessful at meeting his war aims, getting the Congress to bend to his will, or even controlling his own administration. As Lincoln biographer David Donald has written:

> ... the same President who so drastically expanded the scope of his office by the assertion of his war powers under the Constitution was an executive who had singularly little impact either upon Congress or upon his own administrative aides. Just after his triumphant reelection in 1864, Lincoln remarked, with as much insight as wit, that he hoped he could exercise some influence with the incoming administration.[31]

During the Civil War, Lincoln practically became the American government. Careful to relate his actions to his "duty as commander-in-chief," Lincoln engaged in actions which were clearly unconstitutional. But Lincoln believed that his authority stemmed from the Constitution itself, and once said that: "As commander-in-chief of the Army and Navy in time of war, I suppose I have a right to take any measure which may best subdue the enemy."[32]

Lincoln seemed to claim a right to act in disregard of or against the Constitution when a national emergency threatened the government. When the Congress was unavailable, so Lincoln's reasoning went, the president had the right—nay, the duty—to act, even if his actions were in violation of the law. Lincoln also suggested that he was justified in his actions because the president possessed certain war powers that allowed him to act in defense of the Union. Since his oath of office called upon him to "preserve, protect, and defend the Constitution," Lincoln's actions were—in his eyes—taken to uphold the oath. His efforts were to preserve the Constitution, and thus his actions were justified (if not strictly legal).

Lincoln's violations of personal liberty were significant. After the outbreak of hostilities, Lincoln decided that the procedures for controlling disloyalty were inadequate. He decided that the right to habeas corpus should be suspended and that civilians should be tried in military courts. Three court cases are of particular interest to us regarding this issue.

Ex Parte Merryman (17 Fed. Cas. No. 9487, 1861). One of the victims of Lincoln's orders was John Merryman. Merryman was a civilian being held under military arrest without the privilege of habeas corpus (he was accused of treason). He petitioned Chief Justice Taney of the Supreme Court for a writ of habeas corpus. Justice Taney, acting alone, defied Lincoln and ordered that the writ be issued. In that decision, Taney suggested that the president had no power to suspend habeas corpus, that the military had no power to detain a civilian (even if ordered by the president), and that Merryman was entitled to an immediate release. The commanding general in this matter, George Cadwalader, refused to honor the chief justice's order on the grounds that he—Cadwalader—was authorized by the president to suspend the writ. Taney was helpless, all he could do was file his opinion, and write: "I have exercised all the power which the constitution and laws confer upon me, but that power has been resisted by a force too strong for me to overcome."[33]

As Clinton Rossiter wrote regarding this case:

> The one great precedent is what Lincoln did, not what Taney said. Future Presidents will know where to look for historical support. So long as public opinion sustains the President, as a sufficient amount of it sustained Lincoln in his shadowy tilt with Taney and throughout the rest of the war, he has nothing to fear from the displeasure of the courts.[34]

Ex Parte Milligan (4 Wallace 2, 18 L. Ed. 281, 1866). L.P. Milligan, along with some associates, was arrested in Indiana by the military and accused of treason. He was sentenced to be hanged, but President Johnson commuted the sentence to life imprisonment. Milligan petitioned the courts, which unanimously held that the military commission was unlawful and that Milligan was to be freed.

On the surface it appears that the Court acted boldly and stood up to the president in its defense of the rights of Mr. Milligan, but did it? When the Court handed down its decision, the war was over, the danger subsided, and Lincoln, the initiator of Milligan's internment, was dead and buried. The Court's decision did not affect the president who ordered the action, and it did not affect the emergency that the Union faced.

The words of the Court in its defense of the rights of Mr. Milligan are certainly grand, but the words do no reflect the realities of the political conflict that developed between the president and the courts; the conflict the courts conveniently avoided until Lincoln had long since left the scene. The words of Justice Davis seem a bit absurd when one considers the context in which they were delivered. Davis's grand statement read, in part:

> The Constitution of the United States is a law for rulers and people, equally in war and peace, and covers with the shield of its protection all classes of men, at all times, and under all circumstances. No doctrine, involving more pernicious consequences was ever invented by the writ of man than that any of its provisions can be suspended during any of the great exigencies of government.[35]

And Rossiter writes:

> As a restraint upon a President beset by martial crisis it was then, and is now, of practically no value whatsoever. It cannot be emphasized too strongly that the decision in this case followed the close of the rebellion by a full year, altered not in the slightest degree the extraordinary methods through which that rebellion had been suppressed, and did nothing more than deliver from jail a handful of rascals who in any event would have probably gained their freedom in short order . . . In sum, *Ex Parte Milligan* is sound doctrine in forbidding the presidential establishment of military commissions for the trial of civilians in areas where the civil courts are open—but it is little else. Its general observations on the war powers are no more valid today than they were in 1866 [sic]. Here again the law of the Constitution is what Lincoln did in the crisis, not what the court said later.[36]

The Prize Cases: 2 Black 635 (1863). The Prize Cases rose out of the president's blockade of the confederacy, which Lincoln ordered in the early days of the Civil War. In this case, four ships had been captured by Union ships, and brought into ports and labeled as "prizes." The Supreme Court was called upon once again to decide a question of presidential power. The Court was being asked whether the president, in a time of war, had the right to order this blockade. The Court, in a 5–4 decision answered yes. Justice Grier wrote:

> If a war be made by invasion of a foreign nation, the President is not only authorized to resist force by force. He does not initiate the war, but is bound to accept the challenges without waiting for any special legislative authority. And whether the hostile party be a foreign invader, or States organized in rebellion, it is nonetheless a war, although the declaration of it be *"unilateral . . ."*
>
> This greatest of civil wars was not gradually developed by popular commotion, tumultuous assemblies, or local unorganized insurrections. However long may have been its previous conception, it nevertheless sprung forth suddenly from the parent brain, a Minerva in the full panoply of *war.* The President was bound to meet it in the shape it presented itself, without waiting for Congress to baptize it with a name; and no name given to it by him or them could change the fact . . .
>
> Whether the President is fulfilling his duties, as Commander-in-chief, in suppressing an insurrection, has met with such armed hostile resistance, and a civil war of such alarming proportions as will compel him according to them the character of belligerents, is a question to be decided by him, and this Court must be governed by the decision and acts of the political department of the Government to which this power was entrusted. He must determine what degree of force the crisis demands. The proclamation of blockade is itself official and conclusive evidence to the Court that a state of war existed which demanded and authorized a recourse to such a measure, under the circumstances peculiar to the case.[37]

The Prize cases serve as yet another example of a court rationalizing presidential extensions of power in emergencies. The president, acting without a congressionally declared war and in the absence of authorizing legislation, ordered the blockade. The courts agreed with this extension of presidential power, and in the future this case would have an important bearing on presidents who sought to expand the boundaries of their power.

If, as Justice Grier wrote, the question of how hostilities will be met must be decided "by him" (the president), then who is to stand up and defend the rights of the citizenry, the Constitution, and the statutes? Justice Grier's view sounds dangerously like a reliance on Locke's "prerogative" power. If the president decides all matters of policy relating to wars and hostilities, there are no safeguards. Here the importance of the Court diminishes in the face of the emergency powers of the president.

Lincoln's actions during the Civil War, his repeated extensions of presidential power, his extraconstitutional, extralegal actions led him to the position, critics charged, of quasi-dictator. The Supreme Court (Justice Taney, sitting as circuit justice), when asked to review the president's actions, responded by making a weak attempt to check the president in the Merryman case; backing away from the president until after the crisis and the president had passed away in the Milligan case; and backing away from the already bloated powers of the president in the Prize cases. The Court's record during the Civil War is not an altogether distinguished one when one looks at the realities of the cases instead of the words with which the Court chose to condemn Lincoln.

The Court's intent in Merryman may have been genuine and well-founded, but it did not attempt to do more than have the chief justice make a lame appeal to the president (What else could it have done?). This was an excellent example of just how weak the courts can be when facing a resolute president. In the Milligan case, the Court's words are strong and well-presented, but they were a few years too late. The Court, in the Civil War, did little to control presidential extensions of power. Perhaps there was little it could have done.

Additional examples of Lincoln's emergency actions can be seen in such acts as the seizure of newspapers, arrest of editors,[38] and the famous Emancipation Proclamation—issued as an example of his powers as commander-in-chief in time of war. During the Civil War (and perhaps because of it), Lincoln acted either in the absence of congressional consent or in disregard of it.[39]

When faced with the domestic crisis of the Civil War, Lincoln became a "Constitutional Dictator." He assumed the "prerogative" power (as Locke

The first reading of the Emancipation Proclamation before the cabinet

described it), and took unto himself powers otherwise reserved for the other branches of government. The Civil War presidency of Abraham Lincoln serves as an excellent example of the differences in power between the "Normal Conditions Presidency," and the "Emergency Presidency."

If Lincoln ranks as one of if not *the* greatest president, it is with good reason. He was a great man and a great president. In the midst of a vicious and divisive Civil War, he appealed to our better angels. His methods may have raised concerns, but his principles and purposes were of the highest order. He stretched the Constitution but preserved the Union. As George Fort Milton noted, no other president "found so many new sources of executive power, nor so expanded and perfected those others had already used."

On Good Friday, April 14, 1865, just five days after the Union victory in the Civil War, Lincoln was killed. "Now he belongs to the ages," Secretary Stanton said. Poet Walt Whitman wrote:

Oh Captain! My Captain! Our fearful trip is done,
The ship has weather'd every rack, the prize we sought is won,
The port is near, the bells I hear, the people all exulting,
While follow eyes the steady keel, the vessel grim and daring;
　But O heart! heart! heart!
　　O the bleeding drops of red,
　　　Where on the deck my Captain lies,
　　　Fallen cold and dead.

The years from Jackson to Lincoln resembled a roller coaster ride for the presidency. Andrew Jackson helped make the president a more direct

The assassination of President Lincoln at Ford's Theatre

and popular representative of the people, adding to the arsenal of presidential power. But the congressional reaction against Jackson's successors diminished the executive as Congress reasserted its power. While Polk was able to grab some power, most of the presidents of this era served the will of Congress.

Then came Lincoln! The Civil War opened a window of opportunity for executive aggrandizement, and Lincoln as commander-in-chief in time of war took full use of the opportunity. He was arguably the most powerful president to date, and he used his great power to preserve the Union and expand democracy.

4

Reaction and Shrinking/
The World Stage
Andrew Johnson to Woodrow Wilson

In the aftermath of the Civil War and the powerful presidency of Abraham Lincoln, Congress reasserted itself and chained in and shrank the presidency. A series of weak presidents followed Lincoln until the rise of the American empire in the late 1800s. A limited nation required a limited presidency. But as the economy of the United States grew and as the U.S. became a world power, the presidency began to change. Empire and power called forth a strong presidency. By the end of this period, the presidency again returned to center stage in the American political drama.

After the Civil War, the pace of expansion and settlement picked up. People headed west. By 1876, the U.S. had grown to 38 states. By 1901, the U.S. had grown to fill its continental borders.

Andrew Johnson
1865–1869

The reaction against executive power that followed the Civil War led to a dramatic shrinking of executive power, as congressional government characterized the American system for 30 years. Congress could have had no better foil in beginning this process than the stubborn, rigid, and abrasive Andrew Johnson.[1]

Johnson's Senate opponent, Stewart of Nevada, described Johnson as "the most untruthful, treacherous, and cruel person who had ever held a place of power in the United States." No sooner did Johnson take the oath of office than clashes broke out between the new administration and a Congress determined to reassert its power and shape the coming Reconstruction.

President Johnson played a pivotal role in the deconstruction of the presidency. He inherited a powerful wartime presidency but, in the aftermath of war, failed to successfully defend the prerogatives of the institution, and left the office weaker and more vulnerable to the will of Congress.

Johnson became embroiled in a divisive battle with Congress over Reconstruction. Johnson followed Lincoln's lead in promoting a mild recon-

Andrew Johnson

struction designed to restore Union quickly. But the Republican leadership in Congress, the "radicals," led by Senator Charles Sumner of Massachusetts, were determined to extract a harsh price from the southern states.

The separation of powers often sets up a tug-of-war between the executive and Congress for control of policy. The Republican Congress of the Reconstruction era had little patience for Johnson and was determined to undermine his efforts and grab control of policy. It did so on Reconstruction, and, after the Republicans won a convincing victory in the 1866 midterm elections, passed measure after measure designed to strip the presidency of its powers.

Johnson seemed helpless in the face of the Congress. Determined to protect the authority of his office, Johnson fought back. The Radicals in Congress were livid when Johnson, during a congressional recess in December 1865, proposed a lenient reconstruction policy. When Congress reconvened, President Johnson announced that Reconstruction was complete and that every rebel state met his qualifications for readmission to the Union. However it was anything but finished.

The Democrat Johnson and the Republican Congress engaged in open warfare. Congress dumped the president's plan for Reconstruction, replacing it with one of its own, a harsher peace than the president preferred. Congress pushed for the Fourteenth Amendment to the Constitution, which would forbid any state to deny any citizen "due process" or "equal protection" of the law. Johnson pressed southern states to reject the amendment, but it passed anyway.

Johnson took his case directly to the people. His appeals fell mostly on deaf ears. Johnson engaged in bombast and name-calling. *The Nation* magazine characterized Johnson's charges as "vulgar, egotistical and occasionally profane."

When the congressional Radicals passed the Tenure of Office Act, a blatant effort to reclaim the power possessed by the president to fire certain executive branch employees without the consent of the Senate, Johnson reacted. He fired Secretary of War Edwin M. Stanton (who barricaded himself in his office in an effort to stave off removal), and claimed the act was an unconstitutional invasion of his power. This was just what the Congress needed to begin impeachment proceedings against Johnson.

The Senate as a court of impeachment for the trial of Andrew Johnson

The clashes between Johnson and the Congress grew angrier and angrier, with both sides putting their worst foot forward. Efforts began in the House to develop articles of impeachment against Johnson. Finally, eleven articles of impeachment were brought against the president.

The impeachment effort against Andrew Johnson was a largely partisan, rather wooly affair. *New York Tribune* editor, Horace Greeley, called Johnson "an aching tooth in the national jaw, a screeching infant in a crowded lecture room," adding "There is no peace or comfort till he is out." Johnson's Republican congressional critics denounced him as "an ungrateful, despicable, besotted traitorous man—an incubus." Another said he dragged the robes of office through "the purloins and filth of treason." And Johnson's advisors were referred to as "the worst men that ever crawled like filthy reptiles of the footstool of power." No accusation was too wild for the Johnson-bashers. He was accused of aiding in the assassination of Abraham Lincoln, of fathering an illegitimate son, of conspiring to help the Confederacy rise again. The House voted to recommend articles of impeachment to the Senate. But after a Senate trial, the conviction failed by one vote: that of Kansas Republican Senator Edmund Ross. In the next election Ross was thrown out of office, but history remembers him as a hero who stood up for justice. In his prize-winning book, *Profiles in Courage,* John F. Kennedy praised Ross as a case study of integrity in the face of unyielding pressure.

Impeachment proceedings were instituted against President Johnson by the House of Representatives on February 24, 1868, with the following resolution: "Resolved: that Andrew Johnson be impeached of high crimes and misdemeanors." The charges brought against him included usurpation of the law, corrupt use of the veto power, interference at elections, and misdemeanors. Probably the most revealing was Article 10, which said it was an impeachable offense for the president to speak ill of Congress "with a loud voice."

After hearings on the charges, the House voted 126–47 to impeach Johnson, the first time in history a president had been impeached. This moved events to the Senate, where Chief Justice Salmon P. Chase was to preside over the trial against the president.

Associate Justice Samuel Nelson of the Supreme Court administered the following oath to the Chief Justice: "I do solemnly swear that in all things appertaining to the trial of the impeachment of Andrew Johnson, President of the United States, now pending, I will do impartial justice according to the Constitution and laws. So help me God." This oath was then administered by the Chief Justice to the 54 members of the Senate.

The impeachment trial of Andrew Johnson lasted six weeks. The case against the president was weak and politically motivated.

The vote on May 16, 1868, to convict Johnson was 35 guilty, 19 not guilty, one short of the two-thirds needed to convict a president. The trial ended on May 26, 1868 with Johnson acquitted. But the president and the presidency had been put in its place. If Johnson had been convicted, the independence of the executive might have been all but destroyed. As it was, the presidency was severely weakened. Senator Trumball, who voted not guilty gave his reasoning:

> Once set the example of impeaching the President, for what, when the excitement of the hour shall have subsided will be regarded as insufficient causes, . . . and no future president will be safe who happens to differ with a majority of the House and two-thirds of the Senate on any measure deemed by them important, particularly if of a political character. Blinded by partisan zeal, with such an example before them, they will not scruple to remove out of the way any obstacle to the accomplishment of their purposes, and what then becomes of the checks and balances of the Constitution, so carefully devised and so vital to its perpetuity? They are all gone.[2]

All was not tragedy for Andrew Johnson. His most valuable achievement was the purchase of Alaska from Russia for $7.2 million in 1867. Derisively referred to as "Seward's Folly," "Seward's Icebox," or "Johnson's Polar Bear Garden," (Seward was secretary of state and chief negotiator of the deal), it was not long before the benefits of this purchase became clear.

Navigating the choppy waters of the post-Civil War era required tact, subtleness, nuance, and flexibility—qualities Johnson lacked in abundance. He could not bend, so Congress decided to try to break him.

Some historians give Johnson credit for protecting the authority of the presidency by preventing a coup by the Radicals in Congress. But the reality is probably that he much weakened the presidency by intemperate behavior and bad decision making, and invited a harsh response by a Radical Congress that was looking for an opportunity to humble the president and limit the presidency. Johnson gave them the opportunity.

Ulysses S. Grant
1869–1877

After the turmoil of Civil War, impeachment, and years of strife, the voters turned to a popular military hero for leadership. But Ulysses S. Grant,[3] a stocky, hard-drinking, politically inexperienced executive, proved unfit for the task of being president.

In the post-Civil War years, the U.S. experienced an unparalleled period of growth. The railroads opened the West, and agriculture and industry flourished. Immigration also expanded greatly. The age of the Robber Barons ensued, and the Congress as well as the Supreme Court lent support to corporate expansion and development. During this period, government grew as well.

The shrinking of the presidency continued during the Grant years. But unlike his predecessor, who fought unsuccessfully to protect the authority of the presidency, Grant seemed more than willing to play the role of ob-

Ulysses S. Grant

server in the political pageant unfolding before him. After the executive-congressional hostility of the Johnson years, Grant made peace with Congress—but on Congress's terms.

Politically inept and managerially lax, Grant saw the presidency as a purely administrative office, not as a vehicle for national leadership. That suited the Congress just fine. During the Grant years, congressional power reached its zenith.

It was also during the Grant years that the first woman candidate for president emerged. Victoria Woodhull (1838–1927), spiritualist, first woman to open a Wall Street brokerage firm, and newspaper publisher, ran for president in 1872 as the nominee of the newly formed Equal Rights Party. Lamentably, on election day Woodhull was in jail facing charges ranging from slander to adultery. Running as Woodhull's vice president was Fredrick Douglass, the first black vice presidential candidate.

Grant's limited view of his role as president not only fostered weak political leadership but allowed abuses of power and corruption to overwhelm his administration. A series of scandals plagued Grant's administration, including the Whisky Ring scandal, bribery of cabinet officials, the Credit Mobilier scandal, and others. All attest to Grant's weak management of his own administration.

Grant was personally honest but irretrievably inept. He was never himself implicated in the scandals of the administration, but his lax management and naive views allowed those whom he trusted to take advantage of their positions and to poison the administration.

During Grant's term Reconstruction continued, civil service reform was promoted (unsuccessfully), and troubling military clashes with Native-American tribes escalated. In 1873, an economic panic brought about a financial crash.

Grant left the presidency in 1877, after two terms. His last State of the Union message was an astonishing admission of failure. It began, "It was my fortune, or misfortune, to be called to the office of Chief Executive without any previous political training. From the age of 17, I had never even witnessed the excitement attending a Presidential campaign but twice antecedent to my own candidacy, and at but one of them was I eligible as a voter." Because of his political inexperience, "it is but reasonable to suppose that errors of judgement must have occurred." He did not shoulder all the blame: "It is not necessarily evidence of blunder on the part of the Executive because there are these differences of views. Mistakes have been made, as all can see and I admit. . . . " He went on to place the blame indirectly on himself; saying that the mistakes were "oftener in the selections made of the assistants appointed to aid in carrying out the various duties of administering the Government" than in his own actions.

Grant is considered a failure as president. His limited view of the office, limited experience, and limited abilities all contributed to this failure, as did the rise of congressional assertiveness. He is most remembered for the scandals that took place during his tenure, a time snidely referred to as the Era of Good Stealing.

Rutherford B. Hayes
1877–1881

After the failed presidencies of Johnson and Grant, in the midst of congressional ascendency, Rutherford B. Hayes[4] came along and arrested, but did not reverse, the trend toward congressional dominance. Grant left the

Rutherford B. Hayes

presidency at perhaps its lowest ebb ever. Hayes, at 5′8″, with a long beard, governed during what was called the Gilded Age. It was a time of economic growth, a rise in immigration, harsh labor-business disputes, and a growing women's movement.

Henry Adams said of Hayes, "He is a third-rate nonentity whose only recommendation is that he is obnoxious to no one." But Hayes was much more than this. His motto, "He serves his party best who serves his country best" is an admirable sentiment in any age.

The weakness of the presidency in this period was noticed by the observant Englishman Walter Bagehot, who found fault with the American constitutional system and the weakness of the presidency, writing: "The executive is crippled by not getting the law it needs, and the legislature is spoiled by having to act without responsibility; the executive becomes unfit for its name, since it cannot execute what it decides on; the legislature is demoralized by liberty, by taking decisions of which others [and not itself] will suffer the effects."[5]

Hayes came to the presidency after the hotly contested and harshly disputed election of 1876. One of the dirtiest campaigns in history featured two of the cleanest candidates ever. Samuel J. Tilden, Governor of New York, won 51 percent of the popular vote and Hayes conceded defeat to a reporter. But Republicans charged voter fraud in three southern states, and the disputed election went to the House of Representatives for resolution. Congress named a special commission to recommend a solution to the dispute. After a bizarre back and forth process, the commission awarded Hayes all the disputed votes, and he won the election. In "exchange," Republicans in Congress agreed to withdraw all federal troops from the South and end Reconstruction. Hayes was president. But charges of a stolen election hounded him, and opponents referred to Hayes as RutherFRAUD B. Hayes, and His Fraudulency.

Hayes kept to the Republican deal and ended Reconstruction. He also promoted civil service reform and good government. He stood firm in asserting the rights of the executive in the face of Congressional pressure. While his accomplishments were few, he stopped the steady draw of power away from the presidency and attempted to reassert some executive authority.

James A. Garfield
1881

James A. Garfield,[6] 6 feet tall, with blue eyes, a full beard, and reddish-brown hair, served as president for only 200 days (80 of which he spent as an invalid). He was the second president to be assassinated, and served the second shortest term ever. He embraced a Whig view of the presidency, and did not intend to lead the Congress. "My God," he proclaimed on assuming office, "what is there in this place that a man should even want to get into it?" Grant said of him, "Garfield has shown that he is not possessed of the backbone of an angleworm." And Rutherford Hayes said of Garfield, "He was not executive in his talents—not original, not firm, not a moral force. He leaned on others—could not face a frowning world; his habits suf-

James A. Garfield

fered from Washington life. His course at various times when trouble came betrayed weakness."

A polished orator, Garfield was, however, a weak man who often bent to the pressure of party bosses. In the summer of 1881, after only four months in office, he was shot twice in the back by a disgruntled office-seeker. He died two months later, on September 19.

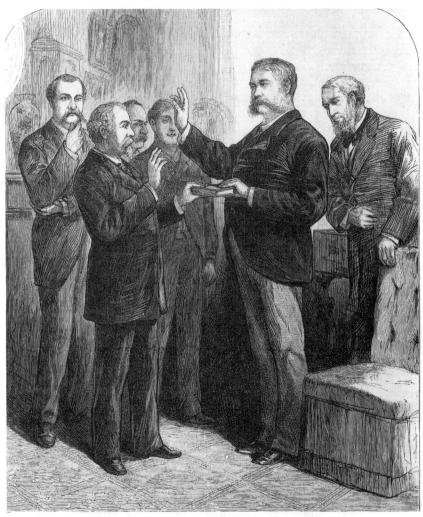

The death of President Garfield—Judge Brady administering the Presidential oath to Vice-President Arthur, at his residence in New York, September 20th

Chester A. Arthur
1881–1885

At 6′2″, sporting full side whiskers and a mustache, Chester A. Arthur[7] cut an imposing figure. Nicknamed "The Gentleman Boss," Arthur was a machine politician whom *The Nation* referred to as "a mess of filth." Woodrow Wilson called him "a non-entity with side whiskers."

The Congress continued to dominate in this age of smaller presidents, but forces were brewing that would soon contribute to an enlarging of the presidency and a shrinking of the Congress. The United States was emerg-

Chester Arthur

ing as an economic force in the world, and soon the U.S. would take a more prominent place on the world stage.

Institutional tugs-of-war aside, the presidency, even in this period of congressional ascendency, was continuing to be subtly transformed. In 1881, William Graham Sumner noted that "the intention of the constitution-makers has gone for very little in the historical development of the presidency."

To Sumner, "the office has been moulded by the tastes and faiths of the people."[8] President Garfield's assassination enflamed public passions against machine politics and the spoils, or patronage, system. Surprisingly, Arthur supported and worked for civil service reform, culminating with the passage of The Pendelton Act.

Grover Cleveland, (I and II)
1885–1889 and 1893–1897

The only president to serve two nonconsecutive terms, Grover Cleveland,[9] 5'11", 260 pounds, rotund, with a dropping mustache, was, given the revelations of his personal character foibles, an unlikely president at best.

In the election of 1884, Cleveland had a sizable lead over his opponent James G. Blaine. But the *Buffalo Evening Telegraph*, blared in huge headlines, "A Terrible Tale," and followed it with the accusation: Cleveland was the father of an illegitimate child! Surprisingly, rather than dissemble, Cleveland took full responsibility. Blaine supporters mocked Cleveland with the taunt "Ma, Ma, where's my Pa?", to which Cleveland's supporters retorted, "Gone to the White House, ha, ha, ha!"

The scandal turned the tide toward Blaine. But shortly before the election a group of Protestant Clergyman visited Blaine. One of the clergymen referred to the Democrats as the party of "rum, Romanism and rebellion." Blaine did not disavow the remark, and it backfired on him. Cleveland won the election.

In the 1880s, government began to grow and services expanded. We often think of the New Deal Era (1930s) as the time when the federal government expanded its size and responsibilities, and that is true. But the expansion began in the 1880s, and was the result of both industrialization and the rise of U.S. global power. (Table 4.1).

Cleveland attempted to defend the authority of the presidency against an aggressive Congress, and he fought for tariff reform. He was known as the "veto president" because of his record 301 vetoes in his first term, with 584 in his two terms (all previous presidents combined vetoed only 132 bills).

In his second term, an economic panic hit—the Depression of 1893. A year later, there was the Pullman strike. Cleveland used federal troops to break up the strike just outside of Chicago (over the objection of the governor), a significant extension of presidential power (later endorsed by the Supreme Court in *In re Debs*).

In 1893, President Cleveland was diagnosed with cancer of the mouth, the growth necessitating the removal of his upper left jaw. The operation was performed on July 1, 1893, aboard Commodore E.C. Benedict's yacht *Oneida* on Long Island Sound. In a second secret operation, on July 17,

Grover Cleveland

other parts of the growth were removed, and the President was fitted with an artificial jaw of vulcanized rubber.

Cleveland was the first president to use the veto power freely. He restored some of the president's power, even added to it. While not a great president, he did assert presidential authority and maintain some independence in the executive.

TABLE 4.1 Public Spending, 1890–1990

Year	Percent of GNP GNP	Expenditures per person in 1958 dollars			
		All Government	Federal	State-Local	Federal Social Welfare
1890	7	$ 56	$ 20	$ 36	$ 7
1913	8	109	33	76	7
1927	12	188	59	129	10*
1940	20	352	173	179	59
1962	31	893	575	318	155
1980	36	1,584	1,020	564	500
1990	40	2,025	1,271	754	623

*For 1929

Source: U.S. Bureau of the Census

Benjamin Harrison
1889–1893

Benjamin Harrison,[10] grandson of President William Henry Harrison, was a "dark horse" presidential candidate (a surprise candidate who seemingly rose out of nowhere). Harrison was president at the end of the era of westward expansion. Soon the nation would look beyond its borders to extend its influence. As the nation changed, so too did the government. Two noticeable shifts were taking place: an increase in the size and scope of government at home; and a growing concern for the world abroad. Both forces played into the growth of the presidency.

Theodore Roosevelt called Harrison "a cold-blooded, narrow-minded, prejudiced, obstinate, timid old psalm-singing Indianapolis politician." Known as "Little Bee" by his Civil War troops, Harrison was ill-equipped and ill-suited to the presidency. Every member of his cabinet was a Presbyterian, as was Harrison. Harrison, 5′6″, with full beard and blue eyes, the first president to watch a professional baseball game (Cincinnati 7, Washington 4, in 11 innings) was president during the waning days of congressional dominance, when party control of Congress was still able to exert its power. But this too was at the back end of an approaching new era.

The Congress's domination of the presidency prompted scholar Woodrow Wilson to proclaim in 1885 that "Unquestionably the predominant and controlling force, the center and source of all motive and of all regulative power is Congress."[11] Harrison seemed quite content to let Congress have its day. Harrison willingly surrendered power to Congress, and the presidency seemed in full retreat. While we would soon witness the reversal of this trend, during Harrison's term, the presidency continued to sink in power.

In 1890 Congress passed the Sherman Antitrust Act, the first piece of antitrust legislation aimed at curbing monopolistic practices in business. In

Benjamin Harrison

the same year, the Dependent and Disability Pensions Act, the Sherman Silver Purchase Act, and the McKinley Tariff Act were passed.

Excessively formal, even dour, Harrison was described by a visitor to the White House as having a handshake "like a wilted petunia." Harrison's very limited view of the president's authority led him neither to propose nor dispose. He saw himself more as a figurehead than leader. He once complained, "When I came to power, I found that the party managers had taken it all to themselves. I could not name my own cabinet. They had sold every place to pay the election expenses."

Ironically, Harrison complained of the spoils system at the moment reformers were challenging it. But rather than champion this cause, the president retreated. In an age when money called most of the shots in politics, Harrison missed his opportunity to focus attention on reform. The Senate of the age was known as "the Millionaire's club," and Kansas newspaper editor William Allen White complained that a Senator represented "something more than a state, more even than a region. He represented principalities and powers to business." But Harrison's self-restricted view of his office prevented him from engaging in a battle for reform.

As one of the late Whiggish presidents, Harrison was in office toward the end of the era of congressional supremacy. Content to let Congress rule, Harrison exerted little direction or leadership. But events would soon overwhelm this model of government. The United States was experiencing massive social, cultural, political, and economic changes. These changes, brought on by industrialization and America's new role as a major player on the world stage, demanded a stronger central government. And a stronger central government meant a stronger presidency.[12]

William McKinley
1897–1901

The presidency of William McKinley,[13] 5'7" and about 200 pounds, marked the beginning of a shift away from congressional government towards a presidency-centered system.

McKinley was something of a paradox. Frequently portrayed as personally weak, he nonetheless (albeit reluctantly) exerted presidential and American power on the world stage. In some ways he displayed a regressive brand of conservatism, promoting high tariffs and embracing jingoistic imperialism. Yet, he also led the nation into the global arena, declaring, "Isolation is no longer possible or desirable." He expanded American and presidential power and began the nation's venture into empire and imperial conquest. He helped transform the role of president from National Clerk to National Leader.

In truth, McKinley was more swept up by events than in control of them. It was a time of growth and change. Henry Jones Ford, whom scholar Edward S. Corwin called "the real herald of the twentieth-century presidency," wrote the influential book, *The Rise and Growth of American Politics,* in 1898. Ford predicted the rise of presidential power:

> It is the product of political conditions which dominate all the departments of government, so that Congress itself shows an unconscious disposition to aggrandize the presidential office . . .
>
> The truth is that in the presidential office, as it has been constituted since Jackson's time, American democracy has revived the oldest political institution of the race, the elective kingship. It is all there: the precogni-

William McKinley

tion of the notables and the tumultuous choice of the freemen, only conformed to modern conditions.

A passive president was no longer possible. Events demanded bolder, more assertive leadership. As America became a global power, it became a presidential nation. Thus, some historians refer to William McKinley as the first modern president.

McKinley, aided by his experience as a congressman, developed a sound working relationship with Congress. But it was not executive-legislative relations alone that marked a change in power. Dramatic changes in foreign relations brought forth a new presidency.

The Spanish-American War, in 1898, was a major transforming event in the life of the nation. The war itself, referred to as "the splendid little war," lasted only a few months, but its impact was revolutionary. After the U.S. victory, Spain lost nearly all its colonial interests in the Americas, and the U.S. became a recognized world power—an imperial power that controlled and occupied nations outside its borders. The U.S. now controlled the fate of Cuba, the Philippines, and Puerto Rico. As a result of the Paris Peace Treaty in December 1898, the U.S. had become an imperial or colonial power.

McKinley was unsure what to do about these new responsibilities. "I don't know what to do with them" he confessed. Rudyard Kipling advised McKinley to "Take up the White man's burden" and civilize the Filipinos. Perplexed, the president turned to God. "I walked the floor of the White House night after night until midnight; and I am not ashamed to tell you . . . I went down on my knees and prayed almighty God for light and guidance more than one night. And one night it came to me this way—I don't know how it was, but it came." Giving the islands back to Spain "would be cowardly and dishonorable." Transferring them to France or Germany "would be bad business and discreditable." The Filipinos were, he said, "unfit for self-government—and they would soon have anarchy and misrule over there worse than Spain's was." He concluded "that there was nothing left for us to do but take them all, and to educate the Filipinos, and uplift and civilize and Christianize them, and by God's grace do the very best we could by them, as our fellow-men for whom Christ also died." And so, McKinley decided to keep the Philippines to bring Christianity to the natives. When told that the Filipinos were already Roman Catholics, McKinley said, "Exactly."

During the McKinley presidency a significant shift in power occurred. The Congress declined and the executive rose. The Constitution's meaning changed as well, as McKinley, along with Teddy Roosevelt and Woodrow Wilson, would extend presidential power to fill America's new global role. In the area of foreign affairs, McKinley greatly enhanced presidential authority. He conducted a presidential war, largely on his own, claimed authority; he acquired the Philippines (using an Executive Agreement and bypassing the Senate); he and the Secretary of State John Hay established an Open Door policy for China; in 1900, without congressional approval, he dispatched 5,000 troops to China to suppress the Boxer Rebellion. By waging war, acting unilaterally, bypassing Congress, establishing an empire, and doing this "solely" on executive authority, McKinley shifted the balance of power (especially in foreign affairs) in favor of the presidency.

In September 1901, McKinley traveled to Buffalo, New York, to open the Pan-American Exposition. As he greeted visitors, he noticed a man whose hand was wrapped in a bandage. As McKinley reached out to shake the man's other hand, two shots rang out from a pistol concealed beneath the bandages. A week later, the president died. "Good Lord," exclaimed Sen-

Assassination of President McKinley

ator Mark Harerce, "that Goddamn cowboy is President of the United States."

Theodore Roosevelt
1901–1909

"It is," Theodore Roosevelt[14] wrote to a friend, "a dreadful thing to come into the Presidency this way; but it would be a far worse thing to be morbid about it. Here is the task, and I have got to do it to the best of my ability; and that is all there is about it."

Puffy face, droopy mustache, pince-nez eyeglasses with thick lenses, prominent teeth, and a high voice, Theodore Roosevelt (TR) helped transform the presidency and convert the office into a truly national leadership institution. It was in the Roosevelt era that the presidency began to resemble the institution with which we are familiar today.

TR was an activist who stamped his personality onto his age. The sheer force of his will compelled action. Roosevelt exerted policy leadership as a "conservative-progressive" à la Disraeli. He transformed the presidency into a more public office, using (some would say abusing) the "bully pulpit" to elevate the rhetorical presidency to new heights, and developing a more sophisticated relationship between the president and the press.

Theodore Roosevelt

At the turn of the century, the presidency was a mere suggestion of what it was to become. McKinley did not fully exploit the opportunity to gain power afforded by the rise of the U.S. as a world power.[15] TR would not let the opportunity slip through his hands. He loved power, relished in its exercise, and sought to dominate. He seized power. The result, he later boasted, was that "I did and caused to be done many things not previously done by the President and the heads of the departments. I did not usurp power, but I did greatly broaden the use of executive power. In other words,

I acted for the public welfare, I acted for the common well-being of all our people, whenever and in whatever manner was necessary, unless prevented by direct constitutional or legislative prohibition." Under TR, the presidency became the center of the political universe. His gravitational pull, his flair for self-dramatization, allowed the president to direct the government and set the political agenda.

Louis Hartz called TR "America's only Nietzschean president." A contemporary of Roosevelt's said, "At every wedding, Theodore wants to be the bride. At every funeral he wants to be the corpse." "He is," said Henry James, "the very embodiment of noise." And muckraker Ida Tarbell wrote of TR, "I felt his clothes might not contain him, he was so steamed up, so ready to go, to attack anything, anywhere." Roosevelt's need to lead every parade compelled him to exert himself, even force himself to center stage. He courted and cultivated public opinion; he was the president as "national celebrity." Did any other president delight in the exercise of power as much as Teddy Roosevelt? Few presidents *needed* power as much as TR. Few *needed* to achieve greatness as much as TR. But conditions, as he recognized, were not ripe for greatness. "If there is not the great occasion," he noted, "you don't get *the* great statesman; if Lincoln had lived in times of peace no one would have known his name now." Oh how he needed power and greatness. "If this country could be ruled by a benevolent czar," he wrote in 1897, "we would doubtless make a good many changes for the better."

TR had an obsession with masculinity bordering on the pathological. As Bruce Miroff writes, "He portrayed a world divided between the timid men of words, sitting in the stands and carping at their betters, and the heroic men of action, gladiators in the political arena."[16] In a 1910 speech at the Sorbonne in Paris, Roosevelt said:

> It is not the critic who counts; not the man who points out how the strong man stumbles, or where the doer of deeds could have done them better. The credit belongs to the man who is actually in the arena, whose face is marred by dust and sweat and blood; who strives valiantly; who errs, and comes short again and again, because there is no effort without error and shortcoming; but who does actually strive to do the deeds."

He "reserved his greatest contempt for 'emasculated sentimentalists'."[17] TR believed in the strenuous life. He once said of his sons, "I would rather one of them should die, than have them grow up weaklings." In Roosevelt, masculinity merged with moral righteousness to form "an ego of heroic proportions."[18]

TR was among a mere handful of presidents who greatly increased the authority and responsibility of the office. He may have built on the foundation of predecessors, but few presidents did as much as TR to fundamentally alter the presidency. He changed the office whereas others held it. He led where others presided.

The America of Roosevelt's era was a more urban, industrial nation; a nation ready to take its place on the world stage. In 1890, there were 63,000,000 Americans. By 1900, the U.S. population was over 75,000,000. When TR left office, the number had risen to over 90,000,000.

It was also an age of political change. The Progressive Movement was sweeping America, promoting activist government, presidential leadership, more open political participation, and control of corporate capitalism. Roosevelt fit perfectly in this new era.

Roosevelt had an expansionist view of presidential power, to say the least. He *personalized* the office, linking policy to personality. In his *Autobiography* (1913), TR described the theory that guided his behavior as president:

> My view was that every officer, and above all every executive officer in high position, was a steward of the people bound actively and affirmatively to do all he could for the people, and not to content himself with the negative merit of keeping his talents undamaged in a napkin. I declined to adopt the view that what was imperatively necessary for the Nation could not be done by the president unless he could find some specific authorization to do it. My belief was that it was not only his right but his duty to do anything that the needs of the Nation demanded unless such action was forbidden by the Constitution or by the laws.

In his first annual message to Congress, TR summed up his view of how American society had changed and how the role of government needed to change as well.

> When the Constitution was adopted, at the end of the eighteenth century, no human wisdom could foretell the sweeping changes, alike in industrial and political conditions, which were to take place at the beginning of the twentieth century. At that time it was accepted as a matter of course that the several States were the proper authorities to regulate, so far as was then necessary, the comparatively insignificant and strictly localized corporate bodies of the day. The conditions are now wholly different and wholly different action is called for.

If the president was to be the "steward of the people," he was also to be the centerpiece of political action. Roosevelt not only changed the way the presidency was viewed but also changed the way it operated, establishing a very close and personal relationship between the president and the public. This connection may have had its roots with Andrew Jackson, but it came into full bloom with TR. He helped turn the executive into a personal presidency and a people's presidency, using the "bully pulpit" to reach out to the people. Here, the rhetorical presidency was born. And TR scoffed at his critics:

> While President I have *been* President, emphatically; I have used every ounce of power there was in the office and I have not cared a rap for the criticisms of those who spoke of my "usurpation of power"; for I knew that the talk was all nonsense and that there was no usurpation. I believe that

the efficiency of this Government depends upon its possessing a strong central executive, and wherever I could establish a precedent for strength in the executive . . . I have felt not merely that my action was right in itself, but that I was establishing a precedent of value.[19]

TR extended executive authority farther than any other peacetime president. His linking of the president to the public established a new theory of government. The president, to Roosevelt, was the chief spokesman for the people. As political scientists Milkis and Nelson note:

> The rise of the rhetorical presidency signified a dramatic transformation of the founding theory and the early history of the executive. The Framers of the Constitution had explicitly proscribed popular leadership. Thus, during the nineteenth century, direct presidential efforts to rouse public opinion in support of policy initiatives were considered illegitimate, a form of demagogy that was beneath the dignity of the office. Roosevelt's "stewardship" theory of the executive, however, demanded that a stronger popular connection be forged. Accordingly, on a number of occasions TR appealed directly to the people to bring pressure to bear on members of Congress who were reluctant to support his policies.[20]

Roosevelt was a whirlwind who sought to dominate events utterly, and he often did. He asserted a claim that the president should be the nation's chief legislator, and pushed himself deeper into the legislative arena than any of his predecessors. TR outlined his proposals in public speeches and messages to Congress. He even went so far as to draft bills and send them to Congress. In the past, this was done behind the scenes for fear that the presidents might be accused of overstepping their separation-of-power bounds. But Roosevelt was very open about this. He also worked very hard lobbying Congress on behalf of his legislative proposals. "A good executive," he asserted "under the present conditions of American political life, must take a very active interest in getting the right kind of legislation." (He once lamented, "Oh, if I could only be President and Congress together for just ten minutes!"). To Roosevelt, the president was not only the voice of the people, but of the legislature as well.

In 1904–1905, Roosevelt added a critical tool to the president's power when he intervened militarily in Santo Domingo. Done ostensibly to protect the interests of U.S. companies, Roosevelt defended his decision on grounds that the U.S. had a right to establish and guarantee hemispheric order. The United States was to be sheriff of the hemisphere. "It is our duty," he said, "when it becomes absolutely inevitable to police these countries in the interest of order and civilization." This act—the Roosevelt corollary to the Monroe Doctrine—added a significant weapon to the president's already enlarging arsenal. In a speech directed to the U.S.'s Latin American neighbors, Roosevelt said:

> It is not true that the United States feels any land hunger or entertains any projects as regards the other nations of the western hemisphere save such

as for their welfare. All that this country desires is to see the neighboring countries stable, orderly and prosperous . . . if a nation shows that it knows how to act with reasonable efficiency and decency in social and political matters, if it keeps order and pays its obligations, it need fear no interference by the United States. Chronic wrongdoing, or an impotence which results in a general loosening of the ties of civilized society may in America, as elsewhere, ultimately require intervention by some civilized nation, and in the western hemisphere the adherence of the United States to the Monroe Doctrine may force the United States, however reluctantly, in flagrant cases of such wrongdoing or impotence, to the exercise of an international police power.

Roosevelt's ambitious legislative agenda, referred to as the Square Deal, included antitrust legislation, the Hepburn Act, conservation, the creation of a Department of Commerce and Labor, and a host of other ideas.

If TR was innovative in the domestic arena, he was even more activist and controversial in foreign affairs. McKinley introduced America to the world stage; Roosevelt was determined to dominate it. He talked of speaking softly but carrying a big stick; he increased the size of the Navy, imposed a deal that led to the building of the Panama Canal; and brokered a peace agreement, ending the Russo-Japanese War (for which he was the first American president to receive a Nobel Peace Prize). When the Senate refused to ratify a treaty with the Dominican Republic, TR merely ignored the will of the Senate and signed an Executive Agreement! Roosevelt defended this decision: "The Constitution did not explicitly give me power to bring about the necessary agreement with Santo Domingo," Roosevelt wrote in 1913. "But, the Constitution did not forbid my doing what I did. I put the agreement into effect, and I continued its execution for two years before the Senate acted; and I would have continued it until the end of my term, if necessary, without any action by Congress."[21] Teddy Roosevelt was no wallflower.

Teddy Roosevelt changed the Constitution: not the wording, but the interpretation and understanding of the scope and nature of executive power. He stretched the constitutional elastic further than any president since Lincoln, and in doing so, helped invent a "new" institution. He redefined the presidency.

TR was a dynamo, a bundle of energy, a man of action. He left the presidency bigger than when he arrived. Future presidents could lay claim to roles of chief legislator, tribune of and spokesman for the people, world leader, steward of the people, and national leader. Not all did, but TR paved the way for those who embraced an expansive view of presidential power.

More than anything, TR wanted to be a great president. But governing in a period of relative calm did not allow for the opportunity for true greatness. But he did change and enlarge the presidency. The presidency TR left behind contained the capacity to do good, but the enlarged presidency could also be used for unsavory ends. One of the dilemmas of the twentieth century was how to empower yet control the presidency.

Upon leaving office TR said: "No President has ever enjoyed himself as much as I have enjoyed myself, and for the matter of that I do not know any man of my age who has had as good a time . . ."

William Howard Taft
1909–1913

A newspaper of the day said Taft looked "like an American bison—a gentle, kind one." Six feet, 350 pounds, with deep-set eyes and a turned-up mustache, William Howard Taft[22] was the largest, though not one of the best, presidents in history. So large was Taft that once he got stuck in the White House bathtub! After being pulled out, a new, larger tub was installed. Taft loved playing golf, but was so rotund he couldn't bend down to place the ball on the tee. His caddy had to do it for him. During Taft's prepresidential stint as governor-general of the Philippines, he cabled Secretary of War Root with news of his illness, adding, "Took long horseback ride today. Feel fine" to which Root wired back: "How is the horse?"

Until running for president as Teddy Roosevelt's handpicked successor, Taft had never been through an election. He was the first president to throw out the opening ball of the baseball season (Walter Johnson threw a one-hitter, and the Washington Senators beat the Philadelphia Athletics, 3–0).

Anyone who followed Teddy Roosevelt into the White House would have had trouble filling TR's enormous shoes. Taft actually never wanted to be president, but prodded by his ambitious wife, he finally agreed to run. He found the presidency "the lonesomest place in the world." Several years after leaving the presidency, President Harding nominated Taft Chief Justice of the Supreme Court. A poor president, Taft was a good justice.

Taft had a much more limited conception of presidential power than TR. A public accustomed to presidential leadership expected more of Taft. The mood of the age was progressive, but Taft was a status quo president. He strongly opposed Roosevelt's theory that the president has a large, unspecific "residuum of powers." Addressing his arguments toward Roosevelt, he wrote in 1916:

> My judgment is that the view of . . . Mr. Roosevelt, ascribing an undefined residuum of power to the President is an unsafe doctrine and that it might lead under emergencies to results of an arbitrary character, doing irremediable injustice to private right. The mainspring of such a view is that the Executive is charged with responsibility for the welfare of all the people in a general way, that he is to play the part of a Universal providence and set things right, and that anything that in his judgment will help the people he ought to do, unless he is expressly forbidden not to do it. The wide field of action that this would give to the Executive one can hardly limit.

William H. Taft

Taft argued for a strict construction of Article II. The executive should exercise only power that is expressly or implicitly granted by the Constitution. After leaving office he wrote:

> The true view of the executive function . . . is that the president can exercise no power which cannot be reasonable or fairly traced to some specific grant of power or justly implied or included within such express grant as necessary and proper to its exercise. Such specific grant must be either in the Constitution or in an act of Congress passed in pursuance thereof.

There is no undefined residuum of power which he can exercise because
it seems to be in the public interest . . .

Where TR loved politics, Taft hated the political fray: "I don't like politics," he once said, "especially when I am in it." Taft did not attempt to exert executive domination, and while dedicated to a fairly ambitious agenda,
he was much more reluctant than TR about promoting it.

During his presidency, the Payne-Aldrich Tariff Act passed, as did the
Maw-Elkins Act. Also, the sixteenth amendment to the Constitution (which
gave Congress the power to levy an income tax) was approved. An independent Department of Labor was established, and more antitrust suits were
launched by Taft than TR. Abroad, Taft promoted what was known as "Dol-
lar Diplomacy" (in which U.S. military intervention was used to promote
American corporate interests).

Teddy Roosevelt became restless and, disappointed in Taft's leadership,
began openly to challenge the president. Finding a new, more radical message, in 1912 TR announced his candidacy for the Republican presidential
nomination. But the Old Guard controlled the party machinery and ma-
neuvered the nomination toward Taft. Not to be deterred, Roosevelt bolted
the party and ran as a Progressive or Bull Moose candidate. Taft and Roosevelt viciously attacked each other (TR called Taft a "fathead" with "brains
less than that of a guinea pig," and Taft called Roosevelt a "demagogue"
who "can't tell the truth.") Taft and Roosevelt split the vote, and Democrat
Woodrow Wilson became president.

As ex-president, Taft lamented, "for all the sins of omission and of commission of society, the president cannot make clouds to rain, he cannot
make the corn to grow, he cannot make business to be good."

Woodrow Wilson
1913–1921

The only president to earn a Ph.D. (from Johns Hopkins University),
Woodrow Wilson,[23] who was president of Princeton University and reform
governor of New Jersey, resumed the activist tone of presidential leadership established by Teddy Roosevelt. At 5'11", 170 pounds, at times aloof,
withdrawn, and temperamental, Wilson, like TR, added to the presidency
and cemented the role of world leader onto the office.

Wilson was a progressive, activist reformer, who used party and popular leadership to move Congress. He was also a wartime president who not
only exerted extraconstitutional leadership in war, but in the aftermath of
the war promoted an expansive and idealistic peace.

TR called Wilson "a Byzantine logothete" (look it up!). One of the most
complex and fascinating presidents in U.S. history, Wilson seemed motivated by a mix of Puritan idealism, burning ambition, and intellectual su-

Woodrow Wilson

periority. He saw the world in starkly simplistic terms as a struggle between good and evil. This made it difficult for Wilson to compromise.

In a way there were three different Wilson presidencies: the very successful domestic reformer of the first term; the very successful war president during World War I; and the idealistic, but in the end tragic, crusader for world peace toward the end of his presidency.

Woodrow Wilson was a political scientist who got the opportunity to put his academic theories of the presidency into practice (and wouldn't all countries be better off if political scientists ran things . . .). In his twenties he wrote: "the President is at liberty, both in law and conscience, to be as big a man as he can." A quarter century later, Wilson had a chance to do just that.

Congressional Government (1885), Wilson's first book, was critical of the Founding Fathers and of the Constitution. They had so distributed power and responsibility as to make leadership virtually impossible:

> The forms of government in this country have always been unfavorable to the easy elevation of talent to a station of paramount authority; and those forms in their present crystallization are more unfavorable than ever to the toleration of the leadership of the few.

The president Wilson saw in the 1890s was a clerk; Wilson wanted him to be a leader. At the turn of the century, Wilson's thinking underwent a change. In a new edition of *Congressional Government*, written in 1900, Wilson argued that the war with Spain had set in motion changes in the distribution of power that altered his earlier ideas. The war had brought the United States into global politics and:

> When foreign affairs play a prominent part in the politics and policies of a nation, its Executive must of necessity be its guide: must utter every initial judgement, take every first step of action, supply the information upon which it is to act, suggest and in large measure control its conduct. The President of the United States is now, as of course, at the front of affairs.

When Wilson delivered the lectures that were to be published in 1908 as *Constitutional Government in the United States* he was more optimistic about the possibilities of leadership. He saw the role of the president as:

> The leader of his party and the guide of the nation in political purpose, and therefore in legal action.

> [The president was now seen] as the unifying force in our complex system.

> [The president's] is the only national voice in our affairs. Let him once win the admiration and confidence of the country and no other single force can withstand him . . . If he rightly interprets the national thought and boldly insists upon it, he is irresistible; the country never feels the zest for action so much as when its President is of such insight and calibre. Its instinct is for unified action and it craves a single leader.

> [The President's] office is anything he has the sagacity and force to make it.

> The Constitution bids him speak, and times of stress and change must more and more thrust upon him the attitude of originator of policies. His is the vital place of action in the system.[24]

Wilson broke precedent by personally addressing a special session of Congress—the first time this occurred since the presidency of John Adams.

This was the beginning of an annual tradition, when the president delivers his State of the Union to Congress himself.

In 1913, shortly after his inauguration, Woodrow Wilson held the first presidential press conference. Soon, the press conference became institutionalized. Wilson used these press conferences to promote both himself and his policies.

Wilson aggressively pursued his legislative agenda in Congress. In his first term, he used party and popular leadership as a source of domestic reforms, known as the New Freedom. Legislation to break monopolies, assist unions, and lower tariffs were passed. Child labor laws, a newly created Federal Reserve, and a series of other laws all were passed as well. Wilson noted that "It is only once in a generation that a people can be lifted above material things. That is why conservative government is on the saddle two-thirds of the time." Thus, when he became president he pushed and pushed hard to achieve as much as possible. But there was also a dark side to his leadership. Wilson's attitude about race relations led him further to impose segregation in several government department, and his administration engaged a massive internal repression during World War I.

A Supreme Court test of the president's removal power was decided in *Myers v. United States*.[25] In that case, Frank S. Myers was named a first-class postmaster by President Woodrow Wilson in 1917. In 1920, Wilson asked for Myers's resignation, but Myers refused. In February of that year, Myers was removed from office by order of the Postmaster General, acting under direction of President Wilson. Myers protested, citing the act of Congress of July 12, 1876, which said that removal of a first-class postmaster could be effective only if the president acted with the consent of the Congress. Wilson neither requested nor received such consent.

The Supreme Court, with Chief Justice Taft writing the majority opinion, denied Myers's claim (brought by his heirs) and ruled in favor of the president's act of removal. Taft based his decision on the premise that this point was thoroughly argued by the First Congress (many of whom participated in the Constitutional Convention), and they had decided that the president did have the removal power. Taft argued that:

> ... The ordinary duties of officers prescribed by statute come under the general administrative control of the President by virtue of the general grant to him of the executive power, and he may properly supervise and guide their construction of the statutes under which they act in order to secure that unitary and uniform execution of the laws which Article II of the Constitution evidently contemplated in vesting general executive power in the President alone ... Finding such officers to be negligent and inefficient, the President should have the power to remove them.

Wilson's great success as a reformer during his first term led to easy re-election, as Wilson promised to keep the U.S. out of war in Europe. But war was in the cards, and Wilson soon became a war president. During the war, Wilson demonstrated skill and determination. On January 8, 1918, he delivered his "Fourteen Points" speech to Congress, a comprehensive post-war plan for peace, calling for greater justice for small nations, self-determination for "enslaved" nations, and arbitration of international dispute.

After the war, Wilson went to work building a lasting peace. He went to Europe to negotiate not only a settlement to the war, but a plan for peace as well. The result was the Treaty of Versailles, which Wilson brought back to the U.S. for Senate approval. (He won a Nobel Peace Prize for his efforts). But the Senate, now controlled by Republicans, balked at the plan, rejecting Wilson's scheme, along with the League of Nations the president was proposing.

Wilson took his case directly to the people. World War I was to "make the world safe for democracy," and Wilson was not about to let the Senate interfere with his ambitious and idealistic plans for a League of Nations and post-war peace. Wilson was too rigid to compromise. He wanted it all, and would settle for nothing less. His inability or unwillingness to compromise with Senate Republicans doomed the treaty.

As matters went from bad to worse, Wilson became more and more rigid. He took an exhausting national tour on behalf of "his" treaty. Soon fatigue and illness overtook him. Finally, he suffered a stroke that left him bedridden.

During his incapacitation, Edith Wilson, his wife, all but ran the country, leading critics to protest, 'We have a petticoat government." The physically weakened Wilson remained uncompromising about the League of Nations. His all-or-nothing attitude led to nothing. Wilson's presidency ended with a debilitated and disappointed president, unable to achieve his final and biggest victory.

If failure marked the end of the Wilson presidency, we should not forget how much success there was: major domestic reforms, victory in war, an idealistic (if unsuccessful) hope for the future. "Whatever his failings," writes historian John Morton Blum, "he phrased and symbolized some of the best hopes of liberalism and its possibilities for the country and the world."[26] Wilson played the part of president as prime minister, leading party, public, and legislature. He expanded and strengthened the presidency. He demonstrated that the presidency could truly be a place of moral leadership.

Conclusion

Reaction against the strong presidency of Abraham Lincoln followed the Civil War, and an era of congressional dominance ensued. Andrew Johnson was impeached and nearly convicted in a power struggle between the executive and legislative branches.

Several rather weak presidents followed Johnson, but as the United States became a world industrial and military presence, the power of the presidency rose. Teddy Roosevelt with his bully pulpit, and Woodrow Wilson with his progressive idealism and wartime leadership, once again established a strong, even heroic model of presidential power.

5

Republicanization and Retreat/
Birth of the Modern
Warren Harding to Franklin D. Roosevelt

After the frenetic leadership of Teddy Roosevelt, the activist leadership of Wilson, and World War I and its contentious aftermath, the American public was ready to relax and catch its breath. The "Roaring Twenties," a self-interested period bordering on the narcissistic, and a post-war economic boom contributed to a turning away from public concerns. The U.S. was emerging as a world military and economic leader, but the nation retreated into isolationist tendencies. For a decade, America turned away from public purposes and instead focused on private concerns.

Warren Gamaliel Harding
1921–1923

Warren G. Harding[1] promised a "Return to Normalcy." An unlikely choice for president, Harding once confessed: "I like to go out into the country and bloveate" (loaf). At 6 feet tall, handsome, and charming (he looked like a president), Harding was passive and uninterested in the details of government. His nomination was so much of a surprise that *The New York Times* called Harding's Senate record "faint and colorless." The *Times* added, "We must go back to Franklin Pierce if we would seek a President who measures down to his political stature." Harding was once employed as a schoolteacher but soon quit, saying it was the hardest job he ever had.

Harding was the first president to broadcast a speech over radio (dedicating the Francis Scott Key Memorial at Fort McHenry, in Baltimore, Maryland, on June 14, 1922) and the first to win an election in which women voted. His inauguration was the first ever described over radio. A British reporter described Harding's inaugural address as "the most illiterate statement ever made by the head of a civilized government." He is considered by many historians as the worst president in history.

Harding, a one time small-town Ohio newspaper editor, had a strange way with words. He often left transitive verbs hanging mysteriously without the aid of direct objects: "I would like the government to do all it can to mitigate"; he invented words like "re-revealment"; and he often spoke in

Warren G. Harding

trite banalities: "Despite all the depreciation, I cannot bring myself to accept the notion that the inter-relation among our men and women has departed." H. L. Mencken dubbed these gems "Gamalielese," and said of Harding, "No other such a complete and dreadful nitwit is to be found in the
pages of American history." Poet e. e. cummings called Harding "The only
man woman or child who wrote a simple declarative sentence with seven
grammatical errors. . . ."

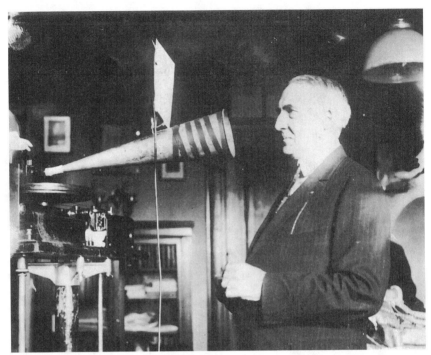

President Harding's voice has been preserved in phonograph records in the government archives.

A poor manager and disinterested president, Harding saw his role as primarily ceremonial. He did not attempt actively to lead Congress. This allowed Congress, determined to reassert its authority after TR and Wilson, to take command during the Harding years. Harding once admitted, "I am a man of limited talents from a small town. I don't seem to grasp that I am President." He once confessed to his secretary, "Jud, you have a college education, haven't you? I don't know what to do or where to turn . . . Somewhere there must be a book that tells all about it . . . But I don't know where that book is, and maybe I couldn't read it if I found it! . . . My God, but this is a hell of a place for a man like me to be in!" His wife, Florence, kept a "little red book" in which she listed her husband's enemies (Nixon wasn't the first!).

Harding preferred women and gambling to politics and policy. He had a weakness for women, and had several long- and short-term "relationships." His father once said of him, "If you were a girl, Warren, you'd be in the family way all the time. You can't say 'No.'"

During the Harding years, American participation in the League of Nations died when the president announced he would not support U.S. membership in the League. Under Harding, the 1921 Washington Conference for the Limitation of Armament limited the spread of the arms race. The

Bureau of the Budget was created in 1921, and the president was required to submit a federal budget proposal to Congress.

The most noteworthy and notorious event of the Harding years centered around corruption. The Harding scandals ran deep. Harding himself was never implicated in these scandals, but he was guilty of lax management. Harding appointed friends and cronies, but he did not properly supervise them. Seeing that Harding was asleep at the wheel, they felt that they could take advantage of the president—and did.

Among the numerous scandals that plagued the Harding administration, the biggest was Teapot Dome. Harding's secretary of the interior, Albert B. Fall, was convicted of accepting a $100,000 bribe for granting oil leases under value to some "friends." He was the first cabinet member ever convicted of a crime while in office.

Fraud in the Veterans Bureau, graft in the Office of Alien Property Custodian, criminal conspiracy in the Justice Department (which was known as the "Department of Easy Virtue"), suicides, and a slew of other crimes and scandals haunted the administration. Harding's "friends" from the Ohio Gang used a weak and indifferent president to feather their financial nests. And the president remained blissfully unaware and pleasantly disinterested.

After being victimized by so many of his underlings, an exasperated Harding opined: "My god, this is a hell of a job! I can take care of my enemies all right. But my damn friends, my god-damn friends They're the ones that keep me walking the floor nights!" He finally admitted, "I am not fit for this office and should never have been here."

On a trip to the West, Harding contracted several "unspecified" illnesses. He died in August of 1923. After his death, his wife, Florence Harding, refused to permit an autopsy (fueling endless speculation of foul play).

After Harding's death, investigations into administrative corruption revealed a dark underbelly to the Harding team. Three high officials went to jail. One of the president's friends committed suicide, and a series of crimes was revealed. Until the Nixon years, the Harding administration was considered the most corrupt in U.S. history.

Calvin Coolidge
1923–1929

Calvin Coolidge,[2] thin and standing 5′9″, known as "Silent Cal" due to his quiet, taciturn, even mundane manner, was probably America's first "feel good" president. "Keep Cool With Coolidge" was his motto, and Coolidge kept cool by sleeping more than any other president in U.S. history. He seemed convinced that the less a president did, the better. H. L. Mencken said: " . . . while he yawned and stretched the United States went slam bang down the hill—and he lived just long enough to see it fetch up with a horrible bump at the bottom." The chronically shy Coolidge was a man of few

Calvin Coolidge

words. George Creel said he was "distinguishable from the furniture only when he moved."

During the 1924 campaign, a reporter asked him: "Have you any statement on the campaign?" "No," replied Coolidge. "Can you tell us something about the world situation?" asked another. "No." "Any information about Prohibition?" "No." As the reporters started to leave, Coolidge said solemnly: "Now, remember—don't quote me." At a White House social event, a woman approached Coolidge: "You must talk to me, Mr. President," she said. "I made a bet today that I could get more than two words out of you." "You lose" was the reply. Foreign diplomats said Coolidge "can be silent in five languages."

In a way Coolidge fit the mood of the times. "I think the American public wants a solemn ass as a president. And I think I'll go along with them," he once said. And humorist Will Rogers said, "He didn't do nothing, but that's what we wanted done."

Coolidge was straight-laced and a man of unbending grayness, a man newspaper editor William Allen White referred to as "a Puritan in Babylon." TR's daughter, Alice, said Coolidge "looked like he had been weaned on a pickle."

In 1921, automobile registration in the U.S. was at 9.3 million. By 1929, that number soared to 26.7 million. The telephone was revolutionizing communication. Radio was introduced. And moving pictures became a popular pastime. In 1922, 40 million movie tickets were sold per week. By 1929, the number climbed to 100 million. And in 1920, women won the right to vote.

Coolidge rejected the activist view of the presidency and was deferential to congressional leadership. One of his few strongly held beliefs was that "the business of the American people is business," and Coolidge vowed nonintervention in the affairs of business. This gave the commercial interests in America a free hand to pursue their goals unencumbered by government supervision.

Coolidge was president in the midst of the "Roaring Twenties." Prohibition was in force, *The Jazz Singer* was released, Sacco and Vanzetti were executed, Babe Ruth went on his home run binge, Al Capone and Mickey Mouse captured the popular imagination, Charles Lindbergh flew the first solo flight across the Atlantic, and an economic boom swept the land. It was a time of individualism and materialistic extravagance. And Silent Cal was president during the Roaring Twenties—it was a paradox that made sense.

Silent Cal let Congress do the talking. Other than proposing tax reductions, Coolidge had virtually no legislative agenda. In this way, he more closely resembled nineteenth- than twentieth-century presidents. Having abandoned the role of legislator-in-chief, he chose instead to use the veto pen to limit legislative activity.

During the Coolidge years, the Harding scandals were exposed, Congress passed the Immigration Act of 1924 (which limited the number of Italians and Jews who could enter the country, raised quotas for northern Europeans, and excluded Japanese; "America must be kept American," Coolidge said), the Revenue Acts of 1924 and 1926 (tax cuts) were enacted, the Veteran's Bonus Act of 1924 was passed (over Coolidge's veto), the McNary-Haugen Bill of 1927 was passed (over Coolidge's two vetos), and in *Myers v. United States* (1926) the Supreme Court gave constitutional sanction to a broad interpretation of the president's removal power. In foreign affairs, the Pact of Paris (the Kellogg-Briand pact) of 1928 was approved.

Coolidge's reluctance to regulate business in spite of some early warning signs helped lead to the Great Depression, which hit six months after he left office. Coolidge, committed to a *laissez faire* approach, decided to leave business alone. He ignored the mounting economic troubles that would soon plunge the nation into a deep depression.

Coolidge built up a meager record as president. He probably wanted it that way. He shrunk the presidency and left several key problems unaddressed. His failure to supply leadership, to recognize and even anticipate problems, contributed to the Great Depression.

"Silent Cal" died of a heart attack on January 5, 1933. On hearing the news of Coolidge's death, writer Dorothy Parker asked, "How can they tell?"

Herbert Hoover
1929–1933

If one could create a person with all the qualities essential for a great president, you might invent Herbert Hoover.[3] His prepresidential career reveals one success after another. The "Great Engineer," as Hoover was called, brought to the presidency a reputation for skill, accomplishment, and public service that was truly impressive. He was food administrator during Wilson's presidency, secretary of commerce under Harding and Coolidge, an able administrator, and a man of integrity. Few presidents stood so high in public esteem as they entered office. Yet this same man who had accomplished so much, and from whom so much was expected would, four years later, leave office amid scorn and abuse. This dramatic reversal is due to one thing: the Great Depression of 1929.

In presidential politics, as in life, much hinges on luck—good and bad. Napoleon, when choosing generals, would say "find me a man who is lucky." Herbert Hoover had the great misfortune to become president a few months before the depression of 1929 struck. As the old blues song goes: "If it wasn't for bad luck, I wouldn't have no luck at all."

In October 1929, the stock market plunged. From a high of 469, it sunk to 85 by 1932. Unemployment soared. Some estimates put the unemployment rate at 35 percent. Businesses failed, banks closed, the poor took to the streets and to the roads.

Hoover at first responded with pep talks designed to instill confidence in the midst of chaos. "Prosperity is just around the corner," he would say. When that failed he turned to intervention in the economy, launching public works programs, tax reductions, and the establishment of a Reconstruction Finance Corporation. These small steps also failed. Ex-President Coolidge visited the White House and discussed the administration's efforts at reversing the depression. Coolidge told Hoover he could not understand why Hoover's relief efforts were so ineffective and why the president's critics were so vehement. "You can't expect to see calves running in the field the day after you put a bull to the cows," Coolidge said. "No," replied Hoover, "but I would expect to see contented cows."

As the depression deepened, a "Bonus Army" comprised of thousands of World War I veterans marched on Washington demanding help. They set up shacks, and their makeshift town became known as a "Hooverville," in which they kept warm with "Hoover blankets" (discarded newspapers).

Herbert Hoover

In July of 1932, Hoover ordered the army to tear down the makeshift huts. U.S. troops went in carrying rifles with fixed bayonets, and they used tear gas and flamethrowers on the demonstrators, demolishing the Hooverville. The nation, seeing this in movie-house newsreels, was stunned. Hoover appeared heartless as well as helpless.

Herbert Hoover was a talented, sincere man, overcome by events. He was the victim, not master of these events. In the face of the depression, Hoover sometimes seemed lost. "This office is a compound hell," he said towards the end of his presidency.

Franklin Delano Roosevelt
1932–1945

Considered one of the three greatest presidents in history, Franklin D. Roosevelt[4] (FDR) brought the nation through two crises: a depression, and a world war, and he transformed the nation and the presidency in the process.

FDR is credited with creating the "modern presidency." Roosevelt transformed the presidency from a rather small, personalized office, into a massive institution. (In 1931, there were 600,000 federal employees; by 1941, that number topped 1.4 million). Facing the crises of the Depression and World War II, FDR contributed to the creation of both the welfare state and the warfare state. When Roosevelt died during his fourth term, he left America a vastly different nation than when he took office in 1933.

Roosevelt was tall (6'1"), handsome, had riveting blue eyes, and came from an aristocratic background. With his privileged background came training in duty to community and a sense of noblesse oblige. In the midst of a promising political career, Roosevelt contracted polio (1921) and lost the

Franklin Delano Roosevelt

use of both legs. His political career seemed over, but FDR refused to give in. Rather than defeating him, his illness transformed him. His polio was a defining event in his life. Going through a long, difficult rehabilitation, he also went through a deeply personal journey of introspection and reinvention. His depth of character was forged in personal crisis. It transformed him from a wealthy politician with a large ego and grand ambitions to a man of substance and character. Frances Perkins, FDR's secretary of labor, believed that in facing illness, Roosevelt went through a "spiritual transformation," which helped him understand "the problem of people in trouble."

Roosevelt had a radiant, buoyant personality. Charming, witty, optimistic, and enthusiastic, FDR loved life and loved the give-and-take of politics. His jaunty smile, soothing voice, and confident manner inspired hope and trust. Winston Churchill said that meeting Roosevelt was like opening a bottle of champagne. But he was no angel. He could be duplicitous and manipulative. But he was also open, flexible, and willing to experiment.

FDR was less a thinker than a doer, and Oliver Wendell Holmes, Jr. said he was "A second-class intellect—but a first-class temperament." And that is one of the keys to Roosevelt's success. FDR loved politics, and he exuded confidence and optimism. As FDR noted: "the country said, and, unless I mistake its temper, the country demands bold, persistent experimentation. It is common sense to take a method and try it. If it fails, admit it frankly and try another. But above all, try something." He later said: "You know I am a juggler, and I never let my right hand know what my left hand does."

FDR was a leader. He became the model of the modern president. All successors have been compared (unfavorably) to him. He cast, as historian William Luchtenberg noted, "a giant shadow."

Roosevelt needed to get off to a fast start. Nearly 15 million men were unemployed; 4,600 banks failed; industrial production fell below 50 percent of the 1929 level. His inaugural address called the nation to noble enterprise to meet the challenge of depression:

> It is hoped that the normal balance of executive and legislative authority may be wholly adequate to meet the unprecedented task before us . . . But in the event that . . . the national emergency is still critical . . . I shall ask the Congress for one remaining instrument to meet the crisis—broad executive power to wage a war against the emergency, as great as the power that would be given to me if we were in fact invaded by a foreign foe.

On his first day in office he declared a "Bank Holiday;" four days later he proposed the Emergency Banking Bill. It was the beginning of one of the most extraordinary times in American politics: The Hundred Days. From March 9 to June 15, an unrelenting succession of bills was passed by Congress.

FDR took his case for action directly to the people in the form of "Fireside Chats," radio addresses in which the president forged a close and direct link to the American people. Not only were the addresses informative and reassuring, they also were used to link presidential power to popular power, with the aim of leading Congress. Roosevelt spoke *directly* to the people; he acted *firmly* in the political arena; and he exuded *confidence* in the political future.

The president demanded "action; and action now." A national emergency required the president to act, and thus was born FDR's New Deal, the birth of the welfare state, and the beginnings of the modern presidency.

The New Deal was a combination of legislation, executive orders, and presidential proclamations. They dealt with banking reform, social security, public relief, public works projects, and a slew of other programs. Designed to put people back to work, to renew hope, and to prime the economic pump, this hodgepodge of programs was more the result of trial and error than any clear economic philosophy. While the New Deal did not end the Depression, it did renew hope for most and give jobs to some.

The increasing demands on government led to calls for greater institutional support for the presidency. Mushrooming responsibilities led to the need for increased staff. It was in this context that the presidency was transformed from a small, personalized office to a large, "impersonal" institution. At the prodding of the Brownlow Committee, which argued that "the president needs help," an Executive Office of the President was established, and thus was born the institutional presidency. (Administrative Reorganization Act, 1939).

Roosevelt began to attack the problem of the depression with a series of proposals designed to meet the economic crisis. He entered office with large Democratic majorities in both houses and with a great deal of public support. In what was to be called his "hundred days," Roosevelt set out to move the nation and the economy out of its state of depression. In addition to immediately declaring a temporary bank holiday, FDR suspended gold exports and foreign exchange operations. There soon followed a flood of legislation coming from the White House, which was quickly passed by the Congress. Acts such as the Emergency Banking Act, National Recovery Act, Agricultural Adjustment Act, and the Gold Reserve Act set the stage for presidential domination of the legislative process.

These programs met with strong public approval, and while no sudden or dramatic improvement in the economy occurred, a new hope emerged. Many of these programs began to reach the courts for judicial review. The courts acted on these bills with what appeared to be a vengeance. Conservatives were generally distressed at Roosevelt's actions during this period, but little in the way of opposition could come from the Congress (heavily controlled by the Democrats) or the public (overwhelmingly in favor of the Hundred Day legislation). The last hope was the Anti-Majoritarian Supreme Court. The conservatives had some reason for hope when looking to the Supreme Court. Dominated by conservatives, the Supreme Court Justices were not thought to be in political sympathy with the New Deal legislation. The question was, would their political preferences be translated into judicial decisions? The answer was a swift and a loud yes.

By the end of 1936, the Supreme Court had declared unconstitutional 9 of the 16 laws which were at the heart of Roosevelt's New Deal legislation.

The Hughes Court, which struck down the New Deal legislation, was an anti-majoritarian Court, made up mostly of Republican holdovers from previous administrations. Only two of the nine justices were appointed by a Democrat (McReynolds and Brandeis).

The Court's decisions were met with a great deal of criticism by the president, members of Congress, and the general public as well. Hughes, who once said (prior to his appointment as chief justice) that "the Court has found its fortress in public opinion" went directly against public opinion and struck down many of Roosevelt's most important New Deal bills.

Roosevelt felt that he had the political clout to do something about the "unresponsive" Court. He was ready to fight back. After his landslide re-election victory in the 1936 election, Roosevelt struck. Viewing his 1936 election as an endorsement of his New Deal policies, on February 5, 1937, Roosevelt unveiled what was to become his "court-packing plan." This scheme marked an attempt by Roosevelt to force the Supreme Court to change its position and become more amenable to the New Deal legislation.

But Roosevelt had overestimated his electoral mandate, and he overestimated his political strength. His court-packing plan ran into a great deal of trouble in the Congress and in the minds of the public. In Congress, the court-packing plan hastened the development of the soon to become powerful "Conservative Coalition," and in the public, support for the judicial reorganization plan was weak.

Roosevelt had clearly lost the battle, but what of the war? His court-packing plan was doomed, but in losing this battle he won the war with the Supreme Court. Between March and June, the Court gave in to Roosevelt on a number of New Deal issues. The Court approved of the Farm Mortgage Act of 1935, the amended Railway Labor Act of 1934, the National Labor Relations Act of 1935, a state minimum wage law, and the Social Security Act of 1935.

By the early 1940s, the Supreme Court had done an almost complete reversal, with control of the court passing from the Republican, anti-majoritarians to the majoritarian Democrats. The Courts' philosophy also changed. Now Roosevelt had a Court more sympathetic to the New Deal. It was indeed Roosevelt's Court. The earlier Court had made a "great retreat," and Roosevelt, who had lost the battle over court packing, had won the war over legislation. The Court recognized the superior political power the president could wield, and after an initial show of defiance, the Court backed down. It was probably a wise decision on the part of the Court. Once again, the Court half-heartedly tries, and ultimately fails, to stand up to a resolute president. It is yet another lesson in the ultimate ineffectiveness of the Supreme Court when faced by a determined president.

If an economic depression were not enough, war was looming in Europe. Roosevelt saw the war in Europe coming, but the U.S. was self-absorbed and isolationist, with no interest in the problems abroad.

FDR, ever sensitive to the limits imposed by public opinion, could not move too far too fast. To get too far ahead of public opinion was dangerous in a democracy. So Roosevelt acted—usually behind the scenes—to help England (e.g., lend-lease), while carefully trying to change public opinion.

On Sunday, December 7, 1941, the Japanese launched a surprise attack on Pearl Harbor, Hawaii. On December 8, Roosevelt asked Congress for a declaration of war against Japan. Three days later, war was declared on Germany and Italy.

If the presidency emerged from the depression stronger and more central to American politics, the second world war placed Roosevelt and the presidency at the pinnacle of power. Roosevelt was aided in this by the Supreme Court.

In 1936, the Supreme Court, in *U.S. v. Curtiss-Wright Export Corp.*, upheld a 1934 measure authorizing the president to embargo arms sales to countries engaged in conflicts. In and of itself this is not a terribly significant decision. But the language of the Court's opinion in *Curtiss-Wright* was, to most constitutional scholars, excessive if not downright wrong. The Court referred to the president as the "sole organ" of foreign policy; the executive's authority over foreign affairs was a "plenary and exclusive power." The sweeping (and questionable) language of *Curtiss-Wright* has been used by nearly every president since Roosevelt to claim extended, if not exclusive, powers over making foreign policy.

A 1937 case, *U.S. v. Belmont* legitimized the legal authority of executive agreements. In 1942 (*United States v. Pink*), the Court reaffirmed this view. These cases, with their expansive views of the president's foreign affairs powers all but made the president the nation's foreign policy czar.

The Supreme Court was faced with another test of the president's removal power in *Humphrey's Executor v. United States*. William E. Humphrey was chairman of the Federal Trade Commission and President Roosevelt asked for his resignation because, as Roosevelt said: "I do not feel that your mind and my mind go along together on either the policies or the administering of the Federal Trade Commission, and, frankly, I think it best for the people of this country that I should have a full confidence."

Humphrey refused to resign, and Roosevelt fired him. Humphrey sued, claiming that the president did not possess unlimited powers of removal over the executive departments and that the act by Roosevelt was purely political (the statute upon which Humphrey based his claim specified "inefficiency, neglect of duty, or malfeasance in office" as grounds for removal by a president). The Supreme Court, in the Humphrey case, decided against the President, and ruled that the terms of removal for certain officers could be defined by the Congress. The Court said:

Whether the power of the President to remove an officer shall prevail over the authority of Congress to condition the power by fixing a definite term and precluding a removal except for the cause, will depend upon the character of the office; the *Myers* decision, affirming the power of the President alone to make the removal, is confined to purely executive officers and that a Federal Trade Commissioner was not such an officer.[5]

When war came, Roosevelt, bolstered by public and Supreme Court support, articulated an expansive view of the president's power. In a Labor Day speech of September 7, 1942, Roosevelt asserted inherent executive prerogative:

I ask the Congress to take . . . action by the first of October. Inaction on your part by that date will leave me with an inescapable responsibility to the people of this country to see to it that the war effort is no longer imperiled by threat of economic chaos.

In the event that the Congress should fail to act, and act adequately, I shall accept the responsibility, and I will act . . .

The President has the powers, under the Constitution and under congressional acts, to take measures necessary to avert a disaster which would interfere with the winning of the war . . .

The American people can be sure that I will use my powers with a full sense of responsibility to the Constitution and to my country. The American people can also be sure that I shall not hesitate to use every power vested in me to accomplish the defeat of our enemies in any part of the world where our own safety demands such a defeat.

When the war is won, the powers under which I act automatically revert to the people—to whom they belong.

Congress caved in.

During wartime, the Constitution can be, to a degree, ignored. Presidents need not adhere to the letter or, even at times, the spirit of the law. World War II brought what Edward Corwin called:

. . . the most drastic invasion of civil rights in the United States which this war has evoked, the most drastic invasion of the rights of citizens of the United States by their own government that has thus far occurred in the history of our nation.[6]

Corwin's harsh comments derive from the actions taken by the government based upon Executive Order 9066, issued on February 19, 1942.

Based upon this order, over 112,000 Japanese-Americans (more than 80,000 of whom were American citizens) were evacuated from their homes and herded into what were called "relocation centers" situated in the western states. "The War," allowed the government to ignore the guarantees within the Constitution and Bill of Rights, and to place American citizens in these detention centers.

The Supreme Court was asked to review the legality of the government's actions, and it did so in a number of cases. The first of these cases was *Hirabayashi v. United States.* Hirabayashi was convicted in federal court of violating the curfew and with failure to report to his designated Civil Control Station. The Supreme Court decided this case on a very narrow question, avoiding the more important question of the constitutionality of the establishment of the internment centers. In a unanimous decision, the court ruled that the president and Congress could order a curfew, and thus the conviction of Hirabayashi was upheld. The chief justice wrote:

> We cannot close our eyes to the fact, demonstrated by experience, that in time of war residents having ethnic affiliations with an invading enemy may be a greater source of danger than those of different ancestry. Nor can we deny that Congress, and the military authorities acting with its authorization, have constitutional power to appraise the danger in light of facts of public notoriety. We need not now attempt to define the ultimate boundaries of the war power. In this case it is enough that circumstances within the knowledge of those charged with the responsibility for maintaining the national defense afforded a rational basis for the decision which they made. Whether we would have made it is irrelevant.[7]

In *Korematsu v. United States,* the validity of the evacuation was once again faced by the Court. Mr. Korematsu, a resident of San Leandro, California, refused to leave his home and go to one of the relocation centers. The Court was faced with the question: was the establishment of the relocation centers a proper exercise of power? The Court answered yes. In *Hirabayashi,* the Court avoided the question, and thus avoided a possible clash with the president. In *Korematsu,* the Court rationalized this extension of presidential power. In the *Korematsu* decision, Justice Black wrote:

> We are not unmindful of the hardships imposed ... upon a large group of American citizens. But hardships are part of war, and war is an aggregation of hardships. All citizens alike, both in and out of uniform, feel the impact of war in greater or lesser measure. Citizenship has its responsibilities as well as its privileges, and in time of war the burden is always heavier. Compulsory exclusion of large groups of citizens from their homes, except under circumstances of direct emergency and peril, is inconsistent with our basic governmental institutions. But when under conditions of our modern warfare our shores are threatened by hostile forces, the power to protect must be commensurate with the threatened danger.[8]

The third case, *Ex Parte Endo,*[9] decided on the same day as *Korematsu,* upheld the right of a Japanese-American girl whose loyalty to the United States had been established, to a writ of habeas corpus. This writ freed her from her relocation center—two and one-half years after she had filed her petition. But once again, the Court avoided a direct ruling on the constitutionality of the confinement program.

Throughout the war, and in all constitutional crises, be they wars, economic crises, or internal insurrections, the president has "come to the rescue" of the system of government. Presidents have come to be looked upon as our saviors. The knight on the white horse has been the chief executive. In such crisis periods, the power of the president has been expanded to an extent which seems to violate the precepts of democratic government. The situation during the Second World War was one such crisis. Roosevelt was "given" extraconstitutional powers (or he simply assumed them), and the system revolved around him.

During the war, Roosevelt masterfully led the Allies to victory over the Axis powers. Exercising expansive executive authority, Roosevelt's war leadership further contributed to the developing "president-centric" trend of government. The dual emergencies of the depression and world war not only placed the presidency at center stage, but Roosevelt was so adept at the uses of power that a heroic presidency image came to dominate the public imagination.

From that point on, the public looked to the president for leadership. The "Clerk" president of the Adams, Madison, Monroe eras was now the leader of the nation. A "Superman" image grew around the presidency. FDR

Crimean Conference—Prime Minister Winston Churchill, President Franklin D. Roosevelt, and Marshal Joseph Stalin at the palace in Yalta, where the Big Three met

was the model, and all subsequent presidents were expected to live up to his elevated status. The U.S. had become a "presidential republic."[10]

The president was not only leader-in-chief, he was also a national shaman. Through the use of words and symbols, the president was expected to provide meaning, articulate a vision, and define reality for the public. The rhetorical presidency emerged as central to the American system. Recognizing that "the greatest duty of a statesman is to educate," Roosevelt used his public voice to lead as well as to follow public opinion. "The presidency," he told a reporter, "is predominantly a place of moral leadership," and FDR used his office to speak to, talk with, and, on occasion, lead the public. After Roosevelt, "Presidential leadership became, by definition, public leadership."[11]

After Roosevelt, the minimalist state and the minimalist presidency were no longer possible. He utterly transformed America. Serving as president during two of the most difficult periods of American history, facing two major crises, Roosevelt redefined both the role of the federal government and the job of the president. He was the architect of a New Deal coalition—a resilient and long-term political realignment—that made the Democrats the nation's majority party, which dominated the political landscape for half a century.

Roosevelt served longer than any other president. He appointed the first woman to the cabinet (Frances Perkins, Secretary of Labor), officially recognized the U.S.S.R., broke the "no third term" taboo, fought through the depression, led the nation through World War II, supervised the building of the atomic bomb, and established the presidency as the center of political action. The Roosevelt years mark the high point of executive authority in America.

"The essence of Roosevelt's Presidency," wrote political scientist Clinton Rossiter, "was his airy eagerness to meet the age head on." This helped give a frightened and defeated nation the hope necessary to go on. As Roosevelt himself said

> The Presidency is not merely an administrative office. That is the least of it. It is pre-eminently a place of moral leadership.
>
> All of our great Presidents were leaders of thought at times when certain historic ideas in the life of the nation had to be clarified. Washington personifies the idea of Federal Union, Jefferson practically originated the party system as we now know it by opposing the democratic theory to the republicanism of Hamilton. This theory was reaffirmed by Jackson.
>
> Two great principles of our government were forever put beyond question by Lincoln. Cleveland, coming into office following an era of great political corruption, typified rugged honesty. Theodore Roosevelt and Wilson were both moral leaders, each in his own way and for his own time, who used the Presidency as a pulpit.
>
> That is what the office is—a superb opportunity for reapplying, applying to new conditions, the simple rules of human conduct to which we always go back. Without leadership alert and sensitive to change, we . . . lose our way.

Franklin Delano Roosevelt earned his place as one of America's Mount Rushmore presidents. He became an American icon, along with Washington, Jefferson, and Lincoln. He enlarged the presidency and expanded the scope of government. He was an event-making president.

As was so often the case, the strong presidencies of TR and Wilson were followed by rather weak presidents. But, as is also often the case, the age of weak leaders did not last.

In the midst of the depression, the nation demanded strong leadership, and Franklin Roosevelt supplied that leadership in abundance. His accomplishments are breathtaking, leading the nation through the crisis of an economic depression and a massive world war. In the process, FDR established what many refer to as the "modern presidency," a strong, activist model of leadership most of his successors felt compelled to try to emulate.

⚘ 6 ⚘

The Cold War/Heroic Presidency
Harry S Truman to John F. Kennedy

The United States emerged from World War II as the dominant or hegemonic power of the West. As the "only" superpower, the U.S. had sobering responsibilities, as well as exciting opportunities.

It wasn't long before U.S. world leadership was challenged. The Soviet Union, while not having the superpower status of the U.S., nonetheless began to clash with the U.S. over the shape of the post-war world. A bipolar conflict, known as the Cold War, quickly enveloped the globe.

To meet the challenge of the Cold War, the U.S. set up a permanent wartime economy, created a national security state, and gave to the president vast powers to fight this ongoing cold war. The Republic had been overtaken by Empire, and the United States was the new hegemonic power.

In the space of 50 years, the U.S. went from a small, provincial, isolationist nation to the world's mightiest superpower, with a large standing army, a nuclear arsenal of awesome destructive power, and responsibility for world stability. Meeting the burdens of empire required a strong, centralized leader. The Cold War presidency evolved.

The U.S. of the Cold War era was a vastly different nation from the one FDR governed in 1933. The depression and New Deal led to the acceptance of a more positive governmental approach to economic intervention and management. World War II centralized production and put the economy on a war footing; the public had also come to expect, even demand, strong, assertive presidential leadership. When in the immediate aftermath of World War II, the Cold War engulfed the world, it seemed only natural to once again turn to the institution "created" by FDR to see us through the new crisis.

Harry S Truman
1945–1953

Harry Truman[1] inherited the presidency toward the end of World War II. If the end was in sight, the war was far from over. Important decisions about the conduct of the war had yet to be made. And once the war ended, the U.S. was thrust into a position of global leadership and had to respond to the growing conflict with the Soviet Union.

Harry S Truman

Barely 5'10", nearsighted, he spoke in rough, direct language. He had a common touch and a simple way about him. Union leader Al Whitney called him "a ribbon clerk." He had served just 82 days as vice president when Roosevelt died. And yet this unassuming man would make some of the most momentous decisions in history. If FDR refashioned the presidency, Truman gave focus and direction to the post-war era. Few presidents had a greater impact on world history than Harry S Truman.

On April 12, 1945, Vice President Harry Truman walked to the basement office used by House Speaker Sam Rayburn for an end-of-the-day conversation and a glass of bourbon with some of his friends in Congress. As he entered he was told that Steve Early, Roosevelt's press secretary, wanted him to call the White House. Early's pained voice and instructions for coming to the White House gave a clear indication of what had happened. Truman proclaimed, "Jesus Christ and General Jackson" as he put down the phone. When he entered the White House he was informed by Eleanor Roosevelt as she put her arm on his shoulder, "Harry, the president is dead." For a moment, Truman was unable to speak. Then he said, "Is there anything I can do for you?" "Is there anything we can do for you," Mrs. Roosevelt replied, "for you are the one in trouble now."

Roosevelt had been president for so long that for most people, thinking of someone else in the office was all but impossible. And yet here was Truman, asked to fill the giant shoes of an American icon. Few believed he was up to the task.

At his first cabinet meeting as president Truman said, "I feel like I have been struck by a bolt of lightning." The next day, while visiting the Capitol he told a group of reporters, "Boys, if you ever pray, pray for me now."

His new responsibilities were awesome. Not only was he expected to bring a successful conclusion to the war, but he also had to decide what to do with "the bomb," how to guide the nation to demobilization, how to deal with the post-war fallout in Europe and create a new post-war world, how to respond to a new antagonist, and how to fill FDR's shoes.

Clement Attlee, Harry Truman, and Joseph Stalin

When Germany surrendered on May 8, 1945, it became clear that the Soviet Union intended to continue to occupy Eastern Europe and maintain control of the eastern portion of Germany. In July 1945, Truman met with Stalin at the Potsdam Conference to discuss this and other issues, but there was no resolution. During the meeting, Truman gave the go-ahead to use the atomic bomb on Hiroshima and, if necessary, Nagasaki, to hasten Japanese surrender. The bombings, on August 6 and August 9, killed over 120,000 and forced the Japanese into unconditional surrender on August 14, 1945.

As the problems of the world war ended, the problems of the cold war began. Soviet leader Joseph Stalin quickly imposed communist governments in Eastern Europe. Several Western European nations appeared on the verge of collapse. In an effort to bolster noncommunist governments, in March 1947, Truman promised support for any nation struggling against communist takeover.

The *Truman Doctrine*, as it was called, initially involved emergency aid to Greece and Turkey. The *Marshall Plan* followed, an ambitious effort to rebuild Western Europe. Then the North Atlantic Treaty Organization (NATO) was born, a U.S.-Western European security pact. This was the beginning of a "containment" policy designed to contain the spread of Soviet influence around the globe. This containment policy was followed, more or less, by every president until the collapse of the Soviet Union in 1989. It was this program, established by Harry S Truman, that ended up winning the Cold War.

Out of the Cold War, a national security state was established. The National Security Act of 1947 reorganized the military under the control of the secretary of defense and created the National Security Council and the Central Intelligence Agency. The president was at the head of the new (and potentially dangerous) national security state. In order for the presidency to grow in power, presidents needed to institutionalize, that is, build into the minds of the public and Congress an institutional set of expectations regarding the new powers of the office. The creation and institutionalization of the national security state, greatly expanded the powers, responsibilities, and independence of the presidency in dealing with foreign affairs. "I make American foreign policy," Truman told the Jewish War Veterans in 1948. It was a preposterous claim of independent power, made all the more preposterous by its accuracy.

Since a hot war between the Soviet Union and the United States was, in a nuclear age, far too dangerous even to contemplate, smaller surrogate wars were fought around the globe.

One of the first such clashes took place in Korea. North Korea, controlled by the communists, invaded South Korea in 1950. Truman called for "police" action to repel the North. Truman chose to order U.S. forces into combat on his own claimed authority, and did not ask Congress for a declaration of war.

Senator James P. Kem (R., Missouri) rose in the Senate chamber, "I notice that in the president's statement he says, 'I have ordered the fleet to prevent any attack on Formosa.' Does that mean he has arrogated to himself the authority of declaring war?"

Indeed, that is precisely what Truman had done. In the tense atmosphere of the cold war, the president grabbed power and claimed a new, unilateral authority. The war power now seemed to belong to the president.

But the Korean War was a stalemate, and soon the president and General Douglas MacArthur were at odds. As MacArthur became more public in his criticism of Truman, directly challenging the president, Truman felt he had no other option than to fire the popular general. He did so. A political firestorm about the MacArthur firing swept the nation, but Truman stuck to his guns. In his diary, Truman called the public reaction to his firing of MacArthur "Quite an explosion." But with or without public approval, Truman knew he was right—a general could not undermine the commander-in-chief. Truman said:

> I wonder how far Moses would have gone if he had taken a poll in Egypt?
>
> What would Jesus Christ have preached if He had taken a poll in the land of Israel?
>
> Where would the Reformation have gone if Martin Luther had taken a poll?
>
> It isn't polls or public opinion alone of the moment that counts. It is right and wrong, and leadership—men with fortitude, honesty and a belief in the right that makes epochs in the history of the world.

In 1952, the Korean War raged, and in an effort to avoid a steel strike that might have affected the war effort, President Truman issued an executive order calling for the seizure of steel mills. A major constitutional controversy ensued. Claiming "implied" or inherent powers during an (undeclared) emergency, Truman felt confident that the Supreme Court would uphold the seizure.

But the Supreme Court, in *Youngstown Sheet & Tube Co. v. Sawyer* (1952), found against Truman. Justice Hugo Black argued in his opinion for the Court that Truman's order was a de facto statute and that the Constitution did not provide the president with the lawmaking power:

> In the framework of our Constitution, the President's power to see that the laws are faithfully executed refutes the idea that he is to be a lawmaker. The Constitution limits his functions in the lawmaking process to the recommending of laws he thinks wise and the vetoing of laws he thinks bad. And the Constitution is neither silent nor equivocal about who shall make laws which the President is to execute. The first section of the first article says that "All legislative powers herein granted shall be vested in a Congress of the United States . . ."

After the Court decision, Truman needed the Congress; he could not act alone. The Court's rebuff of a claim of presidential authority was significant, for rarely did it curb presidential power in the realm of foreign affairs, especially during war, declared or otherwise. There were, after all, limits on the expansive Cold War presidency.

If the president possessed sweeping (but on occasion limited) powers in foreign affairs, what of his domestic power? Truman, following Roosevelt, further extended the president's powers over domestic affairs.

During the Truman administration several new executive agencies were created and institutionalized, including the Council of Economic Advisers, the Atomic Energy Commission, the National Security Council, the Central Intelligence Agency, and the National Science Foundation. These agencies strengthened the president's control over policy decisions and gave him access to expertise and information so vital to controlling the political agenda.

After World War II, Truman showed himself to be a reformer in the tradition of FDR. He proposed an ambitious and progressive series of reforms known as the Fair Deal. Many of his proposals failed to be passed by Congress, but he kept the heat on and demonstrated that it was the president's agenda that mattered most.

One of the seminal domestic acts was the *Employment Act of 1946*, which formalized the federal government's promise to maintain a healthy economy. The law stated, "it is the continuing policy and responsibility of the Federal Government . . . to promote maximum employment, production, and purchasing power."

Truman also, at great risk, was the first modern president to attempt civil rights reforms. In 1948, he issued an executive order ending racial discrimination in federal government employment. Further, he created the President's Committee on Civil Rights, created a civil rights division in the Department of Justice, ordered the secretary of defense to eliminate racial discrimination in the armed services, created fair-employment guidelines in the executive branch, and advocated several legislative reforms (which the Congress did not pass).

There was also a "dark side" to Truman's usual progressivism. Pushed by the anticommunist hysteria of the times and in an effort to head off criticism, Truman authorized a "loyalty program" in federal employment. Designed to weed out communists from the federal government, this program, along with other reactionary actions of the age, led to significant violations of constitutional rights and liberties.

Truman reaffirmed the modern presidency created by Roosevelt. He exercised bold, innovative leadership in tough times. To Truman, the president was the center of the American (and international) universe. A sign on his White House desk read: "The Buck Stops Here."

On the evening of January 15, 1953 Truman delivered a televised farewell address.

> "I suppose," he said, "that history will remember my term in office as the years when the 'cold war' began to overshadow our lives. I have hardly had a day in office that has not been dominated by this all-embracing struggle . . . And always in the background there has been the atomic bomb."

> "Starting an atomic war," he declared, "is totally unthinkable for ratio-nal men."

He added:

> "The President—whoever he is—has to decide. He can't pass the buck to anybody . . . I want you to realize how big a job, how hard a job it is—not for my sake, because I am stepping out of it—but for the sake of my suc-cessor . . . Regardless of your politics, whether you are Republican or De-mocrat, your fate is tied up with what is done here in this room."

"I wasn't one of the great Presidents," Truman said after leaving the White House, "but I had a good time trying to be one, I can tell you that."

In his day, Truman was not a very popular president. (In his day, it was popular to joke, "To err is Truman"). However, he is considered to be a Near Great president by most historians. The size of the problems he faced, his handling of those problems, and the long-term impact of his decisions, all lead to a very high rating.

During Truman's presidency, Germany and Japan surrendered, the U.S. dropped the first atomic bombs, the post-World War II world of the Cold War and containment were created, Europe was rebuilt, communism was resisted, NATO was created, the Marshall Plan and Truman Doctrine were implemented, and civil rights became a national issue. But there were also frustrations and mistakes. The Korean War was a stalemate, Truman had rough going with the Republican Congress, Joseph McCarthy threatened American liberties, and China fell to the Communists.

Truman took America and the West into a new and dangerous age, pro-moted America's interests, protected the world's fragile democracies, held the ambitions of the Soviet Union in check, and pressed for reforms at home. "I must confess, Winston Churchill told Truman at the end of his presi-dency, "I held you in very low regard . . . I loathed you taking the place of Franklin Roosevelt. I misjudged you badly . . . you more than anyone have saved Western civilization."

Dwight D. Eisenhower
1953–1961

After 20 years of Democrats in control of the White House, the Republicans regained the presidency with the election of Dwight D. Eisenhower.[2] Many Republicans believed Ike would reverse both the policies of his predeces-sors and the president centeredness of politics. While Eisenhower was not an activist president in the Rooseveltian sense, he was also not a reactionary, and in his eight years as president, he maintained rather than reversed the drive toward presidential government.

Dwight D. Eisenhower

Thin, partly bald, with an engaging smile and a way of murdering the syntax of a sentence, Eisenhower wanted to preside rather than lead. Thin on oratorical skills and not adept at the politics of horse trading, Ike nonetheless did a very credible job as president. The nation wanted a calm, apolitical executive, and Ike provided it for them. The era was, as economist John Kenneth Galbraith said unkindly, one of "the bland leading the bland."

A career military man, Eisenhower also knew Washington and how to move in the corridors of power. Eisenhower was personally conservative in his policy views but felt the Republican party had to move to the "middle of the road" to compete effectively with the Democrats.

Not consumed with a reformer's zeal and not driven by an activist agenda, Eisenhower was not to exercise an aggressive form of political leadership. But he also wasn't about to roll back the New Deal and Fair Deal (much to the chagrin of many of his Republican cohorts). Ike appeared to be nonpolitical, but in reality he often displayed what political scientist Fred Greenstein referred to as a "hidden-hand" style of leadership.[3] Often working behind the scenes, Eisenhower tried to exert soft leadership in nonconspicuous ways.

Sometimes Ike's hidden-hand leadership was a bit too hidden, as when he failed to confront the irresponsible and bullying tactics of fellow Republican Joseph McCarthy, whose attacks on "communists in the government" got progressively more reckless. When McCarthy attacked the patriotism of General George C. Marshall (one of the greatest Americans of the twentieth century), Eisenhower refused to defend his former mentor. Ike did criticize McCarthy "behind the scenes," but there are times when even a hidden hand must be revealed.

Ike's hidden-hand leadership may have insulated him from public criticism, but it also meant that the president would not exert moral leadership when necessary. On the rising civil rights movement, Eisenhower was reluctant to use the moral authority of the presidency to lead or educate. He did (reluctantly) send federal troops to Little Rock, Arkansas to enforce school desegregation; and he did, again somewhat reluctantly, sign the Civil Rights Acts of 1957 and 1960, but he never threw the moral weight of the presidency behind this important issue.

Eisenhower was generally reluctant to intrude too deeply into the affairs of Congress. He did not see himself as "the" chief legislator. But one area where his leadership of Congress *did* make a difference was in initiating the building of the Interstate Highway System in 1956. Over forty thousand miles of roads were built as a result of this legislation.

In foreign affairs Eisenhower, the decorated general, was nonbelligerent and deeply concerned with avoiding war. He negotiated an end to the war in Korea in 1953, used the CIA for a variety of covert operations around the world (Iran, Guatemala, Laos, and Indonesia), oversaw the partition of Vietnam into North and South, spearheaded the creation of the Southeast Asia Treaty Organization (SEATO) in 1954, and witnessed the Communist takeover of Cuba in 1959. The Soviet Union continued to cause problems, as the 1956 invasion of Hungary demonstrated, but the U.S. refused to intervene, determined to avoid a hot war with the Soviets over a secondary interest to the U.S. Ike hoped to reach an accord with the Soviet Union, but when a U.S. spy plane (a U-2 flown by Gary Powers) was shot down over Soviet territory in 1960, such hopes broke down.

Eisenhower's ambitions were more limited than those of his predecessors. He did not wish to extend, nor did he try to reverse the New Deal. He succeeded in bringing the isolationist Republicans into a more internationalist perspective, left behind a powerful CIA (and a dangerous temptation to use secret, covert, and sometimes morally repugnant methods), and added to America's nuclear arsenal. He left a number of key domestic problems, such as civil rights, both unsolved and unattended to. "No president in history," wrote Clinton Rossiter, " . . . failed more poignantly to use his power."

In his 1961 farewell address, Eisenhower surprised the nation by warning of the dangers of the growing "military-industrial complex" that was growing to dominate American politics. He warned the country there would be a "recurring temptation" to solve crises through "some spectacular and costly action" that promised to be "the miraculous solution to all current difficulties." Such a miracle cure, Eisenhower declared, did not exist, nor could "a huge increase" in defense spending find the cure.

John F. Kennedy
1961–1963

If the FDR halo seemed to be in limbo during the Eisenhower years, Ike's successor was determined to pull it out of mothballs. John F. Kennedy,[4] the Camelot president, wanted an activist administration, and after eight years of Eisenhower, the public seemed ready for action. But try as he might, President Kennedy's legislative proposals often fell prey to unresponsive leaders in Congress. Stymied by an intransigent Congress, which took the system of checks and balances quite seriously, the Kennedy legislative record was, at best, mixed. The first Roman Catholic to be elected president, and the youngest ever elected, Kennedy won the presidency by a razor-thin margin in 1960. Kennedy presided over the Bay of Pigs fiasco in Cuba, placed military advisors in Vietnam, and successfully led the nation through the Cuban missile crisis. But his ambitious and progressive domestic initiatives often were blocked by a Congress controlled by conservatives in his own party. Kennedy did achieve tax cuts, actually passed later under LBJ, which stimulated economic growth, and he started the Peace Corps and placed civil rights reform on the presidential agenda, but overall he was stymied by a reluctant Congress.

This led to grumblings among the public and scholars: "how can the Congress stand in the way of progress? . . . there are too many checks on the presidency . . . We need *more* power for the president" went the chants. If the presidency was good and just, it also deserved to be strong, and it was the Congress that stood in the way.

Kennedy was young, attractive, and elegant. He was remarkably photogenic, and he, his children and his glamorous wife, Jackie, became America's royal family. It was the age of Camelot, a romanticized era when anything seemed possible. Kennedy exuded charm and sophistication. Author John Steinbeck remarked, "What a joy that literacy is no longer prima-facie

John F. Kennedy

evidence of treason." Only in later years would we learn of a darker side of Camelot: plots against Castro and the president's private affairs.

Washington reporters knew about President Kennedy's "active" private life, but at that time it was not considered relevant or proper to write about such private matters. Only later would the stories of Kennedy's dalliances become public knowledge.

The transformation of the president from chief clerk to tribune of the people was all but complete by the end of the New Deal. But with the advent of television, the president had a new tool to reach directly to the people. Thus Kennedy could state that "only the president represents the national interest. And upon him alone converge all the needs and aspirations of all parts of the country, all departments of government, all nations of the world." That's quite a job description! And while constitutionally that description should be much in doubt, in practical terms that is precisely how presidents viewed themselves and how much of the public viewed them as well. Presidents did not give up their claim to a constitutional base of power. They merely grafted another power—tribune of the people—onto their already inflated job descriptions.

John Kennedy was president when television first became a factor in presidential politics. He took full advantage of this new tool for reaching out to the public. His televised press conferences were virtuoso performances as he stood there cool, calm, witty, intelligent. The camera "loved him." Politics was beginning to cross the line into entertainment, and the president was becoming a national celebrity.

Kennedy summoned the nation to action. If Eisenhower left much undone, Kennedy was determined to get much done. But he realized that revolutions are not built on thin electoral victories, so he pragmatically pursued a reformist agenda.

The White House, he asserted, "must be the center of moral leadership." But on some of the pressing moral issues of the day, Kennedy was a reluctant reformer. He avoided civil rights until it became politically unacceptable to do so. Was this wisdom or cowardice? As FDR knew, it was dangerous to get too far out in front of public opinion. Kennedy waited until the civil rights issue gained prominence, then became its champion.

As Kennedy took office, the civil rights movement was picking up steam. Several violent confrontations between demonstrators and police officials made headline news. In Mississippi and Alabama, reactionary governors tried to prevent black students from enrolling in state universities. Riots followed. "Freedom riders" flocked into the South, hoping to work for racial equality. At first Kennedy was a "reluctant revolutionary," but as events built to the boiling point, the president intervened. Blacks desperately needed the moral force of the presidency to help their cause. Kennedy obliged. Speaking over national television from the Oval Office, Kennedy said the nation faced a "moral crisis as a country and a people." This cannot be the land of the free "except for the Negroes . . . The heart of the question is whether all Americans are to be afforded equal rights and equal opportunities, whether we are going to treat our fellow Americans as we want to be treated." Then, in an especially moving passage, he said, "We cannot say to 10 percent of the population that you can't have that right; that your children can't have the chance to develop whatever talents they have; that the only way that they are going to get their rights is to go into the streets and demonstrate. I think we owe them and we owe ourselves a better country than that."

Another Kennedy priority was to land a man on the moon. The "space race" with the Soviets pushed Kennedy to promote space exploration, and the president promised to land a man on the moon by the end of the decade (an American landed on the moon by 1969). Kennedy set in motion an ambitious and successful space program that involved new technologies and gave the nation a great sense of accomplishment.

Elsewhere in his domestic program, Kennedy faced frustration after frustration. His efforts at developing a "New Frontier" of domestic programs failed to pass a Democrat-controlled Congress, and Kennedy had to settle for a few meager victories, such as tax cuts and small spending increases in the president's projects.

In foreign affairs, Kennedy began his administration with a blunder. The president approved of plans, drawn up during the Eisenhower administration, for an invasion of Communist-controlled Cuba by Cuban refugees trained and supported by the United States. When the invasion faltered, Kennedy refused to allow the U.S. military to intervene, thereby guaranteeing the failure of the mission. The "Bay of Pigs" taught the young president lessons. "How could I have been so stupid?" he asked. "It's a hell of a way to learn things." He took full public responsibility for the disaster (and his popularity shot up afterwards).

President Kennedy was cautious about committing U.S. combat forces in Vietnam, and he extended but did not guarantee long-term U.S. support of South Vietnam. Kennedy had several successes in foreign policy; the Alliance for Progress in Latin America, protection of Berlin against Soviet threats, the Peace Corps, and, most dramatically, the Cuban missile crisis.

In October 1962, intelligence reports revealed that the Soviet Union was building nuclear missile sites in Cuba. The president demanded their removal and ordered a naval quarantine of the island. After several tense days, when the world was poised on the brink of nuclear war, the Russians backed down and removed the missiles.

The threat of nuclear war changed Kennedy from a belligerent "cold warrior" to a man determined to reduce the risk of nuclear annihilation. In 1963, the U.S. and Soviet Union signed the Nuclear Test Ban Treaty, which barred atmospheric testing of nuclear weapons. It may have been Kennedy's greatest accomplishment. In a speech, he discussed the futility of the arms race: "For in the final analysis, our most basic common link is that we all inhabit this small planet. We all breathe the same air. We all cherish our children's future. And we are all mortal . . . Let us reexamine our attitude toward the cold war, remembering that we are not engaged in a debate, seeking to pile up debating points."

On November 22, 1963, while on a political fence-mending visit to Dallas, Texas, President Kennedy was assassinated. He served as president for only one thousand days. Questions of "what might have been" linger. His charm, elegance, and vision brought a whole generation of young men and women into public service. His call for a caring, compassionate America, his call for sacrifice, and his inspiring image of a better America still animate political action. His achievements as president cannot be measured simply by his accomplishments or his failures (Bay of Pigs, Vietnam). It isn't merely a question of what John Kennedy did, it is also a question of what he brought out in the nation: a spirit of sacrifice, a notion that public service was honorable, a call to be our better selves. As Thomas Cronin has written, "His greatness lies less in what he achieved than in what he proposed and began." Cronin added: "In the end he had an impact on all of us who lived in this country at the time. If nothing else he made people think of politics, the presidency, and government in different ways. His impact has less to do with conventional legislative or administrative achievements than it does with attitudes, values, and symbols. His ultimate contributions were far more than the sum of his record in the White House."[5] And James MacGregor Burns offers this verdict in his book *The Power to Lead*:

> In the longer and broader judgment of history . . . he will be seen as a politician of extraordinary personal qualities who rhetorically summoned the American people to a moment of activism and greatness, who fell back on a conventional politics of brokerage, manipulation, and consensus once he attained office, who found the institutional constraints on action—especially in Congress—far more formidable than he had expected, who was intellectually too much committed to existing institutions to attempt to unfreeze them but lacked the passionate moral commitment necessary to try to transcend the restraints—and then, in his third year in the presidency and his last year on earth, he began to find his true direction and make a moral and political commitment to it.[6]

He may have been a man with personal flaws, but he appealed to the better angels within the American people.[7] He was inspirational and inspiring.

In his book *In Search of History: A Personal History*, Theodore H. White wrote:

> So the epitaph on the Kennedy Administration became Camelot—a magic moment in American history, when gallant men danced with beautiful women, when great deeds were done, when artists, writers and poets met at the White House, and the barbarians beyond the walls held back.
>
> Which is, of course, a misreading of history. The magic Camelot of John F. Kennedy never existed . . . the knights of his round table were able, tough, ambitious men, capable of kindness, also capable of error . . . What made them a group and established their companionship was their leader. Of them all Kennedy was the toughest, the most intelligent, the most attractive—and inside, the least romantic. He was a realistic dealer in men, a master of games who understood the importance of ideas. He assumed his responsibilities fully. He advanced the cause of America at home and abroad. But he posed for the first time the great question of the sixties and seventies: What kind of people are we Americans? What do we want to become?

The onset of the Cold War, and the emergence of the United States as *the* world leader in an age of bipolar competition greatly added to the power of the presidency. Harry Truman helped establish a national security state, and all of his successors more or less followed his containment policy toward the Soviet Union until the end of the Cold War. In this age, the presidency was—especially in foreign affairs—the vital center of American politics.

7

Great Society to Demonization/
Imperial to Imperiled
Lyndon B. Johnson to Ronald Reagan

The untimely death of John Kennedy in 1963 left unattained the legislative agenda of the slain president. But his successor, Lyndon Johnson, was a legislative genius who, exploiting the opportunity, managed not only to pass most of the Kennedy proposals that lay dormant but also even expanded Kennedy's activist program and promoted a more ambitious social agenda, which he called the "Great Society." In 1964 and 1965, Johnson passed bill after bill, far surpassing anything his critics though possible. It seemed the FDR halo and Camelot had merged to produce a protean presidency of power of purpose. We were a nation intoxicated by presidential power.

The FDR halo was truly revived. Lyndon Johnson brought the strong-presidency model back to life. The public could breathe easier knowing that a strong president—a superman—was once again at the helm. Johnson's success confirmed the heroic-presidency model. It was proof positive that a strong presidency was a good presidency, that more presidential power meant greater public good. The public placed its trust in the president, invested its hopes in the office, saw the president as powerful, good, and trustworthy.

But it would soon prove to be misplaced trust, because the seeds of the "imperial presidency" planted in the early Cold War era grew in this period, and it would not be long before public trust turned to disdain. Vietnam and Watergate undermined the heroic presidency and led to an imperial presidency.

Lyndon B. Johnson
1963–1969

The sudden, tragic death of President Kennedy put Lyndon Johnson[1] in the White House. Johnson was an experienced legislator, a big (6'3") burly Texan who seemed larger than life. He was an overbearing, domineering man of monumental ambition, an earthy sense of humor, and a need to be the center of attention.

Lyndon B. Johnson

Johnson's manners tended to be imperious. He often spoke of the "State of My Union Address," and of "My Supreme Court." After reviewing some Vietnam-bound marines, President Johnson started toward a helicopter. An officer stopped him, pointed to another chopper, and said,

"That's your helicopter over there, sir." "Son," said LBJ, "they are all my helicopters."

At a White House luncheon, Bill Moyers was saying grace, when Johnson interrupted; "Speak up, Bill! I can't hear a damn thing." Moyers looked up and said quietly, "I wasn't addressing you, Mr. President."

Lyndon Johnson was a legislative genius. In 1965 and 1966, he and the 89th Congress passed an astounding array of bills: Medicare, Medicaid, the Civil Rights Act, the War on Poverty, the Air Pollution Control Act, the Elementary and Secondary Education Act. They also created the Departments of Transportation and of Housing and Urban Development. The number of major bills passed was truly amazing. While the table may have been set by John Kennedy, it was Johnson who got the bills through Congress.

Johnson's Great Society rivaled the New Deal in size and importance. "There is but one way for a president to deal with the Congress." Johnson said, "and that is continuously, incessantly, and without interruption. If it's going to work, the relationship between the president and Congress has got to be almost incestuous." No other president had Johnson's understanding of the Congress or its members. He knew their strengths, weaknesses, what they liked to drink, and what they did in their spare time. He knew when to push, where to push, how far to push. "I pleaded, I reasoned, I argued, I urged, I warned," said Johnson of his lobbying efforts.

It all seemed so grand. Lyndon Johnson's remarkable legislative achievements in the wake of John Kennedy's tragic assassination seemed to confirm for many the wisdom of the strong-presidency model: the presidency was seen as the seat of wisdom, virtue, and effectiveness, and Lyndon Johnson looked like a Mount Rushmore leader.

But just when the public was lulled into a false sense of complacency and security concerning the benevolence of presidential power, things began to change. And they changed quickly and dramatically. It started with Vietnam.

U.S. involvement in Vietnam began quietly, escalated slowly, and eventually led to tragedy. By 1966, the United States was engaged in a war that it could not win and from which it could not (honorably) withdraw. It was a "presidential war," and it brought the Johnson administration to its knees.

As U.S. involvement escalated, and as victory seemed farther and farther away, blame was placed squarely on the shoulders of President Johnson. Although the Constitution gives the power to declare war to the Congress, in practice since the Truman administration and the "Korean Conflict," presidents have often acted unilaterally in this regard. By the time Johnson came to office, presidents had been setting policy in Vietnam for 20 years, virtually unencumbered by the Congress. As U.S. involvement escalated, it was the president who was calling the shots. The tragedy of Lyndon Johnson is that after such a sterling start, after such great success, the blunder of Vietnam would overwhelm him and the nation. From such great heights, the president fell to such tragic depths. The nation was torn apart.

The glue that bound Americans together had lost its adhesiveness, and in its place, divisiveness and conflict overtook the nation. The strong presidency, so long seen as the savior of the American system, now seemed too powerful, too dangerous, too unchecked—in short, a threat. After years of hearing calls for "more power to the president," by the late 1960s the plea was to rein in the overly powerful "monster" in the White House.

It was a rude awakening. All the hopes, all the trust, all the expectations that had been entrusted to the presidency were being shattered. Johnson was compelled not to seek reelection in 1968 when faced with the near certainty of electoral defeat.

As president, Lyndon Johnson rose to the heights, then hit rock bottom. He had a far-reaching and positive impact on the lives of black Americans. His Great Society programs greatly improved the quality of life for many Americans, especially the poor. But Vietnam haunted the Johnson legacy. It was his glaring weakness.

At first Johnson expanded the power of the presidency and generated high expectations for what the office could and should accomplish. But with Vietnam, support for the presidency went into free-fall. He achieved much: the Civil Rights Act of 1964, the Economic Opportunity Act of 1984, Medicare, Medicaid, the Elementary and Secondary Education Act of 1965, the Higher Education Act of 1965, and the Voting Rights Act of 1965. But he failed mightily as well, in Vietnam and the domestic disturbances of the '60s.

After Johnson announced he would not seek another term as president, he went into a deep depression. "I've never felt lower in my life. How do you think it feels to be completely rejected by the party you've spent your life with, knowing that your name cannot be mentioned without choruses of boos and obscenities? How would you feel? It makes me feel that nothing's been worth it. And I've tried. Things may not have turned out as you wanted or even as I wanted. But God knows I've tried. And I've given it my best all these years. I woke up at six and worked until one or two in the morning every day, Saturdays and Sundays. And it comes to this. It just doesn't seem fair."[2]

In a book about his former boss, President Johnson, published in 1982, Press Secretary George Reedy wrote the following.

> He may have been a son of a bitch but he was a colossal son of a bitch. . . . He also possessed the finest quality of a politician. It was a sense of the direction of political power—the forces that were sweeping the masses. He did not merely content himself by getting ahead of those forces. He mastered the art of directing them . . .
>
> Of all his qualities, however, the most important was that he knew how to make our form of government work. That is an art that has been lost since his passing and we are suffering heavily as a result.

Richard M. Nixon
1969–1974

Brilliant, but deeply flawed. An innovative foreign policy strategist, but a small, hurtful, angry man. Richard M. Nixon,[3] 5'11", with a receding hairline, was deeply insecure, vindictive, a fighter, morally obtuse, the first and only president to resign from office (to avoid impeachment and conviction) for abuse of power and criminal behavior. He remains an enigma and a paradox.

Richard M. Nixon

Richard Milhouse Nixon was a complex, multi-dimensional figure. He was not, as some of his critics suggest, a shallow, one-dimensional person. He was a man of many contradictions. There were, as cartoonist Herblock over-simplified, two Nixons: the good Nixon and the bad Nixon, and they existed side by side within the man.

Simple, easy descriptions do not apply to Richard Nixon. Was he, as Garry Wills suggests, "the least 'authentic' man alive?" the "Market's servant?" "plastic?" Was he, as Irving Grant wrote, "a synthetic figure?" Or was he, as Theodore White has written, "a quintessentially insecure man . . . uncomfortable with people?" Does Henry Kissinger's "the essence of this man is loneliness" apply? Or do Nixon's own "I'm an introvert in an extrovert's profession," and "I'm not a lovable man" apply? Arthur Miller wrote that he "marched instinctively down the crooked path," and George V. Higgins said that he was "a virtuoso of deception." Columnist Murray Kempton wrote that Nixon was "the President of every place in the country which does not have a bookstore." Nixon's own chief of staff, Bob Haldeman, likened Nixon to a piece of quartz crystal, "He was very complex, with all kinds of light and dark faces, depending on where you're looking from."

Longtime Nixon friend and speechwriter Raymond Price sees his former boss as a something of a paradox. Theodore White also noticed the paradoxical quality of Nixon, when he wrote of "the essential duality of his nature, the evil and the good, the flights of panic and the resolution of spirit, the good mind and the mean trickery." And former White House aide William Safire sees Nixon as a complex man with multiple layers, best seen as a layer cake, with the icing (Nixon's public face) "conservative, stern, dignified, proper. But beneath the icing one finds a variety of separate layers which reveal a complex, sometimes contradictory, paradoxical human being." One part of Nixon, Price writes, is exceptionally considerate, exceptionally caring, sentimental, generous of spirit, kind. Another part is coldly calculating, devious, craftily manipulative. A third part is angry, vindictive, ill-tempered, mean-spirited. Price notes that those close to Nixon often referred to his "light side" and his "dark side," and suggests that over the years, the light side and the dark side "have been at constant war with one another." Because of this, Price notes, "he has always needed people around him who would help the lighter side prevail." Interestingly, Price points out "the extent to which the dark side grew not out of his nature, but out of his experiences in public life." The light side-dark side assessment of Nixon is frequently referred to, especially by Nixon insiders. Some staffers (e.g., Bob Finch) appealed to Nixon's better side, while others (e.g., Chuck Colson) appealed to the dark side. For the most part, the latter dominated in the White House. This light side-dark side quality of Nixon made him a sort of Dr. Jekyll, Mr. Hyde character.

Bob Haldeman once described Nixon as "the weirdest man ever to live in the White House," and John Ehrlichman described his former boss as "the mad monk." Nixon has been a fascinating subject for analysis precisely because he is so puzzling. As columnist Hugh Sidey has said, "He is an absolutely sinister human being, but fascinating. I'd rather spend an evening with Richard Nixon than with almost anybody else because he is so bizarre. He has splashes of brilliance. He is obscene at times; his recall is almost total; his acquaintanceship with the world's figures is amazing. He is a fascinating human being."

In foreign affairs, Nixon was an innovative thinker and grand strategist. Understanding that the U.S. was entering an "age of limits"[4] Nixon attempted to refashion U.S. power and position in the world, while maintaining international leadership.

The Nixon years were a time of dramatic, bold, innovative approaches and overtures in the field of foreign affairs. They were years when the conventional wisdom was challenged and conventional solutions eschewed for a new strategic approach to foreign policy.

It was a new era that brought about an opening of relations with China, détente with the Soviet Union, a strategic arms limitation agreement with the Soviets. It was a period when America's military involvement in Vietnam and Southeast Asia was expanded, then ended, and when a relatively new approach and strategic orientation was introduced into American foreign policy thinking.

Under Richard Nixon and Henry Kissinger, a reexamination and reorientation of the United States' role in the world produced a different strategic vision. There was a recognition of the changing role and capacity of the United States, a recognition of the limits of power, and an attempt to match America's strategic vision with its capabilities. Had it not been for Watergate and the self-destruction of the Nixon presidency, there is no telling how the early stages of the Nixon foreign policy revolution might have eventually changed the United States and the world.

In collaboration with Henry Kissinger, Nixon promoted a far-reaching, forward-thinking approach to foreign policy that had a momentous impact on the world. As Crabb and Malcahy note: "Nixon's impact was felt in several ways—in the theoretical framework in which his foreign policy initiatives were cast (the so-called 'Nixon Doctrine'), in the specific content of the policies themselves (for example, in détente and the normalization of Sino-American relations), and in the process by which these policies were formulated, especially regarding the role of Kissinger and his White House staff.[5]

As was the case in so many other aspects of his presidency, the foreign policy Nixon promoted was full of irony and contradiction. How could one of America's premier anticommunists open the door to China and promote détente and arms control with the Soviet Union? How could the politician who kept promoting an "America First" attitude negotiate a deal with the Soviets that effectively granted them equality with the United States? How could a president who promoted American hegemony relinquish economic power and prestige? What accounts for these metamorphoses?

Even Nixon's most skeptical critics recognized that this truly was a different and more sophisticated approach to American foreign policy. Nixon had a vision—a new strategic orientation—and attempted to take the steps necessary to bring that vision to fruition. One could argue that Nixon's vision was inappropriate or incorrect, but that Nixon had an integrated, complex, and sophisticated worldview seems clear.

Nixon had a clearer idea of where he wanted to lead the nation in foreign affairs than in any other area of policy. Nixon felt that the domestic arena could be run by a cabinet, but only the president could lead in foreign policy. Foreign policy was Richard Nixon's domain, the area in which he felt most comfortable, most in command. And Nixon had some definite idea about where he wanted to lead the nation, the Western alliance, and the world.

Nixon came to office at a time when U.S. foreign policy was ripe for reexamination and redesign. The post-World War II consensus that had guided the nation for 25 years was collapsing, and America's role in the world was going through some convulsive changes. By the late 1960s, an era of U.S. foreign policy was coming to an end.

For the two decades immediately following World War II, the United States served as the dominant, hegemonic power of the West. It was the beginning, many thought, of the "American Century," a period in which the United States would provide a benevolent leadership and direction. After the decline of Great Britain in the post-war era, the United States inherited hegemonic control, which placed it in the lead of the Western alliance. This role was challenged by the Soviet Union in the years following World War II, but by virtue of vast military and economic superiority, the United States was able to spread its protective umbrella over Western Europe and eventually over much of the rest of the world.

Empire was costly, but in the 1940s and 1950s, the United States had the resources to spend. We could afford a costly web of military ventures and economic aid to contain the expansion of communism. But by the 1960s, America's role was proving to be a burden—a burden costly in lives and resources. By the time Richard Nixon took office, the American empire seemed to be in the early stages of decline.

The combination of the war in Vietnam and the multiple changes taking place in the world left the United States without an acceptable road map for the future. Strategically the United States was adrift and floundering. The war in Vietnam deeply divided the American people. Relations with the Soviet Union were in flux. As the Soviets approached strategic parity with the United States, questions of how best to deal with the Russians proved confounding. Should the United States continue containment? Search for coexistence? Move to confrontation? These questions confused us at a time when a further Cold War belief was being dispelled. The assumption regarding monolithic communism was being reexamined because of deep rifts between the Soviet Union and China, and trouble with the communist satellite states. Tight bipolarity seemed to be giving way to a kind of global pluralism, and the United States was without a plan for dealing with these changes.

Other changes in the world proved equally perplexing to American policy makers. Members of the Western alliance, which the United States had dominated for 20 years, were showing signs of independence as the European economies rebounded from the war with vigor and American economic dominance was being threatened. The third world and less-developed nations were becoming more independent and nationalistic, the oil-producing nations were forming a cartel, and the post-World War II world seemed to be going through changes that the United States could neither control nor comprehend.

The world was becoming more complex, more interdependent, and less amenable to U.S. dominance. This, at a time when America's resources—military and economic—were declining relative to the demands placed upon the United States. Nothing seemed to be working as it should. The center did not hold. Amidst this policy incoherence and confusion, the time was right for a fundamental change in American foreign policy. But how could the United States respond to this changing world?

Vietnam was the most glaring symptom of America's relative decline. Henry Kissinger recognized this "new" relationship when he wrote in his memoirs:

> We were in a period of painful adjustment to a profound transformation of global politics; we were being forced to come to grips with the tension between our history and our new necessities. For two centuries America's participation in the world seemed to oscillate between over-involvement and withdrawal, between expecting too much of our power and being ashamed of it, between optimistic exuberance and frustration with the ambiguities of an imperfect world. I was convinced that the deepest cause of our national unease was the realization—as yet dimly perceived—that we were becoming like other nations in the need to recognize that our power, while vast, had limits. Our resources were no longer infinite in relation to our problems; instead we had to set priorities, both intellectual and material.[6]

Gone were the days when American power was so preponderate that the United States seemed capable of solving problems by simply overwhelming them with America's superior economic or military power. The world had changed; the United States had changed. Not having overwhelming resource superiority, the United States had to be more careful, more selective. But how does one adjust responsibilities to match declining power while still exerting hegemonic control?

In effect, Nixon and Kissinger attempted to deal with relative decline by developing slightly more modest international commitments (the Nixon Doctrine), developing a new international system (Nixon's ambitious "Grand Design" or "structure of peace"), exerting dramatic international leadership (shuttle diplomacy), and refashioning our relationships with the two most powerful communist nations (détente with the Soviet Union, opening the door to China). Osgood called the new strategy "military retrenchment without political disengagement,"[7] and Nixon attempted to deal with the overextension of American power, not by retreating from American globalism, but in an orderly, controlled readjustment, a measured devolution. In light of the new limits on America's capabilities and resources, the United States could not bear the international burdens it had accumulated for the last 25 years.[8] Now the United States would have to settle for less, set clearer priorities, and redefine the national interest. But could this be done while still playing the role of hegemon?

Nixon attempted to implement a new "Grand Strategy" for foreign affairs, but like so many aspects of his presidency, grand designs gave way to petty politics, and Nixon's ambitious plans were eventually crushed by the weight of the Watergate scandal.

In domestic policy, Nixon was often a reluctant reformer.[9] Pushed by a Congress controlled by the Democrats, Nixon promoted a "New Federalism" to devolve some federal power back to the states, imposed wage and price controls during an economic slump, created the Environmental Protection Agency, and witnessed the first moon landing on July 20, 1969.

Because the opposition party controlled Congress, Nixon devised an "Administrative Strategy" to govern.[10] He attempted, where possible, to bypass Congress and use administrative discretion to the limit and beyond. This administrative strategy was an innovation that would later be used by President Reagan with great success. The swelling of the administrative presidency added to the tools of presidential leadership.

Presidential impoundment of funds had become a major issue in the Nixon years. Due to the claims of power by Richard Nixon, the courts faced a series of cases questioning the legality of impoundment.

The roots of impoundment can be traced to Thomas Jefferson's refusal, in 1803, to spend $50,000 appropriated by Congress. But the issue of impoundment did not reach the Supreme Court until 35 years later when, in *Kendal v. United States ex rel Stokes*, the Court ruled against the executive branch in an instance in which the Postmaster General refused to release funds.

Impoundment as a political issue did not, however, become important until the Nixon Administration. President Nixon made the impoundment of funds a weapon in making policy, even when that policy ran counter to the expressed wishes of Congress. A number of cases reached the courts. Most of these cases were decided against the president.

These impoundment cases serve as an example of the courts standing up to the president. In case after case, courts throughout the country ruled against impoundments, and ordered the president to release congressionally appropriated funds. Arthur Miller once noted that the power of the president to impound funds could be exercised "to the extent that the political milieu in which he operates permits him to do so." In the case of the Nixon Administration, it was an example of presidential overload. The political system could take a lot, but it could not take this many intrusions into the realm of congressional policymaking.

The courts were joined by the Congress, which wanted the funds released, and this coalition was able to halt a president who seemed determined to breach the boundaries of the political milieu in which he was operating.

Watergate was the most serious scandal in the history of U.S. presidential politics. It was unusual in presidential history because for the first time the president himself was deeply involved in the crimes of his administration. Watergate was a different kind of scandal. Richard Nixon was a different kind of president.

The roots of Watergate stem from the war in Vietnam and the divisiveness it caused at home. Richard Nixon was elected president in 1968 in the midst of a long war in Vietnam. He was elected, in part, on his promise to end the war. But when he became president, he realized that getting out of Vietnam would be no easy task. Public protests against the war exerted a great deal of pressure on Nixon to bring the war to an end. But the president could find no way to get out of Vietnam "with honor." The war dragged on, and antiwar protests spread. Out of his determination not to be destroyed by the war, as his predecessor Lyndon Johnson had been, Nixon proceeded on a path of self-destruction.

"Watergate" is a generic term that originally referred only to the break-in at the Democratic National Committee (DNC) headquarters located at the Watergate office complex, but it has come to be an umbrella term, under which a wide variety of crimes and improper acts are included. Watergate caused the downfall of President Nixon. It led to jail sentences for more than a dozen of the highest-ranking officials of the administration. It was a traumatic experience for the nation. Why Watergate? How could it have happened? How could someone as smart and experienced as Richard Nixon behave so criminally *and* so stupidly? How could someone so adroit and practiced in the art and science of politics behave so foolishly? How could a "third-rate burglary" turn into a national disaster? How could Richard Nixon have done it to himself?

In essence, Watergate involved three separate but interconnected conspiracies, centered in four different areas. The first conspiracy was the *Plumbers conspiracy*. This involved a variety of steps taken in Nixon's first term (1969–1973): plugging leaks and going after his political enemies, illegal wiretapping, the break-in at Daniel Ellsberg's (who released the *Pentagon Papers*) psychiatrist's office, and other acts, done in some instances for ostensible "national security" reasons and at other times for purely political reasons. The purpose of this conspiracy was to destroy political enemies and strengthen the president's political position.

The second conspiracy was the *reelection conspiracy*. This grew out of lawful efforts to reelect the president, but degenerated into illegal efforts to extort money, launder money, sabotage the electoral process, spy, commit fraud, forgery, and burglary, play "dirty tricks," and attack Democratic front-runners. The purposes of this conspiracy were to (a) knock the stronger potential Democratic candidates (Senators Hubert Humphrey, Edward

Kennedy, Edmund Muskie, and Henry "Scoop" Jackson) out of the race; (b) accumulate enough money to bury the Democratic opponent by massively outspending him; and (c) thus guarantee the reelection of Richard Nixon. This conspiracy was conscious, deliberate, and organized.

The third conspiracy was the *cover-up conspiracy*. Almost immediately after the burglars were caught at the DNC headquarters in the Watergate office complex in Washington, D.C., a criminal conspiracy began that was designed to mislead law enforcement officers and protect the reelection bid of the president, and then after the election, to keep the criminal investigations away from the White House. To this end, evidence was destroyed, perjury committed, lies told, investigations obstructed, and subpoenas defied. The purpose of the cover-up was to contain the criminal charges and protect the president. This conspiracy was less conscious, almost instinctive. It was deliberate but poorly organized.

One can divide Watergate activities into four categories: the *partisan* activities include acts taken against those of the opposition party and those deemed to be "enemies" of the administration. They include acts such as wiretapping and break-ins; the establishment of the Houston Plan; the Plumbers, and the enemies list; forged State Department cables; and political dirty tricks.

Policy activities include the stretching of presidential power beyond legal or constitutional limits. Examples include the secret bombing of Cambodia, the impoundment of congressionally appropriated funds, attempts to dismantle programs authorized by Congress, the extensive use of executive privilege, and underenforcement of laws such as the Civil Rights Act of 1964. When Nixon's defenders answer charges against the president by saying that "everybody does it," they are most often referring to this area of behavior.

In the *financial* area, both Nixon's political and personal finances deserve mention. On the political front, the "selling" of ambassadorships, extortion of money in the form of illegal campaign contributions, and laundering of money must be included. In Nixon's personal finances, such things as "irregularities" in income tax deductions and questionable "security" improvements in his private Florida and California homes, paid for with tax dollars, are included.

Finally, in the *legal* arena, illegal activities of the Nixon administration include obstruction of justice, perjury, criminal cover-up, interference with criminal investigations, and destruction of evidence. It was the criminal cover-up that eventually led to Nixon's forced resignation.

Categorizing and classifying Watergate behavior does a disservice to the drama and suspense of the unfurling of this political mystery. The story of Nixon's rise and fall, of his choices at several important points in the story, of his ultimate collapse, is what makes this drama so poignant and tragic.

Could a sitting president be indicted in a criminal case? Special Prosecutor Leon Jaworski was unsure, instead naming Nixon an "unindicted co-

conspirator" in the case dealing with the president's top staffers. The people with whom the president conspired were all convicted and sent to prison for Watergate offenses. Nixon received a pardon from Gerald Ford.

As the Watergate investigations drew the noose tighter and tighter around the president's neck, it became clear that Nixon would be impeached by the House and convicted by the Senate. The Supreme Court decision in *U.S. v. Nixon* (1974) compelled the president to release tape recordings (while also adding to the power of the presidency by establishing judicial recognition of limited "executive privilege") that clearly established the fact that Nixon was involved in criminal behavior. From that point on, what little support Nixon had quickly evaporated. In order to escape impeachment, Nixon resigned from office on August 9, 1974. He is the only president to resign his office. The House Judiciary Committee approved three articles of impeachment against President Nixon:

Article I

> In his conduct of the office of President of the United States, Richard M. Nixon, in violation of his constitutional oath faithfully to execute the office of President of the United States and, to the best of his ability, preserve, protect, and defend the Constitution of the United States, and, in violation of his constitutional duty to take care that the laws be faithfully executed, has prevented, obstructed, and impeded the administration of justice, in that:
>
> On June 17, 1972, and prior thereto, agents of the Committee for the Re-election of the President committed unlawful entry of the headquarters of the Democratic National Committee in Washington, District of Columbia, for the purpose of securing political intelligence. Subsequent thereto, Richard M. Nixon, using the powers of his high office, engaged personally and through his subordinates and agents, in a course of conduct or plan designed to delay, impede, and obstruct the investigation of such unlawful entry; to cover up, conceal and protect those responsible; and to conceal the existence and scope of other unlawful covert activities.

Article II

> Using the powers of the office of President of the United States, Richard M. Nixon, in violation of his constitutional oath faithfully to execute the office of President of the United States and, to the best of his ability, preserve, protect, and defend the Constitution of the United States, and in disregard of his constitutional duty to take care that the laws be faithfully executed, has repeatedly engaged in conduct violating the constitutional rights of citizens, impairing the due and proper administration of justice and the conduct of lawful inquiries, or contravening the laws governing the agencies of the executive branch and the purposes of these agencies.

Article III

> In his conduct of the office of President of the United States, Richard M. Nixon, contrary to his oath faithfully to execute the office of President of the United States, and, to the best of his ability, preserve, protect, and de-

fend the Constitution of the United States, and in violation of his constitutional duty to take care that the laws be faithfully executed, has failed without lawful cause or excuse to produce papers and things as directed by duly authorized subpoenas issued by the Committee on the Judiciary of the House of Representatives . . . In refusing to produce these papers and things, Richard M. Nixon, substituted his judgment as to what materials were necessary for the inquiry, interposed the powers of the Presidency against the lawful subpoenas of the House of Representatives, thereby assuming to himself functions and judgments necessary to the exercise of the sole power or impeachment vested by the Constitution in the House of Representatives.

In all of this, Richard M. Nixon has acted in a manner contrary to his trust as President and subversive of constitutional government, to the great prejudice of the cause of law and justice, and to the manifest injury of the people of the United States. Wherefore Richard M. Nixon, by such conduct, warrants impeachment and trial, and removal from office.[11]

The aftermath of Watergate led to a decline of the presidency and a rebirth of congressional power. A transformation began to take place. As a result first of Vietnam, then of Watergate, our superman became an Imperial President. The presidency had become a danger to the republic, using its powers not for the public good but for self-aggrandizement. A new image of the presidency developed.

Watergate turned out to be the final nail in the coffin of the unambiguous acceptance of the strong-presidency model. The twin effects of Vietnam and Watergate led to an era of deep cynicism regarding politics and the presidency. Scholars and the public began to condemn the "excesses" of presidential power characterized as the Imperial Presidency, and called for a corralling of a presidency perceived as acting above the law. It was a presidency-curbing, if not presidency-bashing, period.

Reacting against the excesses of power in the Johnson and Nixon presidencies, the Congress attempted to reassert its power by taking a series of presidency-curbing steps, the most notable being the passage of the *War Powers Act*, which attempted (with little subsequent success) to curb the president's war powers. The presidency-curbing era also ushered in a period in which the public did an about-face regarding their trust in and support of presidents and the presidency. Any and all presidential acts were suspect; virtually no support was given for presidential initiatives; and a weak-presidency model (though not a strong-Congress model) prevailed. In the midterm election of 1974, a new breed of activist Democrats was elected to the Congress. Weaned not on FDR's greatness but on Johnson's and Nixon's excesses, this new generation of legislators was less deferential to presidents, less willing to bow to claims of presidential prerogative, and more willing to challenge presidents directly. As a result, the legislative initiatives of Presidents Ford and Carter would fall victim to the Congress's revised, more suspicious attitude toward presidential power.

Gerald Ford
1974–1977

Gerald Ford[12] was born a King. Actually, he was born Leslie King, but when his mother divorced and later remarried, young Leslie King took the name of his new father and became a Ford. He was the nation's only unelected president, having been appointed vice-president when Richard Nixon's first VP, Spiro Agnew, was forced to resign his office in the face of several crim-

Gerald R. Ford

TABLE 7.1 The Growth of the Federal Budget—Outlays in Billions of Dollars

Years	Dollars
1945	92.7bn
1950	42.6bn
1955	68.4bn
1960	92.2bn
1965	118.2bn
1970	195.7bn
1971	332.3bn
1972	590.9bn

inal charges. When Nixon was forced to resign or face impeachment, Gerald Ford became president.

Square jawed, athletic, friendly and open, Ford was a stark contrast to the suspicious loner, Nixon. But if the presidency was imperial during the Nixon years, it was imperiled in the Ford-Carter years. Ford entered office with the nation deeply polarized over Watergate, and he soon fell victim to the Watergate-inspired backlash against the presidency. A series of presidency-bashing, laws were passed, and Ford could do little but attempt to veto bills he found objectionable.

On assuming office, Ford told the Congress he did not want a honeymoon, he wanted a good marriage. A month later he guaranteed that was not to be by issuing a "full, free, and absolute pardon" to Richard Nixon. From that point on, a kind of open warfare between the president and Congress took place.

If the president and Congress were at each other's throats, this deadlock did not serve to diminish the size of the federal government. During the post-World War II period, the federal government continued to grow during Democrat and Republican administrations (see Table 7.1).

Presidents do not govern in a vacuum. Leadership is contextual. For Ford, as the hand-picked successor to the disgraced Nixon, facing a Democrat-controlled Congress ready to bring the Imperial Presidency down a peg or two and a public grown cynical after Vietnam and Watergate, the

TABLE 7.2 Presidential Vetoes: The Top 10

Franklin Roosevelt	635	Ronald Reagan	78
Grover Cleveland	584*	Gerald Ford	66
Harry Truman	250	Calvin Coolidge	50
Dwight Eisenhower	181	Benjamin Harrison	44
Ulysses Grant	93	Woodrow Wilson	44
Theodore Roosevelt	82		

Tables 7.1–7.5 adapted from Robert Spitzer, *The Presidential Veto* (Albany: SUNY Press, 1988) pp. 72–74.
*Cleveland vetoes 414 bills in his first term, and 170 in his second term.

prospects for active leadership were greatly diminished. Most presidents enter office with a rather limited, even a weak power base. Ford, especially after the pardon of Nixon, found himself deep in a hole, out of which he was unable to climb.

Ford had very few opportunities to exert creative leadership.[13] He was forced to exert a reactive brand of leadership, largely characterized by his use of vetoes to limit the ability of the activist Democrats in Congress to pass what Ford believed were budget-busting bills. Ford issued a total of 66 vetoes, an average of 26.4 per year. This is nowhere near the record for vetoes. FDR issued a total of 635 vetoes, for a 52.9 average per year. While FDR's total is the record, the yearly average record for vetoes goes to Grover Cleveland who, in the first of his two nonconsecutive terms averaged 103.5 vetoes per year. Ford ranked eighth in veto totals, and sixth in yearly average. (See Tables 7.2, 7.3, 7.4, and 7.5).

While Gerald Ford suffered from the fallout of Watergate, he did help restore some dignity to the presidency, and he helped halt the decline in trust in government that took such a steep fall after Vietnam and Watergate. But he was a clerk and not a leader. Circumstances precluded active leadership.

TABLE 7.3 Presidential Vetoes: The 10 Fewest

John Adams	0	James Garfield	0
Thomas Jefferson	0	James Monroe	1
John Quincy Adams	0	Martin Van Buren	1
William Henry Harrison	0	George Washington	2
Zachary Taylor	0	James Polk	3
Millard Fillmore	0		

TABLE 7.4 Overrides of Presidential Vetoes: The Top 10

Andrew Johnson	15	Richard Nixon	7
Harry Truman	12	Woodrow Wilson	6
Gerald Ford	12	Franklin Pierce	5
Franklin Roosevelt	9	Ulysses Grant	4
Ronald Reagan	9	Calvin Coolidge	4
Grover Cleveland	7	Herbert Hoover	3

TABLE 7.5 Presidential Vetoes: Highest Yearly Average: The Top 10

Cleveland (first term)	103.5	Eisenhower	22.6
Cleveland (both terms)	73.0	Grant	11.6
F.D. Roosevelt	52.9	B. Harrison	11.0
Cleveland (second term)	42.5	McKinley	10.5
Truman	31.2	Kennedy	10.5
Ford	26.4		

Jimmy Carter
1977–1981

As part of the continuing fallout of Watergate, the voters rejected Gerald Ford and chose instead an unknown former Governor of Georgia ("Jimmy who?" people asked), who spoke openly in biblical terms and promised "I'll never lie to you." In the wake of Watergate it was just what the voters wanted.

Jimmy Carter

Jimmy Carter,[14] 5'10", with sandy hair and a toothy smile, came out of nowhere to the White House.

No president in the last 50 years had so little experience in government as Carter. But it was a time when being a Washington politician was a liability. The voters wanted an "outsider," someone who was not tainted by the evils of Washington politics. And so Jimmy Carter was the first of two consecutive D.C. outsiders to occupy the White House.

Carter's relaxed informality, ready smile of prominent teeth, and down-home style, convinced people that he was one of them, not a professional politician. Astonished at the public's desire to have a nonpolitician in the nation's most highly politicized job, critics lamented, "If you needed brain surgery you'd go to a professional and experienced brain surgeon; why, when choosing a president do you want an amateur in the White House?" But such concerns were lost in a public grown cynical from years of Vietnam and Watergate.

President Carter set out to de-pomp and demythologize the imperial presidency. But while he was one of the most intelligent men to serve as a president, he never articulated a sense of purpose or overall vision beyond his frequently expressed moralism. "Carterism does not march and it does not sing," said historian Eric Goldman. "It is cautious, muted, grayish, at times even crabbed."[15]

A number of characteristics have been used to describe Jimmy Carter. Aide James Fallows, after departing in 1979, stressed Carter's basic fairness and decency. To Fallows, Carter would be an ideal person to judge one's soul.[16] He also emphasized, however, that Carter seemed to conduct a passionless presidency. Others have pointed to Carter's honesty and forthrightness, self-discipline, and tenacious pursuit of personal goals in all activities, including even sporting contests. Less flattering assessments have also been applied, with an emphasis on his naivete about the nature of government, limited creativity and innovativeness, and tendencies toward self-righteousness and feelings of moral superiority.

Carter's four years as president were difficult and contentious ones. He had trouble leading his party, did a mediocre job at leading Congress, and failed to inspire the public. During his term, inflation rose and productivity faltered.

"I learned the hard way," Carter wrote in his memoirs, "that there was no party loyalty or discipline when a complicated or controversial issue was at stake—none. Each legislator had to be wooed and won individually. It was every member for himself, and the devil take the hindmost!"[17]

In spite of the many setbacks, there were also some impressive victories. Carter's emphasis on human rights had significant long-term effects across the globe. His Camp David Accords between Israel and Egypt were a stunning success; he normalized U.S. relations with China, won the Panama Canal Treaty, pushed Strategic Arms Limitations Talks (Salt II), pushed for the transition to black rule in Zimbabwe; and, on the home front, won civil service reform, appointed the first black women to the cabinet, created both the Energy and Education Departments, and avoided major scandal.

On November 4, 1979, a mob of Iranian youths seized the U.S. embassy in Teheran, taking 63 Americans hostage. Carter saw no way to get the hostages released short of an attack that would have endangered their lives. Negotiations and sanctions failed to move the Iranians.

Carter's inability to resolve this crisis successfully became the dominating event of his presidency. A failed rescue mission in 1980 only made Carter look more helpless. Eventually Carter was able to win the release of all the hostages, but by then it was too late for him. The Iranians released the hostages on the morning Carter left office.

Hedrick Hertzberg, a one-time Carter speechwriter said of his former boss, "He was and is a moral leader more than a political leader," adding "He spoke the language of religion and morality far more, and far more effectively, than he spoke the language of politics."[18] Jimmy Carter was a very good man, but not an especially adept politician. He was the first of several "outsiders" to be elected president in an age of cynicism.

Although Carter avoided many of the excesses of other recent presidents, he was unable to generate sufficient support or to exercise decisive leadership. His presidency ended with Gallup poll ratings in the 20-percent range. Consequently, he was defeated in his 1980 bid for reelection. Not since 1932, with Herbert Hoover in the midst of the depression, has an incumbent president been so totally defeated. As a sign of Carter's low standing, Ronald Reagan, in his 1984 bid for reelection, was still running against the memory of Jimmy Carter!

Ronald Reagan
1981–1989

After the crisis of Vietnam, the scandal of Watergate, the weak presidencies of Ford and Carter, and after drift and despair, the nation began to forget about the problems of presidential power, and a hunger for leadership reemerged. Problems accumulated, and the nation's "leaders" seemed powerless in the face of these hardships. The urge for the strong-presidency model reclaimed center stage.

The people wanted a strong leader, one who could solve problems, one who would flex America's muscles. Enter Ronald Reagan,[19] a presidential knight in shining armor. Tall, handsome, with a compelling presence, he looked and sounded presidential. Reagan seemed to be everything Ford and Carter weren't: strong, self-assured, a leader. He made grand promises, spoke in grand terms, created high expectations. He attempted to return America to an era of grandeur.

Reagan took Washington by storm. Claiming a bold mandate and focusing on several key economic items, Reagan managed to get most of his top agenda items enacted into law. But after an impressive start, Reagan fal-

Ronald Reagan

tered. Initial success in dealing with Congress gave way to frustration and defeat. The president could not overcome the system's roadblocks, and unwilling to accept the limits placed upon the office, he and members of his administration went beyond the law and abused power.

Reagan was a bundle of contradictions. Was he, as Nicholas von Hoffman asserted "a Molieresque madman" (*Harper's* Magazine), or was he, as Bruce Bawer noted "Indiana Jones" (*Newsweek*)? Was he as Carl Bernstein noted in *The New Republic*, "The Huck Finn of American politics," or as Wilson Carey McWilliams said, "the Ted Baxter of American politics?" Was he, as Thomas Cronin asserted, "an interesting combination of John Wayne and Mr. Rogers?" Often he was not what he seemed. He appeared strong but was weak; looked like he was in control but was often manipulated by handlers or his wife; promised greatness but left the American economy and infrastructure in a shambles. He attacked big government, but added to the size of government. He condemned deficits yet presided over the biggest deficit increases ever. He spoke movingly of family values yet was notoriously unconcerned as a father. He spoke tearfully about religion yet rarely attended religious services. He honored the nuclear family yet was the nation's only divorced president. He attacked government welfare yet was a modest giver to charities. For Reagan, appearance did not match reality. He was a Wizard of Oz president. He gave the appearance of strength and power but, when the curtain was pulled away, a rather weak figure was revealed. He ruled by illusion and by manipulating the blind faith placed in him by the public. To compound matters, Reagan, like Nixon, displayed a distinct lack of respect for the law and attempted to impose a new imperial presidency. In the end, his presidency was nearly destroyed by the Iran-Contra scandal.

Reagan's engaging personality and ready wit helped make him popular, and while his borrow-borrow, spend-spend approach to policy may have added to America's military might, it also left the nation on the brink of economic insolvency. The United States went from being the world's largest creditor/lender nation in 1980 to becoming the world's largest debtor/borrower nation in 1988.

Handsome, trained as an actor, more conservative than any president this century, Reagan seemed the ideal candidate for his age. In a time of cynicism, Reagan, blamed big government for all the nations ills; in an age of selfishness, Reagan told people to keep and spend their own money and not give your taxes to "Welfare Queens driving Cadillacs."

One of Reagan's chief characteristics was his confidence and optimism for himself and the nation. An avid storyteller, he was fond of happy endings, even when he had to reinvent reality to come up with them. There was also no doubt in his mind that America's story could continue to be one of unbounded success. Reagan also possessed an excellent sense of humor and an ability to use that trait effectively.

Reagan was the oldest man ever elected president. After he left office he was diagnosed with Alzheimer's disease. Several observers maintain that signs of the disease showed themselves while Reagan was still in office.

In the age of television, Reagan was known as the "Great Communicator." His use of the rhetorical and symbolic powers of the office enhanced his image and added to his power. He had a message to communicate, and he communicated that message with force and clarity.

Reagan came to office challenging the principle of the New Deal. He wanted to undo the Roosevelt revolution and replace it with a Reagan revolution: less government, lower taxes, a bigger defense budget, cuts in social welfare spending, and cuts in government regulations on business.

Initially, Reagan got almost everything he wanted out of Congress. He went to Congress with a clear and simple agenda, pushed hard, drew the public into his orbit, and was able to achieve success in establishing "supply-side economics" (Reaganomics). But a recession soon followed, and Congress reinstated some taxes.

Reagan, like Nixon, asserted an administrative strategy to wrestle control of policy from Congress. He had more success than Nixon, partly because his administration insisted that all appointees pass a rigid litmus test to prove loyalty to Reagan and his program.

In foreign affairs Reagan wanted to reassert American military might. He revived the prerogative of the president unilaterally to deploy military forces abroad. The invasions of Grenada and the bombing of Libyan dictator Mu'ammar Gadhafi's headquarters were examples of unilateral presidential actions.

Reagan sharply increased the military budget, and engaged in a war of words with the Soviet Union, calling them "the evil empire." The president wanted to roll back Soviet influence, especially in this hemisphere. That led

TABLE 7.6 The Public Debt

Year	Net Public Debt (Billions of Current Dollars)
1940	42.7
1945	235.2
1950	219.0
1955	226.6
1960	237.2
1965	261.6
1970	284.9
1975	396.9
1980	709.3
1981	804.7
1982	929.3
1983	1,141.8
1984	1,312.6
1985	1,499.4
1986	1,736.2
1987	1,888.1
1988	2,050.2
1989	2,189.3
1990	2,410.4
1991	2,687.4
1992	2,998.6
1995	3,603.3
1996	3,767.1
1997	3,927.5
1998	3,870.0
1999	3,840.0

Source: U.S. Department of the Treasury and Office of Management and Budget; 1998 and 1999 data are estimated.

him to overreach badly and cause the most serious crisis of his presidency: the Iran-Contra scandal.

In November 1986, a Lebanese publication broke a story accusing the Reagan administration of trading U.S. arms for American hostages being held by Iran. Reagan had publicly condemned dealing with terrorists and pressured U.S. allies not to deal with them.

But the Reagan administration had indeed been trading arms for hostages—or at least trying to do so. Led by the Maxwell Smart-like Lt. Col. Oliver "Ollie" North, the U.S. gave Iran much needed arms, and the Iranians promised to release U.S. hostages. There was only one problem: When the weapons were delivered, the Iranians did not release hostages. So the U.S. sent *more* arms, until the Iranians finally released one hostage. But for every hostage released, another one was taken! The absurd *pas-de-deux* lasted for two years. The U.S. continued to play the fool.

What to do with the illegal profits from these arms sales? The Keystone Cops in the White House decided to use the profits to fund the "Contras," the right-wing Nicaraguan rebels fighting the Sandanista (Marxist) government of Nicaragua. This was done in direct violation of the law. The Boland Amendment prevented any such aid to the Contras. But Reagan disagreed with this law, so. . . .

In a performance worthy of the Marx Brothers, President Reagan went back and forth in his statements about his involvement in the Iran-Contra scandal: On July 8, 1985, he called Iran part of a confederation of "outlaw states run by the strangest collection of misfits, Looney Tunes and squalid criminals since the advent of the Third Reich." Over time, his story kept changing:

"We did not—repeat—we did not trade weapons or anything else for hostages."

—November 13, 1986

"I don't think a mistake was made."

—November 19, 1986

"I'm not going to lie about that. I didn't make a mistake."

—November 24, 1986

"It's obvious that the execution of these policies was flawed, and mistakes were made."

—December 6, 1986

"I told the American people I did not trade arms for hostages. My heart and my best intentions still tell me that's true. But the facts and the evidence tell me it is not . . . What began as a strategic opening to Iran deteriorated in its implementation into trading arms for hostages."

—March 4, 1987

When the Iran-Contra scandal broke, Reagan became—quite literally—paralyzed. He became so withdrawn that chief-of-staff Howard Baker even considered invoking the Twenty-fifth Amendment to remove a disabled president.[20]

In the Iran-Contra scandal, the Reagan administration repeatedly lied to the Congress and the American people; they broke a variety of laws, and—had it not been for his affable ways—Reagan might have been impeached.

As the Iran-Contra scandal faded, Reagan pursued arms control with the Soviet Union. In one of the premier events of his presidency, the U.S. and the Soviets signed the INF (intermediate-range nuclear forces) treaty to reduce the number of nuclear weapons. It was a masterful success—especially for someone who had only a few years earlier called the Soviet Union "the focus of all evil in the world."

Above all other modern presidents, Ronald Reagan used television as a tool of leadership. He attempted a direct connection to the people via carefully crafted speeches, painstakingly stage-managed theatrics, and exploitation of his winning personality. This plebiscitary form of leadership "exposes citizens to the sort of public figures who will exploit their impatience with the difficult tasks involved in sustaining a healthy constitutional democracy."[21]

Ronald Reagan leaves a mixed and confusing legacy. He helped revive the spirit and confidence of the American people. His policies may have accelerated the decline of the Soviet Union, and he used the rhetorical aspects of the presidency to full effect. And perhaps most importantly, he helped shift the center of political discourse to the right of the ideological scale.

But the Reagan years also left astronomical budget deficits, a wider gap between the nation's rich and poor, a legacy of sleaze, the Iran-Contra scandal, and an aloof and disengaged management style. Reagan was a good leader (of a conservative movement), but not a very good president. He asserted a great deal of executive prerogative, but did so in a manner that exceeded the bounds of the acceptable. In the end, he left the presidency and the nation weaker than when he took office.

If the presidency resembled a Superman in the post-World War II era, by the mid-1970s it seemed more a Frankenstein. Vietnam and Watergate damaged the FDR halo, and the presidency went from imperial to imperiled.

The disappointing presidencies of Ford and Carter led to demands once again for strong leadership, and Ronald Reagan "seemed" to provide just that. But budget deficits and the Iran-Contra scandal damaged Reagan and the presidency and left a legacy of difficult problems for his successors.

❦ 8 ❧
The Post Cold War Presidency
George Bush and Bill Clinton

For more than 40 years, the ominous cloud of the Cold War hung over the United States and the world. The Cold War utterly dominated politics and policy in that era. But as the Bush administration began, the Soviet empire devolved and self-destructed, marking the end of bipolar competition and leaving the United States as the world's lone remaining superpower.

But the U.S. was a superpower without a road map. For four decades, the cold war determined policy: containment! Now the U.S. was a superpower without a clear mission. How would the end of the Cold War affect presidential power?

George Bush
1989–1993

George Bush[1] had the best resume in Washington: Congressman, U.S. envoy to China, National Chairman of the Republican party, director of the CIA, and vice-president for eight years. But critics wondered what he had accomplished in all these impressive posts: he left few footprints, they said.

Tall at 6'2", thin, to the manner born, educated at Yale, Bush was a man of uncompromising grayness. He was elected in the afterglow of the Reagan revolution, but he was not a Reaganite true believer. Bush was more cautious, more moderate, more pragmatic than Reagan. Bush was a manager at a time when the nation needed a leader, a status quo president in a time of change, a minimalist in a momentous time. The end of the Cold War opened a window of opportunity to exert creative leadership. But Bush was shackled by a vastly depleted resource base (the legacy of Reagan's economic mismanagement) and an intellectual cupboard that was bare (no vision for a post-Cold War future). Bush often seemed a passive observer in a dramatically changing world.

Bush was at his best when he had a clear goal to achieve (e.g., the Gulf War), a goal imposed upon him by events. But when it came time for him to choose, to set priorities, to decide on a direction, he floundered. As conservative columnist George Will commented, "When the weight of the (presidency) is put upon a figure as flimsy as George Bush, the presidency buckles. . . ."

George Bush

George Bush served as a managerial president, not a leader. In a time that cried out for vision, Bush seemed paralyzed. He appeared to want to be president so as to add another impressive notch on his resume. There was no clear aspiration to accomplish any grand goals. Bush's successes include the Persian Gulf War and a winding down of the Cold War, but his failures—his inability to build on the concept of a New World Order or to counter rising deficits, his lack of a domestic agenda, and his standoffish attitude as the economy tumbled—opened the door to Bush's opponents in the 1992 election. When it came time for the public to render judgment on President Bush, it chose another relative unknown instead of him.

There seemed to be no central core to Bush, no clear set of beliefs. As Bert A. Rockman noted, "Bush seems to be not well anchored by a strong set of personal values that put him in control of his circumstances. Instead, he seems to be largely buffeted by circumstances, making his choices to be more susceptible to a raw calculus of what he personally has to lose or gain from them."[2]

Bush was a reactive president, not an initiator, a caretaker or maintaining president, not a visionary. He had an aimless style,[3] which failed to provide clear direction to his staff or the machinery of government. He often appeared to be a spectator president, content to watch the unfolding of world events but afraid to get involved. By the time he did get involved (for example, the liberation of Eastern Europe, aid to the Soviet republics, the Gulf War) it was either too little too late, or too lame. How could someone with so much government experience, with such an impressive resume, be so devoid of ideas and have so few policy preferences? Although Bush did have the most impressive resume in politics, it is equally true that he left few footprints along the way. Bush was a manager, not a leader; he executed other people's ideas, not his own. When he was elected, Bush had precious few ideas that he was determined to translate into policy. His was not an idea-driven administration. President Bush wanted to better manage the status quo.

Bush was pulled between his temperament, which sought stability and continuity, and the demands of the times, which called for dramatic change. It was not a good fit of leader to times.[4]

The Bush leadership style—cautious, prudent, and managerial—did indeed seem a poor fit for times that begged for vision. The procedural presidency of George Bush turned out to be process centered, but not idea driven. The times called for leadership, yet Bush supplied prudence. As events moved rapidly, Bush moved slowly; as the world shook, Bush sat idly by, watching. Bush liked to play the insider game (he has been referred to as the Rolodex president), not the grand strategy game. He often acted late; therefore, the United States was given less input as events unfolded around the world. Soon, the other powers sensed that they no longer needed to defer to the United States: Germany unified, and the United States watched; China repressed dissidents, and the United States issued a mild reproach; Eastern Europe exploded, and the United States watched. The United States was becoming a less influential player in the game of international politics. It was less feared and less respected. Bush's style of leadership was often criticized as being more reactive than proactive; more adrift than imaginative. Bush's was called the Revlon presidency because of his practice of offering only cosmetic solutions to problems. *U.S. News & World Report* called Bush's first year "The Year of Living Timorously."[5] The Bush team was a fairly small, close-knit group of long-time acquaintances, all highly professional. Bush preferred to work with a few key, close advisers—Secretary of

State James Baker, National Security Advisor Brent Scowcroft, Defense Secretary Dick Cheney, and Joint Chiefs of Staff General Colin Powell—all of whom were strong in foreign affairs, but less interested in domestic policy. Their driving theme seemed to be, in Bert Rockman's words, "to do nothing well."[6] Their primary goal was not to accomplish great things, but to protect and better manage the status quo. This would have been acceptable in normal times, but the world was going through revolutionary convulsions. The times, and U.S. interests, demanded a leader. Instead, the United States got a manager.[7]

Bush had few deeply held policy beliefs. In domestic policy, he alienated conservatives by reneging on his "no new taxes" pledge, helped undo a Reagan-era excess by resolving the savings and loan crisis, and promoted "a kinder, gentler America" than his predecessor. But domestically, his policy was less rather than more.

It was in foreign affairs that President Bush felt most at home. By the late 1980s, the tectonic plates of the international system were shifting dramatically. The Soviet Union was breaking apart, Eastern Europe was achieving independence, democracy was taking root in South America, and new powers in economics (Japan) and politics (a more united Western Europe) were rising. It was a time of extraordinary events that created an opportunity for a visionary leader to shape a new world order.

In his inaugural address, the new president spoke of a new breeze that was blowing around the world, refreshed by freedom. Only the United States, Bush asserted, could provide the leadership necessary to meet the challenges of this new world order. The U.S. had leadership, yes but, Bush noted, it had "more will than wallet."

However, in his first and only term, President Bush proved to be more of a manager than a visionary, more a cautious pragmatist than a bold leader. At a time when events called for leadership, George Bush proved to be an underwhelming president, and the opportunity to exert influence on the shape of the emerging world order slipped through his, and the United States', hands.

It is true that Bush boldly exerted presidential prerogative by unilaterally ordering the invasion of Panama in 1989. The U.S. deposed Manuel Noriega, and brought him to the U.S. for trial on drug charges. But where was the far-reaching vision to animate U.S. policy in this new and changing world?

In 1989, the Soviet Union collapsed. Only China, North Korea, and Cuba remained as Communist strongholds. The West had won the Cold War, and George Bush presided over this seminal event. But what would follow (replace) the Cold War?

In August 1990, Iraq invaded Kuwait. George Bush put together a multilateral coalition, and in January 1991, this coalition invaded Iraq and drove the Iraqis back, out of Kuwait. Bush had done a masterful job of coalition building.

After the successful war, Bush's popularity rose to an unprecedented

90 percent. He seemed all but invincible. But as the economy soured, Bush's popularity fell. Domestic problems replaced the jubilation over the war, and as Bush had no response to the nation's domestic and economic problems, the public grew increasingly impatient.

As president when the Soviet Union's power dissolved and the Cold War ended, Bush had a distinct advantage over his predecessors. Gone was the overwhelming burden of cold war confrontation. But Bush still faced enormous problems, not the least of which was the economic legacy of the Reagan years. Facing economic insolvency, Bush pursued a more cooperative, bargaining, coalition-building style of international leadership. The United States was in the lead on this, but the style of leadership was more one of bargaining than commanding. With Soviet power in retreat, the pressures on Bush were eased, and U.S. minimalist hegemony in a bargaining atmosphere emerged.

Structurally, the bipolar world had collapsed, and either a loose unipolar world (with the United States at the helm) or a diffuse multipolar world (with strong U.S. influence) would emerge. In this new world, the United States had less power to impose its will, but was in a heightened position to persuade. This shift in the nature of U.S. power called for a shift in leadership style. To a degree, Bush was able to make this shift in the early stages of the Gulf crisis. In the end though, he retreated into the foggy certainty of old methods: force and war.

Given the dramatically new circumstances facing George Bush, could we have reasonably expected him to devise a new policy approach and stick with it? Bush's early efforts at developing a new world order reflected a new approach to a new era. However, Bush was afraid he might be wrong, so he abandoned hope for a new model and left it in the ashes of war.

As the Soviet Union collapsed, it became clear that President Bush had an enormous window of opportunity to initiate dramatic change. With high popularity ratings and a weak opposition, he had room to maneuver politically. With the end of the cold war, Bush had more freedom to move in new directions than any of his predecessors since Harry S Truman. He could have set the political agenda for the nation and, perhaps, the world. But Bush was a reactor, not an initiator. To his credit, he reacted well to the Gulf crisis, pursuing a model form of leadership in an age of limits. To his detriment, he could not dream grand dreams, set new standards, or pursue bold changes.[8] This lost opportunity may yet come back to haunt the United States. As Alan Tonelson notes:

> Bush's foreign policy conservatism is exacting considerable and mounting costs on America. It is, after all, a conservatism that is less reasoned than felt—or perhaps, more accurately, learned by rote. Consequently, it is less a strategy than an impulse. Indeed, Bush's incessant, almost ritualistic invocation of cold war ideals—collective security, stability, international law, and above all, United States world leadership—indicates that his conservatism is becoming an intellectual cage, Mantras seem to be in command, instead of ideas.[9]

The tragedy of Bush's term is the tragedy of missed opportunities. Bush was at the helm when the Soviet empire collapsed, when Eastern Europe achieved independence, when Western Europe united, and when Latin America embraced democracy. It was an opportunity to engage in visionary leadership, a chance to create a new world order, and an opportunity to refashion the way the international system operated. Such opportunities come along rarely.

But Bush was the wrong man for the times; a cautious manager when a visionary leader was required. After flirting with transforming leadership (the early days of the Gulf War), Bush quickly retreated into the false security of politics as usual. This was a style of leadership almost totally inappropriate for the times.

Bill Clinton
1993–2001

Bill Clinton[10] was a new president, from a new generation, for a new America. The first president born after World War II, Bill Clinton came from the generation that was inspired by John Kennedy's call to public service, that had witnessed the assassinations of President Kennedy, Martin Luther King, Jr., and Robert Kennedy, that protested the war in Vietnam, marched for Civil Rights, engaged in the cultural revolution of the 1960s, and observed the degradation of Watergate.

The generational shift represented by Bill Clinton made many Americans feel uncomfortable. At 6'2", weighing between 210 and 230 pounds, with sandy gray hair and blue eyes, Clinton was the first Rhodes scholar to become president. He was also the second president to be impeached.

Bill Clinton was a man of contradictions and paradoxes: a policy wonk *and* a people pleaser; a brilliant mind but an adolescent psyche; a disciplined politician but a victim of his robust appetites. Politically, as Elizabeth Drew pointed out, "He was an activist president in a cynical age," an era of hyperpartisanship. He was an "I feel your pain" president in an "in your face" era.

It was hard to get a handle on Bill Clinton's philosophical beliefs. Was he, as journalist E. J. Dionne, Jr., suggested, the founder of an international, neoprogressive "high-wire centrism," or was conservative columnist George Will correct in characterizing Clinton's major achievement as the "transformation of the party of liberalism into the party of conservatism with moist eyes?"[11]

Clinton's public style is that of empathetic preacher/teacher. He used the bully pulpit to help move the nation and examine issues such as racism and violence.

Clinton's presidency was a roller-coaster ride of political ups and downs. His first year saw the most rapid three-month loss of popularity for any president on record. His first year performance also included the passage of a

Bill Clinton

landmark deficit-reduction package and considerable new progressive legislation. His second year saw the embarrassing defeat of his health-care program, charges of White House scandals, and dramatic rejection of his party
in the 1994 midterm election, as the Republicans gained control of both
Houses of Congress, after which Clinton was compelled to insist he was
"not irrelevant!"

After being widely viewed as a one-term president, he outmaneuvered
Republican leaders in Congress on budget politics and a government shut-

down. His opponents incorrectly assumed that he would cave in to their demands. He did not. And the public blamed the Republicans for the shutdown. A year later, against the opinions of pundits and politicians, he became the first Democratic president to gain reelection since FDR, earning Clinton the title "Comeback Kid."

The institutional tug of war between the president and Congress had been growing more bitter, as divided government (one party controlling Congress, the opposition party controlling the White House) became common. When Democrats were the majority party in Congress, investigations into the Nixon, Reagan and Bush administrations uncovered Watergate and exposed the Iran-Contra scandal.

During the Clinton years, the urge to probe reached new heights (or depths). Of course, Clinton's behavior invited some of these investigations, but between the Republican Congress and several special investigators, Clinton was compelled to fend off all sorts of charges, bogus and genuine. So much time, energy, and money was spent by Clinton and his top staff in Clinton's defense that they were less able to perform fully the task of governing—which was largely the intent of his opponents. While accusations and investigations have always been a part of political competition, during Clinton's term they were elevated to a high political art form. The principle seems to be, when you can't beat 'em, investigate 'em, until you either find something on them or tie them in knots and prevent them from governing. This "gotcha" politics has replaced policy debates as a prime form of political competition.

President Clinton began his presidency with big plans. His Kennedyesque rhetoric, however, was not always a good match for a nation that had moved to the political right. Clinton ran in 1992 as a "New Democrat" (more centrist and pragmatic), but once in office he seemed to move left, trying to lift a ban on gays openly serving in the military and proposing a very ambitious health-care reform package. His big plans met with opposition, and when the Republicans took control of both Houses in the '94 midterm elections, President Clinton pulled in his sails and tried to win a series of small reforms that would, he hoped, add up to big changes. This incremental approach proved quite successful and more in tune with the times. He rebounded to win reelection in 1996.

Clinton's successes are impressive: The North American Free Trade Agreement (NAFTA), the 1997 Balanced Budget Agreement, which led to budget surpluses, a very strong economy with low inflation and low unemployment, passage of AmeriCorps (a national service program), proposals to "reinvent government" (streamlining government practices), welfare reform, anticrime bills, the Brady Handgun Bill, the Family Medical Leave Act, telecommunications reform, the Motor Voter bill, the line item veto (later found unconstitutional), an increase in the minimum wage, and the longest peacetime economic boom in history.

In foreign affairs, Clinton sent U.S. troops to Somalia, Bosnia, and Haiti, and brokered peace between Israel and the Palestinians. He helped bring free elections to Haiti, reduced tensions with North Korea, and expanded trade. In 1999, as leader of NATO forces, he orchestrated the bombing of Kosovo in an effort to halt the genocide ordered by Slobodan Milosevic.

But there were also some glaring errors. Failure to pass health-care reform was a major setback for Clinton, as was the loss of majority status in Congress. He also failed to pass campaign finance reform. Failures aside, Clinton has achieved a great deal under trying circumstances.

If policy successes mark Clinton's presidency, scandals and accusations continue to hound him. Most Americans see Clinton as character-challenged, and he has faced an unending string of accusations and investigations. Bill Clinton became the most investigated president in U.S. history.

Throughout his presidency, Bill Clinton was hounded by "the character issue."[12] Accusations about Clinton's extramarital activities surfaced during the 1990 primary season when Gennifer Flowers sold a story to *The Star*, a sensationalist supermarket tabloid, in which she claimed (and which years later the president seemed to confirm) a long-term affair with then-governor Clinton.

Early in his presidency a former Arkansas state employee, Paula Corbin Jones, filed a sexual harassment suit against the president for acts she claimed occurred when Clinton was governor of Arkansas. The suit, subsequently decided in the president's favor, resulted in a settlement in which the president agreed to pay Ms. Jones to end her appeal of the case.

On top of this, an independent counsel investigated Clinton's business dealings as governor. This investigation, initially into the Whitewater land deal, was later expanded to include a variety of other topics, such as the suicide of aide Vince Foster (Clinton's critics alleged he, Clinton, had Foster murdered), firings in the White House travel office, and, later, charges of an improper sexual relationship with a White House intern. Special investigator Kenneth Starr spent more than five years and $50 million, but was unable to bring charges against the president for any of the original accusations. But it was the sexual relationship with intern Monica Lewinsky that finally led to impeachment proceedings.

Ken Starr expanded his investigation to look at charges of sex in the White House. This investigation led to charges filed with the House of Representatives, which called for the impeachment of President Clinton. The president was charged with lying under oath about the sexual relationship, getting Lewinsky a job to keep her quiet, and covering up the sexual relationship.

The Republicans were the majority party in the House and Senate. The House Judiciary Committee held impeachment hearings and ultimately passed—along party lines—four articles of impeachment against the president. Articles I and II related to *perjury* (false statements under oath), Article III dealt with *obstruction of justice* (getting Lewinsky a job to "buy" her silence), and article IV dealt with *abuse of power* (failure to cooperate with the House investigation).

The committee charged that "William Jefferson Clinton has undermined the integrity of his office, has brought disrepute on the Presidency, has betrayed his trust as President, and has acted in a manner subversive of the rule of law and justice, to the manifest injury of the people of the United States." Yet in poll after poll, more than 60 percent of the public was against impeachment.

In December 1998, the full House took up the question of impeachment. A simple majority was necessary to report articles of impeachment to the Senate for trial of the president. "Impeachment," the ultimate sanction against a sitting president, is no trivial matter. Yet as journalist Elizabeth Drew notes, "by 1998, numerous House Republicans were treating impeachment as an almost casual matter."[13] For only the second time in the nation's history, the House voted to impeach a president, as Articles I (perjury) and III (obstruction of justice) passed in a largely straight-line partisan vote.

As with the last impeachment (of Andrew Johnson in 1869), the president was a Democrat and the House was controlled by Republicans. In January 1999, the trial of William Jefferson Clinton was to begin in the U.S. Senate.

The Senate trial, presided over by Chief Justice William Rehnquist, was contentious and, in the end, the Republican-controlled Senate could not muster even a simple majority (a two-thirds vote is necessary to convict a president) for either article of impeachment.

Bill Clinton survived an impeachment trial in the Senate, but what were the effects of impeachment on the presidency? In the course of the impeachment proceedings, several presidential powers were diminished. Due to court decisions, the president now may face civil trial while in office (*Clinton v. Jones*, 1997), his Secret Service guards and White House attorneys can be compelled to testify against him in court, and the president's executive privilege has been eroded.[14] Clinton has left a diminished and defensive presidency to his successors. The tragedy of Bill Clinton is that here is a man of enormous skill and possibility who could not control his darker impulses. He demeaned himself and his office.

Conclusion

The collapse of the Soviet Union led to the end of the cold war, but the United States had little time to celebrate. Reagan had left a mountain of debt and a number of unsolved problems to his successors. Getting the nation's economic house in order was the first priority.

But as Bush and Clinton attempted to solve the nation's economic problems, a far greater threat emerged: the savaging of political opponents in the age of "the politics of personal destruction." Clinton, a man who invited many of his own problems, was nonetheless savaged by personal attacks in what can be called an age of cynicism. The politics of the end of the twentieth century were highly personalized, excessively partisan, and deeply hurtful. And the presidency became a smaller, less dignified office.

⌘ 9 ⌘
Conclusion
The Presidency in the New Millennium

As this book demonstrates, the presidency changes from season to season, occupant to occupant, issue to issue. We may never unravel most of the paradoxes of the American presidency. Strong individuals, in demanding times, with the support of Congress and the public, can greatly expand the parameters of the office and its powers. Less skilled or less powerful presidents, in less demanding times, especially when facing an uncooperative Congress and an unconvinced public, can be weak and helpless. The presidency is a dynamic, elastic office. Its shape and powers change over time.

Perhaps, then, we should celebrate the work of the inventors of this unique office. Is the genius of the framers that they created an office capable of adapting to the needs and demands of an ever-changing world? They invented an office just ambiguous enough, just flexible enough to adapt, yet not so loose and undefined that it could easily overwhelm the delicate balance of the separation of powers.

The office of the presidency has an enormous, larger-than-life quality. In spite of the dramatic ups and downs of the office in the past 50 years, it does seem to be, in Arthur Schlesinger's words, "the indestructible institution."[1] It is at once the most powerful and the weakest executive office in the world. The great opportunity to do good is matched by the equally strong capacity to do great harm. The constitutional design of the office was left vague enough to give presidents an opportunity to shape and mold the office to conform, in part, to the needs of the time, the level of political opportunity, and the skills of each incumbent. But it was also an office encumbered by obstacle after obstacle. As political scientist James David Barber reminds us:

> The Presidency is much more than an institution. It is a focus of feelings. . . . The Presidency is the focus for the most intense and persistent emotions in the American polity. The President is a symbolic leader, the one figure who draws together the people's hopes and fears for the political future. On top of all his routine duties he has to carry that off—or fail.[2]

But if there were Washingtons, Jeffersons, Jacksons, Lincolns, and Roosevelts who stamped their imprints on the office, there were also—and more commonly—Buchanans, Grants, Hardings, Pierces, Coolidges, Fillmores,

190

and Tylers, who were overwhelmed and defeated by the office. In fact, the office ends up defeating most presidents.

Americans have historically had a difficult time deciding what they wanted of their leaders: someone to pull them forward or someone to follow their wishes; someone to act forcefully or someone to execute the people's will. Likewise, Americans have historically had a difficult time reconciling leadership with their democratic aspirations. Having said this, it is equally (though no less problematically) true that "American political thought has not lacked admirers of leadership."[3]

Because of our ambivalence and confusion regarding the proper scope of powers to be invested in the presidency, we swing back and forth between the desire for heroic leaders to "save" us and the desire to contain, if not destroy, the leaders who disappoint us. The pendulum swings back and forth between eras when we invest too much hope in leaders and eras of disposable leaders and the dwarfing of the presidency. As James M. Burns has noted, "We search eagerly for leadership yet seek to cage and tame it."[4] But "power," if it be exercised wisely and in the interests of the people, cannot be so restricted nor so liberated as to make it either ineffectual or dangerous.

Just what do we want of the presidency? Part of the difficulty inherent in such a question stems from a historical dilemma: the Founders themselves were never quite clear as to what they wanted of the institution. Constitutionally, they left the presidency vague and unformed, hoping that the venerated George Washington would set appropriate precedents.[5] But how well do eighteenth-century precedents work as we approach the twenty-first century? Perhaps it is time, in the spirit of Jefferson, who believed that no generation should be enslaved by the dogmas of the past, to ask anew: what do we want of the U.S. presidency? As Jefferson himself noted:

> Some men look at constitutions with sanctimonious reverence and deem them like the Ark of the Covenant, too sacred to be touched. They ascribe to the men of the preceding age a wisdom more than human, and suppose what they did to be beyond amendment. I knew that age well; I belonged to it, and labored with it. It deserved well of its country. It was very like the present, but without the experience of the present; and forty years of experience in government is worth a century of bookreading; and this they would say themselves, were they to rise from the dead. . . . Institutions must advance also, and keep pace with the times. We might as well require a man to wear still the coat which fitted him when a boy. . . . [6]

There is yet another compelling reason to reexamine the scope of presidential power: the end of the cold war. In the cold war era (1945–1989), it was widely believed that the United States, as the hegemonic power of the West, required strong presidential leadership (especially in foreign affairs).[7] But with the collapse of the Soviet empire, we are free from "some" of the burden of power imposed by the dangers of the cold war. Freed of the weight of the cold war we can ask: in the post-cold war world, what powers and limits do we wish to invest in the presidency in this "post-hegemonic era?"[8]

Put another way, as we approach the next century and the new world before us, we must find out "how to empower the president without endangering the system."[9] While the president's formal powers are rather limited, his informal powers may help to overcome the limits of the office, but skill can only go so far. And, paradoxically, there are areas in which the president clearly has too little power (domestic and economic policy) and simultaneously areas in which he has too much power (foreign policy and war).

Our confusion is complicated by the fact that leadership often seems at odds with democracy. We know leadership is important, but can we truly reconcile our need for leadership with our belief in democracy? Thomas E. Cronin believes we must.

> The Challenge, for those who care about our nation and the dreams of constitutional democracy, is to seek ways to reconcile these concepts—leadership and democracy. Whether we like it or not, our democracy will stand or fall on the quality of leaders as well as on the quality of citizens we produce and nurture here.[10]

And Cronin attempts to provide guidance on how we can democratize leadership by calling for a rebirth of citizen politics. As he writes,

> The challenge of reconciling leadership and democracy is part definitional, part attitudinal, and part behavioral. We have too long held a view of leaders that is hierarchical, male, and upon which followers, like subjects or slaves, are dependent. That conception is antithetical to our democratic aspirations. The very word "followers" is a negative and demeaning word and ought, if possible, to be discarded or at least greatly modified. For a nation of subservient followers can never be a democratic one. A democratic nation requires educated, skeptical, caring, engaged, and contentious citizen-leaders—citizens who are willing to lead as well as follow, who are willing to point the way as often as they are persuaded in one way or another, and prize the spirit of liberty and free speech that animates our Bill of Rights.[11]

Only by creating a cadre of citizen-leaders can we hope to democratize (and thereby empower) leadership in the United States. But is this possible in the fractious, divisive, and petty politics of the left versus the right?

Presidents who lead in the democratic spirit create leaders, foster citizen responsibility, and inspire and empower others to assume leadership responsibilities in their communities. Democratic leaders establish a moral vision; pursue egalitarian goals; question, challenge, engage, and educate citizens; and offer hope. Emiliano Zapata said that "strong leaders make a weak people."[12] But strong democratic leaders help create strong citizens. Eugene Debs encapsulated the dilemma when he said: "Too long have the workers of the world waited for some Moses to lead them out of bondage. He has not come; he will not come. I would not lead you out if I could; for if you would be led out, you could be led back again."[13]

Democratic theorists have long wrestled with a particularly vexing question: Is there such a thing as "democratic leadership" or are the two words mutually exclusive, if not contradictory? Thomas E. Cronin has gone so far as to call them "warring concepts."[14] But can any system of government exist without leadership? For those who believe in the superiority of democracy over other forms of government, a way must be found to reconcile these two seemingly warring concepts into a sustainable whole.

The tension between the need for leadership and the demands of democracy was discussed by James Bryce, who reminded us that "perhaps no form of government needs great leaders so much as democracy."[15] But what kind of leadership? The strong, forceful direction of a heroic leader or the gentle, guiding hand of a teacher? Proponents of robust democracy realize, as Bruce Miroff has written, that

> Leadership has rarely fit comfortably with democracy in America. The claim of leaders to political precedence violates the equality of democratic citizens. The most committed democrats have been suspicious of the very idea of leadership. When Thomas Paine railed against the "slavish custom of following leaders," he expressed a democrat's deepest anxiety.[16]

These tensions have not prevented Americans from looking to strong leaders to guide the republic. Especially during a crisis, we turn to our leaders in hopes that strong or heroic leadership can save us. Thus, while we are suspicious of strong leadership, we also admire it. As Arthur M. Schlesinger, Jr., has noted,

> The American democracy has readily resorted in practice to the very leadership it had disclaimed in theory. An adequate democratic theory must recognize that democracy is not self-executing: that leadership is not the enemy of self-government but the means of making it work; that followers have their own stern obligation, which is to keep leaders within rigorous constitutional bounds; and that Caesarism is more often produced by the failure of feeble governments than by the success of energetic ones.[17]

Dilemmas notwithstanding, is there a style of leadership compatible with political democracy? While a tension will always exist between leadership and democracy, there are ways to bring the two into a creative tension that both calls for a role for the leader and also promotes democratic participation and practices among the citizenry.

Just as Abraham Lincoln gave us a succinct, eloquent definition of democracy as "government of the people, by the people, for the people,"[18] so too did one of America's other Mt. Rushmore leaders give us an eloquent, even simple definition of democratic leadership. Thomas Jefferson believed that the primary duties of a leader in a democracy were "to inform the minds of the people, and to follow their will."[19]

There are two key concepts contained in Jefferson's brief definition: *inform minds,* and *follow the people's will.* Informing the minds of the people speaks to the role of leader as educator. In a democracy, the leader has a responsibility to educate, enlighten, and inform the people. He or she must identify problems and mobilize the people to act. By informing or educating the citizenry, the leader also engages in a dialogue, the ultimate goal of which is to involve leader and citizen in the process of developing a vision, grounded in the values of the nation, which will animate future action.

The leader's task in a democracy is to look ahead, see problems, focus the public's attention on the work that must be done, provide alternative courses of action, chart a path for the future, and move the nation in support of his or her ideas. The leader must attempt to mobilize the public around a vision and secure a consensus on the proper way to proceed.

The second component of Jefferson's definition, to "follow their will," suggests that after educating and involving the people, the leader must ultimately follow the will of the people. Several commentators have noted the distinction between the whim of the people (temporary and changing) and the will of the people (deeply held truths that speak to the nation's highest aspirations). The leader's job is to inform, educate, and persuade the public to embrace and work for a vision that taps into the deeper truths and higher purposes of the will of Americans. But whatever their judgment, the leader must serve the people and ultimately follow their direction.

In a democracy, following the will of the people is essential. Any leader who pursues policies contrary to the expressed wishes of the people can be accused of the cardinal sin in a democracy: defying the will of the people. Thus, to be a leader requires, first, that one use all possible means to bring about informed judgments by the people. Then, the leader must serve the people. This form of democratic accountability calls for the leader to play an important role, but it ultimately relies upon the people to make final judgments.

In this sense, Ronald Reagan did not exercise democratic leadership in the case of Nicaragua. Reagan believed that the Sandinistas, who controlled Nicaragua, were a threat to U.S. interests. He attempted to enlighten the public on this issue but failed to change public opinion. Congress, in line with public opinion, passed restrictive legislation, banning U.S. assistance to the rebels (Contras) who were attempting to overthrow the Nicaraguan government. In spite of this, the Reagan administration violated both the law and the public's wish by assisting the Contras. This is the type of leadership that the Founders feared and that contradicts democratic standards.

The best democratic leadership, in Bruce Miroff's words, "not only serves people's interests but furthers their democratic dignity as well."[20] Thus, Thomas Jefferson's vision of a democratic leadership that informs the public, then follows their will, elevates both leader and citizen. Such a form of leadership is difficult, time consuming, and fraught with pitfalls. But it is a style of leadership that builds strong citizens for a strong democracy.

The United States needs a strong presidency and a democratically controlled presidency; a strong presidency and strong citizenship.[21] Benjamin R. Barber notes the difficulty inherent in such a hope:

> At the heart of democratic theory lies a profound dilemma that has afflicted democratic practice at least since the eighteenth century. Democracy requires both effective leadership and vigorous citizenship: yet the conditions and consequences of leadership often seem to undermine civic vigor. Although it cries for both, democracy must customarily make do either with strong leadership or with strong citizens. For the most part, depending on devices of representation in large-scale societies, democracy in the West has settled for strong leaders and correspondingly weak citizens.[22]

James Madison's caution in *The Federalist,* no. 51, speaks volumes in today's world:

> If men were angels, no government would be necessary. If angels were to govern man, neither external nor internal controls in government would be necessary. In framing a government which is to be administered by men over men the great difficulty lies in this, you must first enable the government to control the governed and in the next place oblige it to control itself. A dependence on the people is no doubt the primary control on the government. But experience has taught mankind the necessity for auxiliary precautions.

How can one give power but control it? Can the presidency be empowered but democratized?

Of course, our desire for strong presidential leadership seems contrary to the goal of holding presidents accountable. Leadership implies power; accountability implies limits. Contradictions aside, accountability is a fundamental piece of the democratic puzzle. In essence, it denotes that public officials are answerable for their actions. But to whom? Within what limits? Through what means?

All presidents want to be successful, but what does it mean to be a success? High popularity? A good historical reputation? Achieving one's policy goals? A high congressional box score? Getting one's way?

If success is measured merely by getting one's way, then many bullies are successful. But success in leadership means more than getting what one wants. In determining success, we must always ask "power for what ends?" because power divorced from purpose is potentially dangerous and democratically undesirable.

In a democracy, people tend to get the government they deserve. If we look upon government as the enemy and politics as a dirty word, our anger turns to apathy, allowing power (but not responsibility) to slip through our hands; we look at politics not as a means to achieve public good, but as a necessary evil; we see elections as the choice between the lesser of two evils or the evil of two lessers; we presume that our democratic responsibilities are satisfied merely by the act of voting every so often; or we drop out of politics. In short, if we abandon politics, power abandons us. So we return to a question: How do we bring Hamiltonian energy to the Madisonian system to achieve Jeffersonian ends?[23] If democracies have trouble finding and supporting leaders who seek to democratize power, they have an equally difficult time measuring success. Emerson, answering the question "What is success?" came close:

> To laugh often and love much, to win the respect of intelligent persons and the affection of children; to appreciate beauty; to find the best in others; to give one's self; to leave the world a lot better whether by a healthy child, a garden patch, or a redeemed social condition; to have played and laughed with enthusiasm and sung with exaltation, to know even one life has breathed easier because you have lived—this is to have succeeded.[24]

In a democracy, a successful leader pursues and uses power, not for selfish ends, not to aggrandize his or her own status, but to achieve the goals of empowerment. Democratic leaders are educators, they are visionaries. They move the government in pursuit of the consensus generated from the values of the nation. They appeal to the best in citizens and attempt to lead the nation toward its better self.[25]

Franklin Roosevelt reminded us that the presidency "is preeminently a place of moral leadership."[26] Thus, presidents may use their office as a "bully pulpit" to—when at their best—lead democratically. While the current cynicism and disdain about government sweeps the land—partly the result, I have argued, of the persistence of failed presidencies—let us not forget the great good for which government can and has been used. After all, it was through politics and government that the great social movements of this century helped moved us toward greater racial and gender equality, devised policies to expand education and opportunities to a wider segment of the population, and attempted to protect and expand the rights of citizens. These battles are far from over. As a nation, we have a long way to go before we can truly grant the blessings of liberty and prosperity on all our fellow citizens, but it is through politics—and only through politics—that we can hope to achieve these noble goals. And if we want our politics (our government) to succeed, we must find ways for citizen power to guide, ennoble, and empower presidential leadership.

The presidency is a dynamic, not a static institution. While there are standard role expectations and responsibilities faced by all occupants of the office, such uniformity must be seen as the flip side of the rich variety each president brings to the office. Each president brings a unique set of skills, experiences, goals, and styles to the presidency, yet the office and the requirements of the times place certain demands on every president. Each new president has to emulate the master performances of Washington, Lincoln, and FDR, yet find his or her own voice and identity and invent the kind of approach that will help build a better America. It is this mix of the unique and the expected that makes the presidency such a fascinating institution.

The American presidency, while the subject of much criticism and disappointment, has lasted for over two hundred years. The system created by Madison and the other founders has lasted more or less intact for an amazingly long time, by comparative standards. It is thus time to pay tribute to the framers, but it is also time to honor their memory by reexamining the institution of the presidency, and ask: Is this the best we can do? Is this eighteenth-century document adequate for governing in the twenty-first century?

The framers would most certainly have been pleased to see how the system of checks and balances has thwarted executive tyranny. But they would perhaps have been less pleased with the gridlock that so often characterizes relations between the president and Congress. The founders wanted to limit presidential power, not spay and neuter the office.

"How," Bert Rockman asks in *The Leadership Question,* "can leadership be exerted yet restrained?"[27] It is a question that confounded the Founders and troubles us today.

Is the separation-of-powers model the problem? Does it create a magical gridlock machine? To one who is president, there must be times when it seems so. Woodrow Wilson—writing in 1885, before occupying the White House—saw the separation as creating a massive political escape clause for blame and responsibility:

> Power and strict accountability for its use are the essential constituents of good government. . . . It is, therefore, manifestly a radical defect in our federal system that it parcels out power and confuses responsibility as it does. The main purpose of the Convention of 1787 seems to have been to accomplish this grievous mistake. . . . Were it possible to call together again the members of that wonderful Convention . . . they would be the first to admit that the only fruit of dividing power had been to make it irresponsible.[28]

But on reflection, we are reminded of the positive benefit of separating, sharing, and overlapping power. If one values deliberation, discussion, and debate; if we accept a model of democratic governing based on consensus and cooperation, then the reform agenda will be short. But many see the separation as the likely suspect in the crime of gridlock.

Among reformers, there is a great deal of sympathy for the parliamentary alternative, but it must be admitted that with the American reverence for the Constitution, to make such a dramatic change is out of the question. Even if parliamentary reform were the panacea that some of its proponents suggest, there is simply no way to expect the American people to pursue such a radical restructuring of their system of government.

The problems that plague the presidency (and the American political system) are not entirely new. Past presidents faced many of the antileadership obstacles that have confronted the recent occupants of the White House. Many of the problems inhibiting presidential leadership (e.g., intent of the framers, structure of government) represent historical continuities, not radical departures from the past. All presidents have presided over a system that put leaders in chains. But there are some newer elements to add to the leadership-aversion system that inhibits presidents (e.g., the decline of party support, weakness of congressional leadership, decline of U.S. power). The leadership-aversion system is a constant reality; the components that make up its totality may change over time.

In order to attain progress and not merely change, we must know what to do (vision), how to go about doing it (skill), and hope that the system can be moved in that direction (resources and opportunity).

The United States is usually a presidentially driven system. Without presidential leadership it is difficult for the government to sustain concerted action. While there are times and issues upon which the Congress takes the initiative and leads, this must be seen as the exception rather than the rule.

While the "living" Constitution has evolved to Hamiltonian proportions, the written document still clings to a Madisonian architecture. To modern-day Hamiltonians, the Constitution is an empowering document; to Madisonians, it is a restricting document. In reality, it conforms to Corwin's dictum that it is an "invitation to struggle" for control of power. Since power floats in the American system, someone must grab and hold on to it. But power is slippery. The person best positioned to grab power (if only for a limited time) is the president. Thus, presidential leadership is important, perhaps indispensable, if the machinery of government is to move ahead.

While power is sometimes abused, often misused, and usually poorly used, we should not forget that the office and powers of the presidency are potential powers. And the power to do harm exists with the power to do good. If the presidency of the modern era has not been able to translate power potential into practical good, it must be remembered that it is not power itself that is good or ill, but the uses to which power is put. One could use government power to achieve good ends, but first one must be able to use the power of government.

In this sense, the United States needs presidential power. The president must be a leader, but not just any kind of leader. Presidents must have the power to do good, but the system of checks and balances is important to put a halt to presidents whose actions may be suspect. Presidents need the power to achieve the ideals grounded in the Declaration of Independence and Bill of Rights, but the citizens need the separation of powers to control potential abuse.

Perhaps that is why, as messy, confusing, frustrating, and aggravating as the separation of powers can be, it may still offer us the best available model for governing. If made to work properly—presidential leadership and persuasion moving the public around a vision that in turn leads to presidential influence in Congress—the separation of powers, and the theory of government that animates it, offers an opportunity for the government to be both powerful and democratically accountable.[29] In this way, respect for and reinvigoration of the separation of powers may offer presidents a way to overcome the roadblocks so endemic in the American system.

The Presidents of the United States

President	Born	Birthplace	Political Party	Age at inauguration	Served	Died	College or University	Religion	Vice President
1. George Washington	Feb. 22, 1732	Westmoreland County, Va.	None	57	1789–1797	Dec. 14, 1799		Episcopalian	John Adams
2. John Adams	Oct. 30, 1735	Braintree, Mass.	Federalist	61	1797–1801	July 4, 1826	Harvard	Unitarian	Thomas Jefferson
3. Thomas Jefferson	Apr. 13, 1743	Albemarle County, Va.	Democratic-Republican	57	1801–1809	July 4, 1826	William and Mary	Unitarian	Aaron Burr
4. James Madison	Mar. 16, 1751	Port Conway, Va.	Democratic-Republican	57	1809–1817	June 28, 1836	Princeton	Episcopalian	George Clinton / George Clinton / Elbridge Gerry / Elbridge Gerry
5. James Monroe	Apr. 28, 1758	Westmoreland County, Va.	Democratic-Republican	58	1817–1825	July 4, 1831	William and Mary	Episcopalian	Daniel Tompkins
6. John Quincy Adams	July 11, 17677	Braintree, Mass.	Democratic-Republican	57	1825–1829	Feb. 23, 1848	Harvard	Unitarian	John C. Calhoun
7. Andrew Jackson	Mar. 15, 1767	Waxhaw Settlement, S.C.	Democratic	54	1837–1841	July 24, 1862		Presbyterian	John C. Calhoun / Martin Van Buren
8. Martin Van Buren	Dec. 5, 1782	Kinderhook, N.Y.	Democratic	54	1837–1841	July 24, 1862		Dutch Reformed	Richard Johnson
9. William H. Harrison	Feb. 9, 1773	Berkeley, Va.	Whig	68	1841	Apr. 4, 1841	Hampden-Sydney	Episcopalian	John Tyler
10. John Tyler	Mar. 29, 1790	Greenway, Va.	Whig	51	1841–1845	Jan. 18, 1862	William and Mary	Episcopalian	
11. James K. Polk	Nov. 2, 1795	Near Pineville, N.C.	Democratic	49	1845–1849	June 15, 1849	Univ. N. Carolina	Methodist	George M. Dallas

President	Born	Birthplace	Political Party	Age at inauguration	Served	Died	College or University	Religion	Vice President
12. Zachary Taylor	Nov. 24, 1784	Orange County, Va.	Whig	64	1849–1850	July 9, 1850		Episcopalian	Millard Fillmore
13. Millard Fillmore	Jan. 7, 1800	Locke, N.Y.	Whig	50	1850–1853	Mar. 8, 1874		Unitarian	
14. Franklin Pierce	Nov. 23, 1804	Hillsboro, N.H.	Democratic	48	1853–1857	Oct. 8, 1869	Bowdoin	Episcopalian	William R. King
15. James Buchanan	Apr. 23, 1791	Near Mercersburg, Pa.	Democratic	65	1857–1861	June 1, 1868	Dickinson	Presbyterian	John Breckinridge
16. Abraham Lincoln	Feb. 12, 1809	Near Hodgenville, Ky.	Republican, Union†	52	1861–1865	Apr. 15, 1865		Presbyterian	Hannibal Hamlin Andrew Johnson
17. Andrew Johnson	Dec. 29, 1808	Raleigh, N.C.	Union‡	56	1865–1869	July 31, 1875		Methodist	
18. Ulysses S. Grant	Apr. 27, 1822	Point Pleasant, Ohio	Republican	46	1869–1877	July 23, 1885	U.S. Mil. Academy	Methodist	Schuyler Colfax Henry Wilson
19. Rutherford B. Hayes	Oct. 4, 1822	Delaware, Ohio	Republican	54	1877–1881	Jan. 17, 1893	Kenyon	Methodist	William A. Wheeler
20. James A. Garfield	Nov. 19, 1831	Orange, Ohio	Republican	49	1881	Sept. 19, 1881	Williams	Disciples of Christ	Chester A. Arthur
21. Chester A. Arthur	Oct. 5, 1829	Farfield, Vt.	Republican	51	1881–1885	Nov. 18, 1886	Union	Episcopalian	
22. Grover Cleveland	Mar. 13, 1837	Caldwell, N.J.	Democratic	47	1885–1889	June 24, 1908		Presbyterian	Thomas A. Hendricks
23. Benjamin Harrison	Aug. 20, 1833	North Bend, Ohio	Republican	55	1893–1897	March 13, 1901	Miami	Presbyterian	Levi P. Morton
24. Grover Cleveland	Mar. 13, 1837	Caldwell, N.J.	Democratic	55	1893–1897	June 24, 1908		Presbyterian	Adlai E. Stevenson
25. William McKinley	Jan. 29, 1843	Niles, Ohio	Republican	54	1897–1901	Sept. 14, 1901	Allegheny College	Methodist	Garret A. Hobart Theodore Roosevelt
26. Theodore Roosevelt	Oct. 27, 1858	New York, N.Y.	Republican	42	1901–1909	Jan. 6, 1919	Harvard	Dutch Reformed	Charles W. Fairbanks
27. William H. Taft	Sept. 15, 1857	Cincinnati, Ohio	Republican	51	1909–1913	Mar. 8, 1930	Yale	Unitarian	James S. Sherman
28. Woodrow Wilson	Dec. 29, 1856	Staunton, Vz.	Democratic	56	1913–1921	Feb. 3, 1924	Princeton	Presbyterian	Thomas R. Marshall
29. Warren G. Harding	Nov. 2, 1865	Near Blooming Grove, OH	Republican	55	1921–1923	Aug. 2, 1923		Baptist	Calvin Coolidge
30. Calvin Coolidge	July 4, 1872	Plymouth Notch, Vt.	Republican	51	1923–1929	Jan. 5, 1933	Amherst	Congregationist	Charles G. Dawes
31. Herbert C. Hoover	Aug. 10, 1874	West Branch, Iowa	Republican	54	1929–1933	Oct. 20, 1964	Stanford	Friend (Quaker)	Charles Curtis

No. Name	Born	Birthplace	Party	Age	Term	Died	College	Religion	Vice President
32. Franklin D. Roosevelt	Jan. 30, 1882	Hyde Park, N.Y.	Democratic	51	1933–1945	Apr. 12, 1945	Harvard	Episcopalian	John N. Garner Henry A. Wallace Harry S Truman
33. Harry S Truman	May 8, 1884	Lamar, Mo.	Democratic	60	1945–1953	Dec. 26, 1972		Baptist	Alben W. Barkley
34. Dwight D. Eisenhower	Oct. 14, 1890	Denison, Tex.	Republican	62	1953–1961	Mar. 28, 1969	U.S. Mil. Academy	Presbyterian	Richard M. Nixon
35. John F. Kennedy	May 29, 1917	Brookline, Mass.	Democratic	43	1961–1963	Nov. 22, 1963	Harvard	Roman Catholic	Lyndon B. Johnson
36. Lyndon B. Johnson	Aug. 27, 1908	Near Stonewall, Tex.	Democratic	55	1963–1969	Jan. 22, 1973	SW Texas State	Disciples of Christ	Hubert H. Humphrey
37. Richard M. Nixon	Jan. 13, 1913	Yorba Linda, CA	Republican	56	1969–1974	Apr. 22, 1994	Whittier	Friend (Quaker)	Spiro T. Agnew Gerald R. Ford[P]
38. Gerald R. Ford*	July 14, 1913	Omaha, Neb.	Republican	61	1974–1977		Michigan	Episcopalian	Nelson Rockefeller§
39. Jimmy Carter	Oct. 1, 1924	Plains, Ga.	Democratic	52	1977–1981		U.S. Naval Academy	Baptist	Walter F. Mondale
40. Ronald W. Reagan	Feb. 6, 1911	Tampico, Ill.	Republican	69	1981–1989		Eureka	Disciples of Christ	George H.W. Bush
41. George H.W. Bush	June 12, 1924	Milton, Mass.	Republican	64	1989–1993		Yale	Episcopalian	Dan Quayle
42. Bill Clinton	Aug. 19, 1946	Hope, Ark.	Democratic	46	1993–		Georgetown	Baptist	Al Gore

†The Union Party was made up of Republicans and War Democrats

‡The Union Party was made up of Republican and War Democrats; Johnson was a War Democrat

PInaugurated Dec. 6, 1973, to replace Agnew, who resigned Oct. 10, 1973.

*Inaugurated Aug. 9, 1974, to replace Nixon, who resigned on the same day

§Inaugurated Dec. 19, 1974, to replace Ford, who became president Aug. 9, 1974

Presidential Elections

Year	Winner and Loser	Popular Vote and Percentage	Electoral Vote
1789	George Washington (no party)	Unknown	69
	No opposition		
1792	George Washington (Federalist)	Unknown	132
	No opposition		
1796	John Adams (F)	Unknown	71
	Thomas Jefferson (Democratic-Republican)	Unknown	68
1800	Thomas Jefferson (DR)	Unknown	73
	Aaron Burr (DR)	Unknown	73
	John Adams (F)	Unknown	65
	Charles C. Pinckney (F)	Unknown	64
1804	Thomas Jefferson (DR)	Unknown	162
	Charles C. Pinckney (F)	Unknown	14
1808	James Madison (DR)	Unknown	122
	Charles C. Pinckney (F)	Unknown	47
1812	James Madison (DR)	Unknown	128
	DeWitt Clinton (F)	Unknown	89
1816	James Monroe (DR)	Unknown	183
	Rufus King (F)	Unknown	34
1820	James Monroe (DR)	Unknown	231
	John Quincy Adams (no party)	Unknown	1
1824	John Quincy Adams (no party)	108,740–30.6%	84
	Andrew Jackson (no party)	153,544–43.1%	99
	William H. Crawford (no party)	46,618–13.1%	41
	Henry Clay (no party)	47,136–13.2%	37
1828	Andrew Jackson (D)	647,286–56.0%	178
	John Quincy Adams (NR)	508,064–44.0%	83
1832	Andrew Jackson (D)	687,502–56.5%	219
	Henry Clay (NR)	530,189–43.5%	49
1836	Martin Van Buren (D)	765,483–50.9%	170
	William H. Harrison (W)	549,567–41.8%	73
1840	William H. Harrison (W)	1,274,624–53.1%	234
	Martin Van Buren (D)	1,127,781–46.9%	60
1844	James K. Polk (D)	1,338,464–49.6%	170
	Henry Clay (W)	1,300,097–48.1%	105
1848	Zachary Taylor (W)	1,360,967–47.3%	163
	Lewis Cass (D)	1,222,342–42.5%	127
1852	Franklin Pierce (D)	1,601,117–50.9%	254
	Winfield Scott (W)	1,385,453–44.1%	42
1856	James Buchanan (D)	1,832,955–45.3%	174
	John C Frémont (R)	1,339,932–33.1%	114
	Millard Fillmore (A)	871,731–21.6%	8
1860	Abraham Lincoln (R)	1,865,593–39.8%	180
	Stephen A. Douglas (D)	1,382,713–29.5%	12
	John C. Breckinridge (D)	8488,356–18.1%	72
	John Bell (CU)	592,906–12.6%	39
1864	Abraham Lincoln (NU)	2,206,938–55.0%	212
	George McClellan (D)	1,803,787–45.0%	21

Year	Winner and Loser	Popular Vote and Percentage	Electoral Vote
1868	Ulysses S. Grant (R)	3,013,421–52.7%	214
	Ulysses S. Grant (R)	2,706,829–47.3%	80
1872	Ulysses S. Grant (R)	3,596,745–55.6%	286
	Horace Greeley (D)	2,843,446–44.0%	66
1876	Rutherford B. Hayes (R)	4,036,572–48.0%	185
	Samuel J. Tilden (D)	4,284,020–51.0%	184
1880	James A. Garfield (R)	4,453,295–48.5%	214
	Winfield S. Hancock (D)	4,414,082–48.1%	155
1884	Grover Cleveland (D)	4,879,507–48.5%	219
	James G. Blaine (R)	4,850,293–48.2%	182
1888	Benjamin Harrison (R)	5,447,129–47.9%	233
	Grover Cleveland (D)	5,537,857–48.6%	168
1892	Grover Cleveland (D)	5,555,426–46.0%	277
	Benjamin Harrison (R)	5,182,690–43.0%	145
	James Weaver (P)	1,029,846–8.5%	22
1896	William McKinley (R)	7,102,246–51.0%	271
	William J. Bryan (D)	6,492,559–46.7%	176
1900	William McKinley (R)	7,218,491–51.7%	292
	William J. Bryan (D)	6,356,734–45.5%	155
1904	Theodore Roosevelt (R)	7,628,461–56.4%	336
	Alton B. Parker (D)	5,084,223–37.6%	140
1908	William H. Taft (R)	7,675,320–51.6%	321
	William J. Bryan (D)	6,412,294–43.1%	162
1912	Woodrow Wilson (D)	6,296,547–41.9%	435
	Theodore Roosevelt (Pr)	4,118,571–27.4%	88
	William H. Taft (R)	3,486,720–23.2%	8
1916	Woodrow Wilson (D)	9,127,695–49.4%	277
	Charles E. Hughes (R)	8,533,507–46.2%	254
1920	Warren G. Harding (R)	16,143,407–60.4%	404
	James M. Cox (D)	9,130,328–34.2%	127
1924	Calvin Coolidge (R)	15,718,211–54.0%	382
	John W. Davis (D)	8,385,283–28.8%	136
	Robert M. La Follette (Pr)	4,031,289–16.6%	13
1928	Herbert C. Hoover (R)	21,391,993–58.2%	444
	Alfred E. Smith (D)	15,016,169–40.9%	87
1932	Franklin D. Roosevelt (D)	22,809,638–57.4%	472
	Herbert C. Hoover (R)	15,758,901–39.7%	59
1936	Franklin D. Roosevelt (D)	27,752,869–60.8%	523
	Alfred Landon (R)	16,674,665–36.5%	8
1940	Franklin D. Roosevelt (D)	27,307,819–54.8%	277
	Wendell Wilkie (R)	22,321,018–44.8%	254
1944	Franklin D. Roosevelt (D)	25,606,585–53.5%	432
	Thomas E. Dewey (R)	22,104,745–46.0%	99
1948	Harry S Truman (D)	24,105,812–49.5%	303
	Thomas E. Dewey (R)	21,970,065–45.1%	189
	J. Strom Thurmond (SR)	1,169,063–2.4%	39
	Henry A. Wallace (Pr)	1,157,172–2.4%	0
1952	Dwight D. Eisenhower (R)	33,936,234–55.1%	442
	Adlai F. Stevenson (D)	27,314,992–44.4%	89
1956	Dwight D. Eisenhower (R)	35,590,472–57.4%	457
	Adlai F. Stevenson (D)	26,022,752–42.0%	73
1960	John F. Kennedy (D)	34,227,096–49.5%	303
	Richard M. Nixon (R)	34,108,546–49.4%	219
1964	Lyndon B. Johnson (D)	43,129,484–61.1%	486
	Barry M. Goldwater (R)	27,178,188–38.5%	52
1968	Richard M. Nixon (R)	31,785,480–43.4%	301
	Hubert H. Humphrey (D)	31,275,165–42.7%	191
	George C. Wallace (AI)	906,473–13.5%	46

Year	Winner and Loser	Popular Vote and Percentage	Electoral Vote
1972	Richard M. Nixon (R)	47,169,911–60.7%	520
	George S. McGovern (D)	29,170,383–37.5%	17
	John G. Schmitz (AI)	1,098,482–1.4%	0
1976	Jimmy Carter (D)	40,825,839–50.0%	297
	Gerald R. Ford (R)	38,147,770–47.9%	240
	Eugene J. McCarthy (IND)	680,390–0.8%	0
1980	Ronald Reagan (R)	43,904,153–50.8%	489
	Jimmy Carter (D)	35,483,883–41.0%	49
	John B. Anderson (IND)	5,719,222–6.6%	0
1984	Ronald Reagan (R)	54,450,603–58.8%	525
	Walter F. Mondale (D)	37,573,671–40.6%	13
1988	George Bush (R)	47,917,342–54%	426
	Michael Dukakis (D)	41,013,030–46%	112
1992	Bill Clinton (D)	43,728,275–43%	370
	George Bush (R)	38,167,416–38%	168
	H. Ross Perot (none)	19,237,447–19%	0

Political Control of Congress: 1789–1997

Congress	Years	President and Party		House of Representatives			Senate		
				Majority Party	Minority Party	Other	Majority Party	Minority Party	Other
1st	1789–91	George Washington	Federalist	Fed–38	A-F–26	—	Fed–17	A-F–9	—
2nd	1791–93	George Washington	Federalist	Fed–37	DR–33	—	Fed–16	DR–13	—
3rd	1793–95	George Washington	Federalist	DR–57	Fed–48	—	Fed–17	DR–13	—
4th	1795–97	George Washington	Federalist	Fed–54	DR–52	—	Fed–19	DR–13	—
5th	1798–99	John Adams	Federalist	Fed–58	DR–48	—	Fed–20	DR–12	—
6th	1799–1801	John Adams	Federalist	Fed–64	DR–42	—	Fed–19	DR–13	—
7th	1801–03	Thomas Jefferson	Dem–Rep	DR–69	Fed–36	—	DR–18	Fed–13	—
8th	1803–05	Thomas Jefferson	Dem–Rep	DR–102	Fed–39	—	DR–25	Fed–9	—
9th	1805–07	Thomas Jefferson	Dem–Rep	DR–116	Fed–25	—	DR–27	Fed–7	—
10th	1807–09	Thomas Jefferson	Dem–Rep	DR–118	Fed–24	—	DR–28	Fed–6	—
11th	1809–11	James Madison	Dem–Rep	DR–94	Fed–48	—	DR–28	Fed–6	—
12th	1811–13	James Madison	Dem–Rep	DR–108	Fed–36	—	DR–30	Fed–6	—
13th	1813–15	James Madison	Dem–Rep	DR–112	Fed–68	—	DR–27	Fed–9	—
14th	1815–17	James Madison	Dem–Rep	DR–117	Fed–65	—	DR–25	Fed–11	—
15th	1817–19	James Monroe	Dem–Rep	DR–141	Fed–42	—	DR–34	Fed–10	—
16th	1819–21	James Monroe	Dem–Rep	DR–156	Fed–27	—	DR–35	Fed–7	—
17th	1821–23	James Monroe	Dem–Rep	DR–158	Fed–25	—	DR–44	Fed–4	—
18th	1823–25	James Monroe	Dem–Rep	DR–187	Fed–26	—	DR–44	Fed–4	—
19th	1825–27	John Quincy Adams	Coalition	Co–105	Ja–97	—	Co–26	Ja–20	—
20th	1827–29	John Quincy Adams	Coalition	Ja–119	Co–94	—	Ja–28	Co–20	—
21st	1829–31	Andrew Jackson	Democrat	D–139	NR–74	—	D–26	NR–22	—
22nd	1831–33	Andrew Jackson	Democrat	D–141	NR–58	14	D–25	NR–212	—

Congress	Years	President	Party	House of Representatives			Senate		
				Majority Party	Minority Party	Other	Majority Party	Minority Party	Other
23rd	1833–35	Andrew Jackson	Democrat	D–147	A-M–53	60	D–20	NR–208	—
24th	1835–37	Andrew Jackson	Democrat	D–145	W–98	—	D–27	W–25	—
25th	1837–39	Martin Van Buren	Democrat	D–108	W–107	24	D–30	W–184	—
26th	1839–41	Martin Van Buren	Democrat	D–124	W–118	—	D–28	W–22	—
		William H. Harrison	Whig						
27th	1841–43	John Tyler	Whig	W–133	D–102	6	W–28	D–22	2
28th	1843–45	John Tyler	Whig	D–142	W–79	1	W–28	D–25	1
29th	1845–47	James K. Polk	Democrat	D–143	W–77	6	D–31	W–25	—
30th	1847–49	James K. Polk	Democrat	W–115	D–108	4	D–36	W–21	—
31st	1849–51	Zachary Taylor	Whig	D–112	W–109	9	D–35	W–25	2
		Millard Fillmore	Whig						
32nd	1851–53	Millard Fillmore	Whig	D–140	W–88	5	D–35	W–24	3
33rd	1853–55	Franklin Pierce	Democrat	D–159	W–71	4	D–38	W–22	2
34th	1855–57	Franklin Pierce	Democrat	R–108	D–83	43	D–42	R–155	
35th	1857–59	James Buchanan	Democrat	D–131	R–92	14	D–39	R–205	
36th	1859–61	James Buchanan	Democrat	R–113	D–101	23	D–38	R–262	
37th	1861–63	Abraham Lincoln	Republican	R–106	D–42	28	R–31	D–11	7
38th	1863–65	Abraham Lincoln	Republican	R–103	D–80	—	R–39	D–12	—
39th	1865–67	Abraham Lincoln	Unionist	U–145	D–46	—	U–42	D–10	—
		Andrew Johnson	Unionist						
40th	1867–69	Andrew Johnson	Unionist	R–143	D–49	1	R–42	D–11	—
41st	1869–71	Ulysses S. Grant	Republican	R–170	D–73	—	R–61	D–11	—
42nd	1871–73	Ulysses S. Grant	Republican	R–139	D–104	—	R–57	D–17	—
43rd	1873–75	Ulysses S. Grant	Republican	R–203	D–88	3	R–54	D–19	1
44th	1875–77	Ulysses S. Grant	Republican	D–181	R–107	5	R–46	D–29	1
45th	1877–79	Rutherford B. Hayes	Republican	D–156	R–137	—	R–39	D–36	1

Congress	Years	President	Party						
46th	1879–81	Rutherford B. Hayes	Republican	D-150	R-128	15	D-43	R-33	—
47th	1881–83	James A. Garfield	Republican	R-152	D-130	11	R-37	D-37	2
48th	1883–85	Chester A. Arthur	Republican	D-200	R-119	6	R-40	D-36	—
49th	1885–87	Chester A. Arthur	Republican	D-182	R-140	3	R-41	D-34	—
50th	1887–89	Grover Cleveland	Democrat	D-170	R-151	4	R-39	D-37	—
51st	1889–91	Grover Cleveland	Democrat	R-173	D-156	1	R-47	D-37	2
52nd	1891–93	Benjamin Harrison	Republican	D-231	R-88	14	R-47	D-39	5
53rd	1893–95	Benjamin Harrison	Republican	D-220	R-126	10	D-44	R-38	6
54th	1895–97	Grover Cleveland	Democrat	R-246	D-104	7	R-44	D-39	5
55th	1897–99	Grover Cleveland	Democrat	R-206	D-134	17	R-46	D-34	10
56th	1899–1901	William McKinley	Republican	R-185	D-163	39	R-53	D-26	11
57th	1901–03	William McKinley	Republican	R-198	D-153	6	R-56	D-29	5
58th	1903–05	Theodore Roosevelt	Republican	R-207	D-178	1	R-58	D-32	—
59th	1905–07	Theodore Roosevelt	Republican	R-250	D-136	—	R-58	D-32	—
60th	1907–09	Theodore Roosevelt	Republican	R-222	D-164	—	R-61	D-29	2
61st	1909–11	William H. Taft	Republican	R-219	D-172	1	R-59	D-32	1
62nd	1911–13	William H. Taft	Republican	D-228	R-162	1	R-49	D-42	—
63rd	1913–15	Woodrow Wilson	Democrat	D-290	R-127	18	D-51	R-44	1
64th	1915–17	Woodrow Wilson	Democrat	D-231	R-193	11	D-56	R-39	1
65th	1917–19	Woodrow Wilson	Democrat	D-210	R-216	9	D-53	R-42	1
66th	1919–21	Woodrow Wilson	Democrat	R-237	D-191	7	D-48	R-47	1
67th	1921–23	Warren G. Harding	Republican	R-300	D-132	3	R-59	R-37	—
68th	1923–25	Warren G. Harding	Republican	R-225	D-207	3	R-51	D-43	—
69th	1925–27	Calvin Coolidge	Republican	R-247	D-183	5	R-54	D-40	—
70th	1927–29	Calvin Coolidge	Republican	R-237	D-195	3	R-48	D-47	—
71st	1929–31	Calvin Coolidge	Republican	R-267	D-163	1	R-56	D-39	—
72nd	1931–33	Herbert C. Hoover	Republican	D-216	R-218	5	R-48	D-47	—
73rd	1933–35	Franklin D. Roosevelt	Democrat	D-313	R-117	5	D-59	R-36	1

Congress	Years	President and Party		House of Representatives			Senate		
		President	Party	Majority Party	Minority Party	Other	Majority Party	Minority Party	Other
74th	1935–37	Franklin D. Roosevelt	Democrat	D-322	R-103	10	D-69	R-25	2
75th	1937–39	Franklin D. Roosevelt	Democrat	D-333	R-89	13	D-75	R-17	4
76th	1939–41	Franklin D. Roosevelt	Democrat	D-262	R-169	4	D-66	R-23	4
77th	1941–43	Franklin D. Roosevelt	Democrat	D-267	R-162	6	D-57	R-28	2
78th	1943–45	Franklin D. Roosevelt	Democrat	D-222	R-209	4	D-57	R-38	1
79th	1945–47	Franklin D. Roosevelt	Democrat	D-243	R-190	2	D-57	R-38	1
80th	1947–49	Harry S Truman	Democrat	R-246	D-188	1	R-51	D-45	—
81st	1949–51	Harry S Truman	Democrat	D-263	R-171	1	D-54	R-42	—
82nd	1951–53	Harry S Truman	Democrat	D-234	R-199	2	D-48	R-47	1
83rd	1953–55	Dwight D. Eisenhower	Republican	R-221	D-213	1	R-48	D-46	2
84th	1955–57	Dwight D. Eisenhower	Republican	D-232	R-203	—	D-48	R-47	1
85th	1957–59	Dwight D. Eisenhower	Republican	D-234	R-201	—	D-49	R-47	—
86th	1959–61	Dwight D. Eisenhower	Republican	D-283	R-153	—	D-64	R-34	—
87th	1961–63	John F. Kennedy	Democrat	D-262	R-175	—	D-64	R-36	—
88th	1963–65	John F. Kennedy / Lyndon B. Johnson	Democrat	D-258	R-176	1	D-67	R-33	—
89th	1965–67	Lyndon B. Johnson	Democrat	D-295	R-140	—	D-68	R-32	—
90th	1967–69	Lyndon B. Johnson	Democrat	D-248	R-187	—	D-64	R-36	—
91st	1969–71	Richard M. Nixon	Republican	D-243	R-192	—	D-57	R-43	—
92nd	1971–73	Richard M. Nixon	Republican	D-255	R-180	—	D-54	R-44	2
93rd	1973–75	Richard M. Nixon / Gerald R. Ford	Republican	D-242	R-192	1	D-56	R-42	2

Congress	Years	President	Party	House Majority	House Minority	House Other	Senate Majority	Senate Minority	Senate Other
94th	1975–77	Gerald R. Ford	Republican	D-291	R-144	—	D-60	R-37	2
95th	1977–79	Jimmy Carter	Democrat	D-292	R-143	—	D-61	R-38	1
96th	1979–81	Jimmy Carter	Democrat	D-277	R-158	—	D-58	R-41	1
97th	1981–83	Ronald Reagan	Republican	D-243	R-192	—	R-53	D-46	—
98th	1983–85	Ronald Reagan	Republican	D-268	R-167	—	R-55	D-45	—
99th	1985–87	Ronald Reagan	Republican	D-253	R-182	—	R-53	D-47	—
100th	1987–89	Ronald Reagan	Republican	D-258	R-177	—	D-54	R-46	—
101st	1989–91	George Bush	Republican	D-260	R-175	—	D-55	R-45	—
102nd	1991–93	George Bush	Republican	D-267	R-167	1	D-57	R-43	—
103rd	1993–95	Bill Clinton	Democrat	D-258	R-176	1	D-57	R-43	—
104th	1995–97	Bill Clinton	Democrat	R-230	D-204	1	R-54	D-46	—

Political Party Abbreviations: A-F–Anti-Federalist; A-M–Anti-Masonic; Co–Coalition; D–Democrat; DR–Democratic-Republican; Fed–Federalist; Ja–Jacksonian; NR–National Republican; R–Republican; U–Unionist; W–Whig.

First Ladies and Wives of the Presidents

Name[1]	Dates	Birthplace	Married	Children[2]
Washington, Martha (Dandridge) Castis	1731–1802	New Kent Co., Va.	1759	—
Adams, Abigail Smith	1744–1818	Wrymouth, Mass.	1764	5
Jefferson, Martha (Wayles) Skelton	1748–1882	Charles City Co., Va.	1772	6
Madison, Dorothea "Dolley" (Payne) Todd	1768–1849	Guilford Co., NC	1794	—
Monroe, Elizabeth Kortright	1768–1830	New York, NY	1786	3
Adams, Louisa Catherine Johnson	1775–1852	London, England	1797	1
Jackson, Rachel (Donelson) Robards	1767–1828	Halifax Co., Va.	1791	—
Van Buren, Hannah Hoes	1783–1819	Kinderhook, NY	1807	4
Harrison, Anna Symmes	1775–1864	Morristown, NJ	1795	10
Tyler, Letitia Christian	1790–1842	Cedar Grove, Va.	1813	8
Tyler, Julia Gardiner	1820–1889	Gardiner's Is., NY	1844	7
Polk, Sarah Childress	1803–1891	Murfreesboro, Tenn.	1824	—
Taylor, Margaret Smith	1788–1852	Calvert Co., Md.	1810	6
Fillmore, Abigail Powers	1798–1853	Stillwater, NY	1826	2
Fillmore, Caroline (carmichael) McIntosh	1813–1881	Morristown, NJ	1858	—
Pierce, Jane Means Appleton	1806–1863	Hampton, NH	1834	3
Lincoln, Mary Todd	1818–1882	Lexington, KY	1842	4
Johnson, Eliza McCardle	1810–1876	Leesburg, Tenn.	1827	5
Grant, Julia Dent	1826–1902	St. Louis, Mo.	1848	4
Hayes, Lucy Ware Webb	1831–1889	Chillicothe, Ohio	1852	8
Garfield, Lucretia Rudolph	1832–1918	Hiram, Ohio	1858	7
Arthur, Ellen Lewis Herndon	1837–1880	Fredericksburg, Va.	1859	3
Cleveland, Frances Folsom	1864–1947	Buffalo, NY	1886	5
Harrison, Caroline Lavinia Scott	1832–1892	Oxford, Ohio	1853	2
Harrison, Mary Scott (Lord) Dimmick	1858–1948	Homesdale, Pa.	1896	1
McKinley, Ida Saxton	1847–1907	Canton, Ohio	1871	2
Roosevelt, Alice Hathaway Lee	1861–1884	Chestnut Hill, Mass.	1880	1
Roosevelt, Edith Kermit Crow	1861–1948	Norwich, Conn.	1886	3
Taft, Helen Herron	1861–1943	Cincinnati, Ohio	1886	3
Wilson, Ellen Louise Axson	1860–1914	Savannah, Ga.	1885	3
Wilson, Edith (Bolling) Galt	1872–1961	Wytheville, Va.	1915	—
Harding, Florence (Kling) DeWolfe	1860–1924	Marion, Ohio	1891	—
Coolidge, Grace Anna Goodhue	1879–1957	Burlington, Vt.	1905	2
Hoover, Lou Henry	1875–1944	Waterloo, Iowa	1899	2
Roosevelt, Anna Eleanor Roosevelt	1884–1962	New York, NY	1905	6
Truman, Elizabeth "Bess" Wallace	1885–1982	Independence, Mo.	1919	1

Name[1]	Dates	Birthplace	Married	Children[2]
Eisenhower, Mamie Geneva Doud	1896–1979	Boone, Iowa	1916	2
Kennedy, Jacqueline Lee Bouvier	1929–1994	Southampton, NY	1953	3
Johnson, Claudia Alta "Lady Bird" Taylor	1912–	Marshall, Texas	1934	2
Nixon, Thelma Catherine Patricia "Pat" Ryan	1912–1993	Ely, Nev.	1940	2
Ford, Elizabeth "Betty" (Bloomer) Warren	1918–	Chicago, Ill.	1948	4
Carter, Rosalynn Smith	1927–	Plains, Ga.	1946	4
Reagan, Jane Wyman	1914–	St. Joseph, Mo.	1940	2
Reagan, Nancy Davis	1923–	New York, NY	1952	2
Bush, Barbara Pierce	1925–	Rye, NY	1945	6
Clinton, Hillary Rodham	1947–	Chicago, Ill.	1975	1

[1]Names in parentheses are maiden names of previously married women.
[2]Children by previous marriages are not included. Children who died in infancy are included.

Vice Presidents

Name (party)	Dates	Birthplace	Served under	Took office
1. John Adams (F)	1735–1826	Braintree, Mass.	Washington	1789
2. Thomas (DR)	1743–1826	Shadwell, Va.	John Adams	1797
3. Aaron Burr (DR)	1756–1836	Newark, NJ	Jefferson	1801
4. George Clinton (R)	1734–1812	Little Britain, NY	Jefferson, Madison	1805
5. Elbridge Gerry (R)	1744–1814	Marblehead, Mass.	Madison	1813
6. Daniel D. Tompkins (R)	1774–1825	Fox Meadows, NY	Monroe	1817
7. John C. Calhoun (R)	1782–1850	Abbeville District, SC	J.Q. Adams, Jackson	1825
8. Martin Van Buren (D)	1782–1862	Kinderhook, NY	Jackson	1833
9. Richard M. Johnson (D)	1780–1850	Beargrass, Ky.	Van Buren	1837
10. John Tyler (W)	1790–1862	Charles City Co., Va.	W.H. Harrison	1841
11. George M. Dallas (D)	1792–1864	Philadelphia, Pa.	Polk	1845
12. Millard Fillmore (W)	1800–1874	Cayuga Co., NY	Taylor	1849
13. William R. King (D)	1786–1853	Sampson Co., NC	Pierce	1853
14. John C. Breckinridge (D)	1821–1875	Lexington, Ky.	Buchanan	1857
15. Hannibal Hamlin (R)	1809–1891	Paris, Me.	Lincoln	1861
16. Andrew Johnson (NU)[1]	1808–1875	Raleigh, NC	Lincoln	1865
17. Schuyler Colfax (R)	1823–1885	New York, NY	Grant	1869
18. Henry Wilson (R)	1812–1875	Farmington, NH	Grant	1873
19. William A. Wheeler (R)	1819–1887	Malone, NY	Hayes	1877
20. Chester A. Arthur (R)	1830–1886	Fairfield, Vt.	Garfield	1881
21. Thomas A. Hendricks (D)	1819–1885	Muskingham Co., OH	Cleveland	1885
22. Levi P. Morton (R)	1824–1920	Shoreham, Vt.	B. Harrison	1889
23. Adlai F. Stevenson (D)[2]	1835–1914	Christian Co., Ky.	Cleveland	1893
24. Garret A. Hobart (R)	1844–1899	Long Branch, NJ	McKinley	1897
25. Theodore Roosevelt (R)	1858–1919	New York, NY	McKinley	1901
26. Charles W. Fairbanks (R)	1852–1918	Unionville Center, OH	T. Roosevelt	1905

Name (party)	Dates	Birthplace	Served under	Took office
27. James S. Sherman (R)	1855–1912	Utica, NY	Taft	1909
28. Thomas R. Marshall (D)	1854–1925	N. Manchester, Ind.	Wilson	1913
29. Calvin Coolidge (R)	1872–1933	Plymouth Notch, Vt.	Harding	1921
30. Charles G. Dawes (R)	1865–1951	Marietta, OH	Coolidge	1925
31. Charles Curtis (R)	1860–1936	Topeka, Kan.	Hoover	1929
32. John N. Garner (D)	1868–1967	Red River Co., TX	F. Roosevelt	1933
33. Henry A. Wallace (D)	1888–1966	Adair Co., Iowa	F. Roosevelt	1941
34. Harry S Truman (D)	1884–1972	Lamar, Mo.	F. Roosevelt	1945
35. Alben W. Barkley (D)	1877–1956	Graves Co., Ky.	Truman	1949
36. Richard M. Nixon (R)	1913–1994	Yorba Linda, CA	Eisenhower	1953
37. Lyndon B. Johnson (D)	1908–1973	Near Stonewall, TX	Kennedy	1961
38. Hubert H. Humphrey (D)	1911–1978	Wallace, SD	L. Johnson	1965
39. Spiro T. Agnew (R)	1918–	Baltimore, Md.	Nixon	1969
40. Gerald R. Ford (R)	1913–	Omaha, Neb.	Nixon	1973
41. Nelson A. Rockefeller (R)	1908–1979	Bar Harbor, Me.	Ford	1974
42. Walter F. Mondale (D)	1928–	Ceylon, Minn.	Carter	1977
43. George Bush (R)	1924–	Milton, Mass.	Reagan	1981
44. J. Danforth Quayle (R)	1947–	Indianapolis, Ind.	Bush	1989
45. Albert Gore, Jr. (D)	1948–	Washington, D.C.	Clinton	1993

[1]Andrew Johnson: A Democrat nominated by Republicans and elected with Lincoln on the National Union ticket.
[2]Adlai F. Stevenson: 23rd Vice President. Grandfather of the Democratic candidate for President, 1952 and 1956.

APPENDIX F

James Madison
LETTER TO THOMAS JEFFERSON

New York October 24, 1787

You will herewith receive the result of the Convention, which continued its session till the 17th of September. I take the liberty of making some observations on the subject, which will help to make up a letter, it they should answer no other purpose.

This ground-work being laid, the great objects which presented themselves were (1) to unite a proper energy in the Executive, and a proper stability in the Legislative departments, with the essential characters of Republican Government (2) to draw a line of demarcation which would give to the Central government every power requisite for general purposes, and leave to the States every power which might be most beneficially administered by them (3) to provide for the different interests of different parts of the Union (4) to adjust the clashing pretensions of the large and small States. Each of these objects was pregnant with difficulties. The whole of them together formed a task more difficult than can be well conceived by those who were not concerned in the execution of it. Adding to these considerations the natural diversity of human opinions on all new and complicated subjects, it is impossible to consider the degree of concord which ultimately prevailed as less than a miracle.

The first of these objects, as respects the Executive, was peculiarly embarrassing. On the question whether it should consist of a single person, or a plurality of co-ordinate members, on the mode of appointment, on the duration in office, on the degree of power, on the re-eligibility, tedious and reiterated discussions took place. The plurality of co-ordinate members had finally but few advocates. Governour Randolph was at the head of them. The modes of appointment proposed were various, as by the people at large—by electors chosen by the people—by the Executives of the States—by the Congress, some preferring a joint ballot of the two Houses—some a separate concurrent ballot, allowing to each a negative on the other house—some, a nomination of several candidates by one House, out of whom a choice should be made by the other. Several other modifications were stated. The expedient at length adopted seemed to give pretty general satisfaction to the members. As to the duration in office, a few would have preferred a tenure during good behaviour—a considerable number would have done so in case an easy & effectual removal by impeachment could be settled. It was much agitated whether a long term, seven years for example, with a subsequent & perpetual ineligibility, or a short term with a capacity to be re-elected, should be fixed. In favor of the first opinion were urged the danger of a gradual degeneracy of re-elections from time to time, into first a life and then a hereditary tenure, and the favorable effect of an incapacity to be reappointed in the independent exercise of the Executive authority. On the other side it was contended that the prospect of necessary degradation would discourage the most dignified characters from aspiring to the office, would take away the principal motive to ye faithful discharge of its duties—the hope of being rewarded with a reappointment would stimulate ambition to violent effort for holding over the Constitutional term—and instead of producing an independent administration, and a firmer defence of the constitutional rights of the department, would render the officer more indifferent to the importance of a place which he would soon be obliged to quit forever, and more ready to yield to the encroachmts. of the Legislature of which he might again be a member. The questions concerning the degree of power turned chiefly on the appointment to offices, and the control on the Legislature. An absolute appointment to all offices—to some offices—to no offices, formed the scale of opinions on the first point. On the second, some contended for an absolute negative, as the only possible means of reducing to practice the theory of a free Government which forbids a mixture of the Legislative and Executive powers. Others would be content with a revisionary power, to be overruled by three fourths of both Houses. It was warmly urged that the judiciary department should be associated in the revision. The idea of some was that a separated revision should be given to the two departments—that if either objected two thirds, if both, three fourths, should be necessary to overrule.

APPENDIX G

Alexander Hamilton

FEDERALIST NO. 69

Proceed now to trace the real characters of the proposed Executive, as they are marked out in the plan of the convention. This will serve to place in a strong light the unfairness of the representations which have been made in regard to it.

The first thing which strikes our attention in that the executive authority, with few exceptions, is to be vested in a single magistrate. This will scarcely, however, be considered as a point upon which any comparison can be grounded; for if, in this particular, there be a resemblance to the king of Great Britain, there is not less a resemblance to the Grand Seignior, to the khan of Tartary, to the Man of the Seven Mountains or to the governor of New York.

That magistrate is to be elected for *four* years; and is to be re-eligible as often as the people of the United States shall think him worthy of their confidence. In these circumstances there is a total dissimilitude between *him* and a king of Great Britain, who is an *hereditary* monarch, possessing the crown as a patrimony descendible to his heirs forever; but there is a close analogy between *him* and a governor of New York, who is elected for *three* years, and is re-eligible without limitation or intermission . . .

The President of the United States would be liable to be impeached, tried, and, upon conviction of treason, bribery, or other high crimes or misdemeanours, removed from office; and would afterwards be liable to prosecution and punishment in the ordinary course of law. The person of the king of Great Britain is sacred and inviolable; there is no constitutional tribunal to which he is amenable; no punishment to which he can be subjected without involving the crisis of a national revolution. In this delicate and important circumstance of personal responsibility, the President of Confederated America would stand upon no better ground than a governor of New York, and upon worse ground than the governors of Maryland and Delaware.

The President of the United States is to have power to return a bill which shall have passed the two branches of the legislature for reconsideration; and the bill so returned is to become a law if, upon that reconsideration, it be approved by two thirds of both houses. The king of Great Britain, on his part, has an absolute negative upon the acts of the two houses of Parliament. The disuse of that power for a considerable time past does not affect the reality of its existence; and is to be ascribed wholly to the crown's having found the means of substitution influence to authority, or the art of gaining a majority in one or the other of the two houses, to the necessity of exerting a prerogative which could seldom be exerted without hazarding some degree of national agitation. The qualified negative of the President differs widely from this absolute negative of the British sovereign; and tallies exactly with the revisionary authority of the council of revision of this State, of which the governor is a constituent part . . .

Source: This essay by "Publius" was originally published in the New York Packet, March 14, 1788.

The President is to be the "commander-in-chief of the army and navy of the United States, and of the militia of the several States, when called into the actual service of the United States. He is to have power to grant reprieves and pardons for offences against the United States, *except in cases of impeachment*; to recommend to the consideration of Congress such measures as he shall judge necessary and expedient; to convene, on extraordinary occasions, both houses of the legislature, or either of them, and, in case of disagreement between them *with respect to the time of adjournment*, to adjourn them to such time as he shall think proper; to take care that the laws be faithfully executed; and to commission all officers of the United States." In most of these particulars the power of the President will resemble equally that of the king of Great Britain and of the governor of New York. The most material points of difference are these: *First.* The President will have only the occasional command of such part of the militia of the nation as by legislative provision may be called into the actual service of the Union. The king of Great Britain and the governor of New York have at all times the entire command of all the militia within their several jurisdictions. In this article, therefore, the power of the President would be inferior to that of either monarch or the governor. *Secondly.* The President is to be commander-in-chief of the army and navy of the United States. In this respect his authority would be nominally the same with that of the king of Great Britain, but in substance much inferior to it. It would amount to nothing more than the supreme command and direction of the military and naval forces, as first general and admiral of the Confederacy; while that of the British king extends to the *declaring* of war and to the *raising* and *regulating* of fleets and armies—all which, by the constitution under consideration, would appertain to the legislature . . . *Thirdly.* The power of the President, in respect to pardons, would extend to all cases, *except those of impeachment.* The governor of New York may pardon in all cases, even in those of impeachment, except for treason and murder. Is not the power of the governor, in this article, on a calculation of political consequences, greater than that of the President? . . .

Fourthly. The President can only adjourn the national legislature in the single case of disagreement about the time of adjournment. The British monarchy may prorogue or even dissolve the Parliament. The governor of New York may also prorogue the legislature of this State for a limited time; a power which, in certain situations, may be employed to very important purposes.

The President is to have power, with the advice and consent of the Senate, to make treaties, provided two thirds of the senators present concur. The king of Great Britain is the sole and absolute representative of the nation in all foreign transactions. He can of his own accord make treaties of peace, commerce, alliance, and of every other description.

. . . It must be admitted that, in this instance, the power of the federal Executive would exceed that of any State Executive. But this arises naturally from the sovereign power which relates to treaties. If the Confederacy were to be dissolved it would become a question whether the Executives of the several States were not solely invested with that delicate and important prerogative.

The President is also to be authorised to receive ambassadors and other public ministers. This, though it has been a rich theme of declamation, is more a matter of dignity than of authority. In this circumstance which will be without consequence in the administration of the government; and it was far more convenient that it should be arranged in this manner than that there should be a necessity of convening the legislature, or one of its branches, upon every arrival of a foreign minister, though it were merely to take the place of a departed predecessor.

The President is to nominate and, with the advice and consent of the Senate, to appoint ambassadors and other public ministers, judges of the Supreme Court, and in general all officers of the United States established by law, and whose appointments are not otherwise provided for by the Constitution. The king of Great Britain is emphatically and truly styled the fountain of honour. He not only appoints to all offices, but can create offices. He can confer titles of nobility at pleasure; and has the disposal of an immense number of church preferments. There is evidently a great inferiority in the power of the President, in this particular, to that of the British king; nor is it equal to that of the governor of New York, if we are to interpret the meaning of the constitution of the State by the practice which has obtained under it . . .

Hence it appears that, except as to the concurrent authority of the President in the article of treaties, it would be difficult to determine whether that magistrate would, in the aggregate, possess more or less power than the Governor of New York. And it appears yet more unequivocally that there is no pretence for the parallel which has been attempted between him and the king of Great Britain. But to render the contrast in this respect still more striking, it may be of use to throw the principal circumstances of dissimilitude into a closer group.

The President of the United States would be an officer elected by the people for *four* years; the king of Great Britain is a perpetual and *hereditary* prince. The one would be amendable to personal punishment and disgrace; the person of the other is sacred and inviolable. The one would have a *qualified* negative upon the acts of the legislative body; the other has an *absolute* negative. The one would have a right to command the military and naval forces of the nation; the other, in addition to this right, possesses that of *declaring* war, and of *raising* and *regulating* fleets and armies by his own authority. That one would have a concurrent power with a branch of the legislature in the formation of treaties; the other is the *sole possessor* of the power of making treaties. The one would have a like concurrent authority in appointing to offices; the other is the sole author of all appointments. The one can confer no privileges whatever; the other can make denizens of aliens, noblemen of commoners; can erect corporations with all the rights incident to corporate bodies. The one can prescribe no rules concerning the commerce or currency of the nation; the others is in several respects the arbiter of commerce, and in this capacity can establish markets and fairs, can regulate weights and measures, can lay embargoes for a limited time, can coin money, can authorise or prohibit the circulation of foreign coin. The one has no particle of spiritual jurisdiction; the other is the supreme head and governor of the national church! What answer shall we give to those who would persuade us that things so unlike resemble each other? The same that ought to be given to those who tell us that a government, the whole power of which would be in the hands of the elective and periodical servants of the people, is an aristocracy, a monarchy, and a despotism.

Publius

Alexander Hamilton
FEDERALIST NO. 70

There is an idea, which is not without its advocates, that a vigorous Executive is inconsistent with the genius of republican government . . . Energy in the Executive is a leading character in the definition of good government. It is essential to the protection of the community against foreign attacks; it is not less essential to the steady administration of the laws; to the protection of property against those irregular and high-handed combinations which sometimes interrupt the ordinary course of justice; to the security of liberty against the enterprises and assaults of ambition, of faction, and of anarchy.

There can be no need, however, to multiply arguments or examples on this head. A feeble Executive implies a feeble execution of the government. A feeble execution is but another phrase for a bad execution; and a government ill executed, whatever it may be in theory, must be, in practice, a bad government . . .

The ingredients which constitute energy in the Executive are, first, unity; secondly, duration; thirdly, an adequate provision for its support; fourthly, competent powers.

The ingredients which constitute safety in the republican sense are first, a due dependence on the people; secondly, a due responsibility.

Those politicians and statesmen who have been the most celebrated for the soundness of their principles and for the justice of their views, have declared in favor of a single Executive and a numerous legislature. They have, with great propriety, considered energy as the most necessary qualification of the former, and have regarded this as most applicable to power in a single hand; while they have, with equal propriety, considered the latter as best adapted to deliberation and wisdom, and best calculated to conciliate the confidence of the people and to secure their privileges and interests.

That unity is conducive to energy will not be disputed. Decision, activity, secrecy, and despatch will generally characterize the proceedings of one man in a much more eminent degree than the proceedings of any greater number; and in proportion as the number is increased, these qualities will be diminished.

This unity may be destroyed in two ways; either by vesting the power in two or more magistrates of equal dignity and authority; or by vesting it ostensibly in one man, subject, in whole or in part, to the control and cooperation of others, in the capacity of counsellors to him. Of the first, the two Consuls of Rome may serve as an example; of the last, we shall find examples in the constitutions of several of the States. New York and New Jersey, if I recollect right, are the only States which have intrusted the executive authority wholly to single men. Both these methods of destroying the unity of the Executive have their partisans; but the votaries of an executive council are the most numerous. They are both liable, if not to equal, to similar objections, and may in most lights be examined in conjunction

Wherever two or more persons are engaged in any common enterprise or pursuit, there is always danger of difference of opinion. If it be a public trust or office,

Source: This essay by "Publius" was originally published in the New York Packet, March 14, 1788.

in which they are clothed with equal dignity and authority, there is peculiar danger of personal emulation and even animosity. From either, and especially from all these causes, the most bitter dissentions are apt to spring. Whenever these happen, they lessen the respectability, weaken the authority, and distract the plans and operations of those whom they divide. If they should unfortunately assail the supreme executive magistracy of a country, consisting of a plurality of persons, they might impede or frustrate the most important measures of the government, in the most critical emergencies of the state. And what is still worse, they might split the community into the most violent and irreconcilable factions, adhering differently to the different individuals who composed the magistracy.

Men often oppose a thing, merely because they have had no agency in planning it, or because it may have been planned by those whom they dislike. But if they have been consulted, and have happened to disapprove, opposition then becomes, in their estimation, an indispensable duty of self-love. They seem to think themselves bound in honor, and by all the motives of personal infallibility, to defeat the success of what has been resolved upon contrary to their sentiments . . .

In the legislature, promptitude of decision is oftener an evil than a benefit. The differences of opinion, and the jarrings of parties in that department of the government, though they may sometimes obstruct salutary plans, yet often promote deliberation and circumspection, and serve to check excesses in the majority. When a resolution too is once taken, the opposition must be at an end. That resolution is a law, and resistance to it punishable. But no favorable circumstances palliate or atone for the disadvantages of dissension in the executive department. Here, they are pure and unmixed. There is no point at which they cease to operate. They serve to embarrass and weaken the execution of the plan or measure to which they relate, from the first step to the final conclusion of it. They constantly counteract those qualities in the Executive which are the most necessary ingredients in its composition, —vigor and expedition, and this without any counterbalancing good. In the conduct of war, in which the energy of the Executive is the bulwark of the national security, every thing would be apprehended from its plurality . . .

But one of the weightiest objections to a plurality in the Executive, and which lies as much against the last as the first plan, is that it tends to conceal faults and destroy responsibility. Responsibility is of two kinds—to censure and to punishment. The first is the more important of the two, especially in an elective office. Man, in public trust, will much oftener act in such a manner as to render him unworthy of being any longer trusted than in such a manner as to make him obnoxious to legal punishment. But the multiplication of the Executive adds to the difficulty of detection in either case. If often becomes impossible, amidst mutual accusation to determine on whom the blame, the punishment of a pernicious measure, or series of pernicious measures, ought really to fall . . .

It is evident from these considerations, that the plurality of the Executive tends to deprive the people of the two greatest securities they can have for the faithful exercise of any delegated power, *first*, the restraints of public opinion, which lose their efficacy, as well on account of the division of the censure attendant on bad measures among a number, as on account of the uncertainty on whom it ought to fall; and, *secondly*, the opportunity of discovering with facility and clearness the misconduct of the persons they trust, in order either to their removal from office, or to their actual punishment in cases which admit of it.

In England, the king is a perpetual magistrate; and it is a maxim which has obtained for the sake of the public peace, that he is unaccountable for his administration, and his person sacred. Nothing, therefore, can be wiser in that kingdom, than to annex to the king a constitutional council, who may be responsible to the nation for the advice they give. Without this, there would be no responsibility whatever in the executive department—an idea inadmissible in a free government. But even there the king is not bound by the resolutions of his council, though they are answerable for the advice they give. He is the absolute master of his own conduct in the exercise of his office, and may observe or disregard the counsel given to him at his sole discretion.

But in a republic, where every magistrate ought to be personally responsible for his behavior in office, the reason which in the British Constitution dictates the propriety of a council, not only ceases to apply, but turns against the institution. In the monarchy of Great Britain, it furnishes a substitute for the prohibited responsibility of the chief magistrate, which serves in some degree as a hostage to the national justice for his good behavior. In the American republic, it would serve to destroy, or would greatly diminish, the intended and necessary responsibility of the Chief Magistrate himself.

The idea of a council to the Executive, which has so generally obtained in the State constitutions, has been derived from that maxim of republican jealousy which considers power as safer in the hands of a number of men than of a single man. If the maxim should be admitted to be applicable to the case, I should contend that the advantage on that side would not counterbalance the numerous disadvantages on the opposite side. But I do not think the rule at all applicable to the executive power. I clearly concur in opinion, in this particular, with a writer whom the celebrated Junius pronounces to be "deep, solid, and ingenious," that "the executive power is more easily confined when it is ONE"; that it is far more safe there should be a single object for the jealousy and watchfulness of the people; and, in a word, that all multiplication of the Executive is rather dangerous than friendly to liberty . . .

I will only add that, prior to the appearance of the constitution, I rarely met with an intelligent man from any of the States, who did not admit, as the result of experience, that the UNITY of the executive of this States was one of the best of the distinguishing features of our constitution.

George Clinton

To the Citizens of the State of New York

November 8, 1787

Admitting, however, that the vast extent of America, together with the various other reasons which I offered you in my last number, against the practicability of the just exercise of the new government are insufficient to convince; still it is an undesirable truth, that its several parts are either possessed of principles, which you have heretofore considered as ruinous and that others are omitted which you have established as fundamental to your political security, and must in their operation, I will venture to assert, fetter your tongues and minds, enchain your bodies, and ultimately extinguish all that is great and noble in man.

In pursuance of my plan I shall begin with observations on the executive branch of this new system; and though it is not the first in order, as arranged therein, yet being the *chief*, is perhaps entitled by the rules of rank to the first consideration. The executive power as described in the 2nd article, consists of a president and vice-president—regulates the salary of the president, delineates his duties and powers; and, lastly, declares the causes for which the president and vice-president shall be removed from office.

Notwithstanding the great learning and abilities of the gentlemen who composed the convention, it may here be remarked with deference, that the construction of the first paragraph of the first section of the second article is vague and inexplicit, and leaves the mind in doubt as to the election of a president and every other case, the election of these great officers is expressly provided for; but there is no explicit provision for their election in case of expiration of their offices, subsequent to the election which is to set this political machine in motion; no certain and express terms as in your state constitution, that *stately* once in every four years, and as often as these offices shall become vacant, by expiration or otherwise, as is therein expressed, an election shall be held as follows, &c., this inexplicitness perhaps may lead to an establishment for life.

It is remarked by Montesquieu, in treating of republics, that *in all magistracies, the greatness of the power must be compensated by the brevity of the duration, and that a longer time than a year would be dangerous*. It is, therefore, obvious to the least intelligent mind to account why great power in the hands of a magistrate, and that power connected with considerable duration, may be dangerous to the liberties of a republic, the deposit of vast trusts in the hands of a single magistrate, enables him in their exercise to create a numerous train of dependents; this tempts his ambition, which in a republican magistrate is also remarked, *to be pernicious*, and the duration of his office for any considerable time favors his views, gives him the means and time to perfect and execute his designs, *he therefore fancies that he may be great and glorious by oppressing his fellow-citizens, and raising himself to permanent grandeur*

222

on the ruins of his country. And here it may be necessary to compare the vast and important powers of the president, together with his continuance in office, with the foregoing doctrine—his eminent magisterial situation will attach many adherents to him, and he will be surrounded by expectants and courtiers, his power of nomination and influence on all appointments, the strong posts in each state comprised within his superintendence, and garrisoned by troops under his direction, his control over the army, militia, and navy, the unrestrained power of granting pardons for treason, which may be used to screen from punishment those whom he had secretly instigated to commit the crime, and thereby prevent a discovery of his own guilt, his duration in office for four years: these, and various other principles evidently prove the truth of the position, that if the president is possessed of ambition, he had power and time sufficient to ruin his country.

Though the president, during the sitting of the legislature, is assisted by the senate, yet he is without a constitutional council in their recess; he will therefore be unsupported by proper information and advice, and will generally be directed by minions and favorites, or a council of state will grow out of the principal officers of the great departments, the most dangerous council in a free country.

The ten miles square, which is to become the seat of government, will of course be the place of residence for the president and the great officers of state; the same observations of a great man will apply to the court of a president possessing the powers of a monarch, that is observed of that of a monarch—*ambition with idleness—baseness with pride—the thirst of riches without labor—aversion to truth—flattery—treason—perfidy—violation of engagements—contempt of civil duties—hope from the magistrate's weakness; but above all, the perpetual ridicule of virtue*—these, he remarks, are the characteristics by which the courts in all ages have been distinguished.

The language and the manners of this court will be what distinguished them from the rest of the community, not what assimilates them to it; and in being remarked for a behavior that shows they are not meanly born, and in adulation to people of fortune and power.

The establishment of a vice-president is as unnecessary as it is dangerous. This officer, for want of other employment, is made president of the senate, thereby blending the executive and legislative powers, besides always giving to some one state, from which he is to come, an unjust pre-eminence.

It is a maxim in republics that the representative of the people would be of their immediate choice; but by the manner in which the president is chosen, he arrives to this office at the fourth or fifth hand, nor does the highest vote, in the way he is elected, determine the choice, for it is only necessary that he should be taken from the highest of five, who may have a plurality of votes.

Compare your past opinions and sentiments with the present proposed establishment, and you will find, that if you adopt it, that it will lead you into a system which you heretofore reprobated as odious. Every American Whig, not long since, bore his emphatic testimony against a monarchical government, though limited, because of the dangerous inequality that it created among citizens as relative to their rights and property; and wherein does this president, invested with his powers and prerogatives, essentially differ from the king of Great Britain (save as to name, and locality). The direct prerogatives of the president, as springing from his political character, are among the following: It is necessary, in order to distinguish him from the rest of the community, and enable him to keep, and maintain his court, that the compensation for his services, or in other words, his revenue, should be such as to enable him to appear with the splendor of a prince; he has the power of receiving ambassadors from, and a great influence on their appointments to foreign courts; as also to make treaties, leagues, and alliances with foreign states, assisted by the Senate, which when made become the supreme law of the land: he is a constituent part of the legislative power, for every bill which shall pass the House of Representatives and Senate is to be presented to him for approbation; if he approves of it he is to sign it, if he disapproves he is to return it with objections, which in many cases will amount to a complete negative; and in this view he will have a great share in the power of making peace, coining money, etc., and all the various objects of legislation, expressed or implied in this constitution: for though it may be asserted that the king of Great Britain has the express power of making peace or war, yet he never thinks it prudent to do so without the advice of his Parliament, from whom he is to derive his support, and therefore these powers, in both president and king, are substantially the same: he is the generalissimo of the nation, and of course has the command and control of the army, navy, and militia; he is the general conservator of the peace of the union—he may pardon all offences, except in cases of impeachment, and the principal fountain of all offices and employments. Will not the exercise of these powers therefore tend either to the establishment of a vile and arbitrary aristocracy or monarchy? The safety of the people in a republic depends on the share or proportion they have in the government; but experience ought to teach you, that when a man is at the head of an elective government invested with great powers, and interested in his reelection, in what circle appointments will be made; by which means an *imperfect aristocracy* bordering on monarchy may be established.

You must, however, my countrymen, beware that the advocates of this new system do not deceive you by a fallacious resemblance between it and your own state government which you so much prize; and, if you examine, you will perceive that the chief magistrate of this state is your immediate choice, controlled and checked by a just and full representation of the people, divested of the prerogative of influencing war and peace, making treaties, receiving and sending embassies, and commanding standing armies and navies, which belong to the power of the confederation, and will be convinced that his government is no more like a true picture of your own than an Angel of Darkness resembles an Angel of Light.

November 22, 1787

In my last number I endeavored to prove that the language of the article relative to the establishment of the executive of this new government was vague and inexplicit; that the great powers of the president, connected with his duration in office, would lead to oppression and ruin; that he would be governed by favorites and flatterers, or that a dangerous council would be collected from the great officers of state; that the ten miles square, if the remarks of one of the wisest men, drawn from the experience of mankind, may be credited, would be the asylum of the base, idle, avaricious and ambitious, and that the court would possess a language and manners different from yours; that a vice-president is as unnecessary as he is dangerous in his influence; that the president cannot represent you because he is not of your own immediate choice; that if you adopt this government you will incline to an arbitrary and odious aristocracy or monarchy; that the president, possessed of the power given him by this frame of government, differs but very immaterially from the establishment of monarchy in Great Britain; and I warned you to beware of the fallacious resemblance that is held out to you by the advocates of this new system between it and your own state governments.

And here I cannot help remarking that inexplicitness seems to pervade this whole political fabric; certainly in political compacts, which Mr. Coke calls *the mother and nurse of repose and quietness* the want of which induced men to engage in political society, has ever been held by a wise and free people as essential to their security; as on the one hand it fixes barriers which the ambitious and tyrannically disposed magistrate dare not overleap, and on the other, becomes a wall of safety to the community—otherwise stipulations between the governors and governed are nugatory; and you might as well deposit the important powers of legislation and execution in one or a few and permit them to govern according to their disposition and will; but the world is too full of examples, which prove that to live by one man's will became the cause of all men's misery. Before the existence of express political compacts it was reasonably implied that the magistrate should govern with wisdom and justice; but mere implication was too feeble to restrain the unbridled ambition of a bad man, or afford security against negligence, cruelty or any other defect of mind. It is alleged that the opinions and manners of the people of America are capable to resist and prevent an extension of prerogative or oppression, but you must recollect that opinion and manners are mutable, and may not always be a permanent obstruction against the encroachments of government; that the progress of a commercial society begets luxury, the parent of inequality, the foe to virtue, and the enemy to restraint; and that ambition and voluptuousness, aided by flattery, will teach magistrates where limits are not explicitly fixed to have separate and distinct interests from the people; besides, it will not be denied that government assimilates the manners and opinions of the community to it. Therefore, a general presumption that rulers will govern well is not a sufficient security. You are then under a sacred obligation to provide for the safety of your posterity, and would you now basely desert their interests, when by a small share of prudence you may transmit to them a beautiful political patrimony, which will prevent the necessity of their travelling through seas of blood to obtain that which your wisdom might have secured? It is a duty you owe likewise to your own reputation, for you have a great name to lose; you are characterized as cautious, prudent and jealous in politics; whence is it therefore that your are about to precipitate yourselves into a sea of uncertainty, and adopt a system so vague, and which has discarded so many of your valuable rights? Is it because you do not believe that an American can be a tyrant? If this be the case, you rest on a weak basis: Americans are like other men in similar situations, when the manners and opinions of the community are changed by the causes I mentioned before; and your political compact inexplicit, your posterity will find that great power connected with ambitions, luxury and flattery, will as readily produce a Caesar, Caligula, Nero and Domitian in America, as the same causes did in the Roman Empire.

THE PRESIDENCY AND THE CONSTITUTION

ARTICLE I

SECTION 1. All legislative Powers herein granted shall be vested in a Congress of the United States, which shall consist of a Senate and House of Representatives. . . .

SECTION 2. . . . The House of Representatives shall chuse their Speaker and other Officers; and shall have the sole Power of Impeachment. . . .

SECTION 3. . . . The Vice President of the United States shall be President of the Senate, but shall have no Vote, unless they be equally divided.

The Senate shall chuse their other Officers, and also a President pro tempore, in the Absence of the Vice President, or when he shall exercise the Office of President of the United States.

The Senate shall have the sole Power to try all Impeachments. When sitting for that Purpose, they shall be on Oath or Affirmation. When the President of the United States is tried the Chief Justice shall preside: And no Person shall be convicted without the Concurrence of two thirds of the Members present.

Judgment in Cases of Impeachment shall not extend further than to removal from Office, and disqualification to hold and enjoy any Office of honor, Trust or Profit under the United States: but the Party convicted shall nevertheless be liable and subject to Indictment, Trial, Judgment and Punishment, according to Law. . . .

SECTION 6. . . . No Senator or Represntative shall, during the Time for which he was elected, be appointed to any civil Office under the Authority of the United States, which shall have been created, or the Emoluments whereof shall have been encreased during such time; and no Person holding any Office under the United States, shall be a Member of either House during his Continuance in Office. . . .

SECTION 7. . . . Every Bill which shall have passed the House of Representatives and the Senate, shall, before it become a Law, be presented to the President of the United States; If he approve he shall sign it, but if not he shall return it, with his Objections to that House in which it shall have originated, who shall enter the Objections at large on their Journal, and proceed to reconsider it. If after such Reconsideration two thirds of that House shall agree to pass the Bill, it shall be sent, together with the Objections, to the other House, by which it shall likewise be reconsidered, and if approved by two thirds of that House, it shall become a Law. But in all such Cases the Votes of both Houses shall be determined by Yeas and Nays, and the Names of the Persons voting for and against the Bill shall be entered on the Journal of each House respectively. If any Bill shall not be returned by the President within ten Days (Sundays excepted) after it shall have been presented to him, the Same shall be a Law, in like Manner as if he had signed it, unless the Congress by their Adjournment prevent its Return, in which Case it shall not be a Law.

Every Order, Resolution, or Vote to which the Concurrence of the Senate and House of Representatives may be necessary (except on a question of Adjournment) shall be presented to the President of the United States; and before the Same shall take Effect, shall be approved by him, or being disapproved by him, shall be repassed by two thirds of the Senate and House of Representatives, according to the Rules and Limitations prescribed in the Case of a Bill. . . .

ARTICLE II

SECTION 1. The executive Power shall be vested in a President of the United States of America. He shall hold his Office during the Term of four Years, and, together with the Vice President, chosen for the same Term, be elected, as follows.

Each State shall appoint, in such Manner as the Legislature thereof may direct, a Number of Electors, equal to the whole Number of Senators and Representatives to which the State may be entitled in the Congress: but no Senator or Representative, or Person holding an Office of Trust or Profit under the United States, shall be appointed an Elector.

[The Electors shall meet in their respective States, and vote by Ballot for two Persons, of whom one at least shall not be an Inhabitant of the same State within themselves. And they shall make a List of all the Persons voted for, and of the Number of Votes for each; which List they shall sign and certify, and transmit sealed to the Seat of the Government of the United States, directed to the President of the Senate. The President of the Senate shall, in the Presence of the Senate and the House of Representatives, open all the Certificates, and the Votes shall then be counted., The Person having the greatest Number of Votes shall be the President, if such Number be a Majority of the whole number of Electors appointed; and if there be more than one who have such Majority, and have an equal Number of Votes, then the House of Representatives shall immediately chuse by Ballot one of them for President; and if no Person have a Majority, then from the five highest on the list the said House shall in like Manner chuse the President. But in chusing the President, the Votes shall be taken by States, the Representation from each State having one vote; a quorum for this Purpose shall consist of a Member or Members from two thirds of the States, and a Majority of all the States shall be necessary to a choice. In every Case, after the Choice of the President, the Person having the greatest Number of votes of the Electors shall be the Vice President. But if there should remain two or more who have equal Votes, the Senate shall chuse from them by Ballot the Vice President.]*

The Congress may determine the Time of chusing the Electors, and the Day on which they shall give their Votes; which Day shall be the same throughout the United States.

No Person except a natural born Citizen, or a Citizen of the United States, at the time of the Adoption of this Constitution, shall be eligible to the Office of President; neither shall any Person be eligible to that Office who shall not have attained to the Age of thirty five Years, and been fourteen Years a Resident within the United States.

In Case of the Removal of the President from Office, or of his Death, Resignation, or Inability to discharge the Powers and Duties of the said Office, the Same shall devolve on the Vice President, and the Congress may by Law provide for the Case of Removal, Death, Resignation or Inability, both of the President and Vice President, declaring what Officer shall then act as President, and such Officer shall act accordingly, until the Disability be removed, or a President shall be elected.

*Superseded by Amendment XII, section 2.

The President shall, at stated Times, receive for his Service, a Compensation, which shall neither be encreased nor diminished during the Period for which he shall have been elected, and he shall not receive within that Period any other Emolument from the United States, or any of them.

Before he enter on the Execution of his Office, he shall take the following Oath or Affirmation:—"I do solemnly swear (or affirm) that I will faithfully execute the Office of President of the United States, and will to the best of my Ability, preserve, protect and defend the Constitution of the United States."

SECTION 2. The President shall be Commander in chief of the Army and Navy of the United States, and of the Militia of the several States, when called into the actual Service of the United States; he may require the Opinion, in writing, of the principal Officer in each of the executive Departments, upon any Subject relating to the Duties of their respective Offices, and he shall have Power to grant Reprieves and Pardons for Offenses against the United States, except in Cases of Impeachment.

He shall have Power, by and with the Advice and Consent of the Senate, to make Treaties, provided two thirds of the Senators present concur, and he shall nominate, and by and with the Advice and Consent of the Senate, shall appoint Ambassadors, other public Ministers and Consuls, Judges of the supreme Court, and all other Officers of the United States, whose Appointments are not herein otherwise provided for, and which shall be established by Law: but the Congress may by Law vest the Appointment of such inferior Officers, as they think proper, in the President alone, in the courts of Law, or in the Heads of Departments.

The President shall have Power to fill up Vacancies that may happen during the Recess of the Senate, by granting commissions which shall expire at the End of their next Session.

SECTION 3. He shall from time to time give to the Congress Information of the State of the Union, and recommend to their Consideration such Measures as he shall judge necessary and expedient; he may, on extraordinary Occasions, convene both Houses, or either of them, and in Case of Disagreement between them, with Respect to the Time of Adjournment, he may adjourn them to such Time as he shall think proper; he shall receive Ambassadors and other public Ministers; he shall take Care that the Laws be faithfully executed, and shall Commission all the Officers of the United States.

SECTION 4. The President, Vice President and all Civil Officers of the United States, shall be removed from office on Impeachment for, and Conviction of, Treason, Bribery, or other high Crimes and Misdemeanors . . .

ARTICLE III

SECTION I. The judicial Power of the United States, shall be vested in one supreme Court, and in such inferior Courts as the Congress may from time to time ordain and establish . . .

AMENDMENT XII

(Ratified June 15, 1804)

The Electors shall meet in their respective states and vote by ballot for President and Vice-President, one of whom, at least, shall not be an inhabitant of the same state within themselves; they shall name in their ballots the person voted for as President, and in distinct ballots the person voted for as Vice-President, and they shall make distinct lists of all persons voted for as President, and of all persons voted for as Vice-President, and of the number of votes for each, which lists they shall sign and certify, and transmit sealed to the seat of the government of the United States, directed to the President of the Senate;—The President of the Senate shall, in the presence of the Senate and House of Representatives, open all the certificates and the votes shall then be counted;—The person having the greatest number of votes for President, shall be the President, if such number be a majority of the whole number of Electors appointed; and if no person have such majority, then from the persons having the highest numbers not exceeding three on the list of those voted for as President, the House of Representatives shall choose immediately, by ballot, the President. But in choosing the President, the votes shall be taken by states, the representation from each state having one vote; a quorum for this purpose shall consist of a member or members from two-thirds of the states, and a majority of all the states shall be necessary to a choice. [And if the House of Representatives shall not choose a President whenever the right of choice shall devolve upon them, before the fourth day of March next following, then the Vice-President shall act as President, as in the case of the death or other constitutional disability of the President-]* The person having the greatest number of votes as Vice-President, shall be the Vice-President, if such number be a majority of the whole number of Electors appointed, and if no person have a majority, then from the two highest numbers on the list, the Senate shall choose the Vice-President; a quorum for the purpose shall consist of two-thirds of the whole number of Senators, and a majority of the whole number shall be necessary to a choice. But no person constitutionally ineligible to the office of President shall be eligible to that of Vice-President of the United States . . .

AMENDMENT XX

(Ratified January 23, 1933)

SECTION 1. The terms of the President and Vice President shall end at noon on the 20th day of January, and the terms of Senators and Representatives at noon on the 3rd day of January, of the years in which such terms would have ended if this article had not been ratified; and the terms of their successors shall then begin. . . .

SECTION 3. If, at the time fixed for the beginning of the term of the President, the President elect shall have died, the Vice President elect shall become President. If a President shall not have been chosen before the time fixed for the beginning of his term, or if the President elect shall have failed to qualify, then the Vice President elect shall act as President until a President shall have qualified; and the Congress may by law provide for the case wherein neither a President elect nor a Vice President elect shall have qualified, declaring who shall then act as President, or the manner in which one who is to act shall be selected, and such person shall act accordingly until a President or Vice President shall have qualified.

SECTION 4. The Congress may by law provide for the case of the death of any of the persons from whom the House of Representatives may choose a President whenever the right of choice shall have devolved upon them, and for the case of the death of any of the persons from whom the Senate may choose a Vice President whenever the right of choice shall have devolved upon them.

SECTION 5. Sections I and 2 shall take effect on the 15th day of October following the ratification of this article.

*Superseded by Amendment XX, section 3.

SECTION 6. This article shall be inoperative unless it shall have been ratified as an amendment to the constitution by the legislatures of three-fourths of the several States within seven years from the date of its submission . . .

AMENDMENT XXII

(Ratified February 27, 1951)

SECTION 1. No person shall be elected to the office of the President more than twice, and no person who has held the office of President, or acted as President, for more than two years of a term to which some other person was elected shall be elected to the office of the President more than once. But this Article shall not apply to any person holding the office of President when this Article was proposed by the Congress, and shall not prevent any person who may be holding the office of President, or acting as President, during the term within which this Article becomes operative from holding the office of President or acting as President during the remainder of such term.

SECTION 2. This Article shall be inoperative unless it shall have been ratified as an amendment to the constitution by the legislatures of three-fourths of the several States within seven years from the date of its submission to the States by the Congress.

AMENDMENT XXIII

(Ratified March 29, 1961)

SECTION 1. The District constituting the seat of Government of the United States shall appoint in such manner as the Congress may direct:

A number of electors of President and Vice President equal to the whole number of Senators and Representatives in Congress to which the District would be entitled if it were a State, but in no event more than the least populous State; they shall be in addition to those appointed by the States, but they shall be considered, for the purposes of the election of President and Vice President, to be electors appointed by a State; and they shall meet in the District and perform such duties as provided by the twelfth article of amendment.

SECTION 2. The Congress shall have power to enforce this article by appropriate legislation.

AMENDMENT XXIV

(Ratified January 23, 1964)

SECTION 1. The right of citizens of the United States to vote in any primary or other election for President or Vice President, for electors for President or Vice President, or for Senator or Representative in Congress, shall not be denied or abridged by the United States or any State by reason of failure to pay any poll tax or other tax.

SECTION 2. The Congress shall have power to enforce this article by appropriate legislation.

AMENDMENT XXV

(Ratified February 10, 1967)

SECTION 1. In case of the removal of the President from office or of his death or resignation, the Vice President shall become President.

SECTION 2. Whenever there is a vacancy in the office of the Vice President, the President shall nominate a Vice President who shall take office upon confirmation by a majority vote of both Houses of Congress.

SECTION 3. Whenever the President transmits to the President pro tempore of the Senate and the Speaker of the House of Representatives his written declaration that he is unable to discharge the powers and duties of his office, and until he transmits to them a written declaration to the contrary, such powers and duties shall be discharged by the Vice President as Acting President.

SECTION 4. Whenever the Vice President and a majority of either the principal officers of the executive departments or of such other body as Congress may by law provide, transmit to the President pro tempore of the Senate and the Speaker of the House of Representatives their written declaration that the President is unable to discharge the powers and duties of his office, the Vice President shall immediately assume the powers and duties of the office as Acting President.

Thereafter, when the President transmits to the President pro tempore of the Senate and the Speaker of the House of Representatives his written declaration that no inability exists, he shall resume the powers and duties of his office unless the Vice President and a majority of either the principal officers of the executive department or of such other body as Congress may by law provide, transmit within four days to the President pro tempore of the Senate and the Speaker of the House of Representatives their written declaration that the President is unable to discharge the powers and duties of his office. Thereupon Congress shall decide the issue, assembling within forty-eight hours for that purpose if not in session. If the Congress, within twenty-one days after receipt of the latter written declaration, or, if Congress is not in session, within twenty-one days after Congress is required to assemble, determines by two-thirds vote of both houses that the President is unable to discharge the powers and duties of his office, the Vice President shall continue to discharge the same as Acting President; otherwise, the President shall resume the powers and duties of his office.

Notes

PREFACE

1. Richard E. Neustadt, *Presidential Power* (New York: Mentor, 1960).

2. Alan Wolfe, "Presidential Power and the Crisis of Modernization," *Democracy* 1 no. 2 (1981): 19–3.

3. Wolfe, p. 23.

4. Stephen Skowronek, *The Politics Presidents Make: Leadership from John Adams to George Bush* (Cambridge, MA: Belknap Press, 1993), p. 4.

5. Skowronek, pp. 20–21.

6. Skowronek, pp. 27–28.

7. Thomas E. Cronin and Michael A. Genovese, *The Paradoxes of the American Presidency* (New York: Oxford University Press, 1998).

CHAPTER 1

1. David K. Nichols, *The Myth of the Modern Presidency* (University Park: Pennsylvania State University Press, 1994), p. 6.

2. Fred Greenstein, *Leadership in the Modern Presidency* (Cambridge, MA: Harvard University Press, 1988).

3. Richard Rose, *The Postmodern President* (Chatham, NJ: Chatham House, 1991).

4. Edmund S. Morgan, *Inventing the People* (New York: Norton, 1988).

5. Richard Barry, *Mr. Rutledge of South Carolina* (New York: Duell, Sloan and Pearce, 1942).

6. Bernard Bailyn, *The Ideological Origins of the American Revolution* (Cambridge, MA: Harvard University Press, 1967).

7. Charles C. Thach, *The Creation of the Presidency, 1775–1789: A Study in Constitutional History* (Baltimore, MD: Johns Hopkins University Press, 1922).

8. Thomas E. Cronin, ed., *Inventing the American Presidency* (Lawrence: University Press of Kansas, 1989).

9. Harvey C. Mansfield, Jr., *Taming the Prince: The Ambivalence of Modern Executive Power* (New York: Free Press, 1989).

10. Ralph Ketcham, *Presidents Above Party* (Chapel Hill: University of North Carolina Press 1984), p. 9.

11. Alan Wolfe, "Presidential Power and the Crisis of Modernization," *Democracy* 1, no. 2 (1981): 21.

12. Charles Beard and Mary Beard, *The Rise of American Civilization* (New York: Macmillan, 1933), p. 317.

13. Theodore J. Lowi and Benjamin Ginsberg, *American Government: Freedom and Power* (New York: W. W. Norton, 1990), 243–244.

14. See: Arthur M. Schlesinger, Jr., "The Ultimate Approval Rating," *The New York Times Magazine*, December 15, 1996, pp. 48–49; Robert K. Murray and Tim Bless-

ing, *Greatness in the White House* (University Park: Pennsylvania State University Press, 1994).

15. Thomas E. Cronin and Michael A. Genovese, "Evaluating Presidential Performance," in *The Paradoxes of the American Presidency* (New York: Oxford University Press, 1998), 66–103.

CHAPTER 2

1. Richard Norton Smith, *Patriarch: George Washington and the New Nation* (Boston: Houghton Mifflin, 1993); James Thomas Flexner, *Washington: The Indispensable Man* (Boston: Little, Brown, 1974); Barry Schwartz, *George Washington: The Making of an American Symbol* (Ithaca, NY: Cornell University Press, 1987).

2. Gordon S. Wood, *The Radicalism of the American Revolution* (New York: Vintage Books, 1993), p. 206.

3. Richard Brookhiser, *Founding Father: Rediscovering George Washington* (New York: Free Press, 1996), p. 103.

4. Matthew Spalding, *A Sacred Union of Citizens: George Washington's Farewell Address and the American Character* (Totowa, N.J.: Rowman & Littlefield, 1996).

5. Gordon S. Wood, "The Greatness of George Washington," *The Virginia Quarterly Review*, 68 (spring, 1992), 190.

6. R. Smith, *Patriarch*, p. 215.

7. Richard Norton Smith, *Patriarch: George Washington and the New Nation* (Boston: Houghton Mifflin, 1993); James Thomas Flexner, *Washington: The Indispensible Man* (Boston: Little, Brown, 1974); Richard Brookhiser, *Founding Father: Rediscovering George Washington* (New York: Free Press, 1996).

8. Gordon S. Wood, "Foreword," in John Rhodehamel, ed., *The Great Experiment: George Washington and the American Republic* (New Haven: Yale University Press, 1998), xi.

9. Report of Talleyrand, Minister of Foreign Affairs, on the occasion of the death of George Washington. Vol. 1, nos. 172–173 in the manuscript series ETAT-UNIS, 1799–1800.

10. John Ferling, *John Adams: A Life* (New York: Henry Holt, 1992); Ralph Adams Brown, *The Presidency of John Adams* (Lawrence: University Press of Kansas, 1975); Joseph J. Ellis, *Passionate Sage: The Character and Legacy of John Adams* (New York: Norton, 1993).

11. Quoted in John Ferling, *John Adams: A Life* (New York: Henry Holt, 1992), 306.

12. Ferling, p. 335.

13. Ralph Adams Brown, *The Presidency of John Adams* (Lawrence: University Press of Kansas, 1975).

14. Morton Borden, *Parties and Politics in the Early Republic* (New York: Thomas V. Crowell, 1967).

15. John Ferling, *John Adams: A Life* p. 333.

16. Saul K. Padover, *Jefferson* (New York: Mentor, 1952); Merrill D. Peterson, *Thomas Jefferson and the New Nation* (New York: Oxford, 1970); Noble E. Cunningham, Jr., *In Pursuit of Reason: The Life of Thomas Jefferson* (New York: Ballan-

tine, 1987); Natalie S. Bober, *Thomas Jefferson* (New York: Aladdin, 1988); Willard Steine Randall, *Thomas Jefferson: A Life* (New York: Henry Holt, 1993); and Joseph T. Ellis, *American Sphinx: The Character of Thomas Jefferson* (New York: Random House, 1997).

17. Quoted in Ellis, *American Sphinx* p. 210.

18. Quoted in Norman K. Risjord, *Thomas Jefferson* (Madison, WI: Madison House, 1994), 129–130.

19. Peterson, *Thomas Jefferson and the New Nation* p. 689.

20. 1 Cranch 137 (1803).

21. Ironically, the secretary of state who forgot to deliver the commission was John Marshall, who would soon take office as Chief Justice and write the decision in the Marbury case.

22. Charles Warren, *The Supreme Court in United States History* (Boston: Little, Brown, 1926), Vol 2:169.

23. Thomas Jefferson: letter to Thomas Ritchie, dated December 25, 1820, in: Paul L. Ford, ed., *The Writings of Thomas Jefferson* (New York: G.P. Putnam's Sons, 1899), 170–171.

24. Neal Devins, "The Last Word Debate Revisited," in Robert Spitzer, ed., *Politics and Constitutionalism: The Works of Louis Fisher* (Lawrence: University Press of Kansas, 1999).

25. Ruth Bader Ginsberg, *Speaking in a Judicial Voice,* 67 N.Y.U., L. Rev. 1185, 1198 (1992).

26. See: Christopher N. May, *Presidential Defiance of "Unconstitutional" Laws: Reviewing the Royal Prerogative* (Westport, CT: Greenwood Publishing, 1998).

27. Albert Bergh, ed., Vol. 11 *Writings of Thomas Jefferson,* 215.

28. See: Saul K. Padover, ed., *Thomas Jefferson on Democracy* (New York: Mentor Books, 1939), 63–64.

29. See: Henry J. Abraham, *Freedom and the Court* (New York: Oxford University Press, 1988), 6.

30. Quoted in Cunningham, *In Pursuit of Reason,* p. 242.

31. See: Ellis, *American Sphinx,* pp. 248–250.

32. Thomas Jefferson, letter to Secretary of State, James Madison; see Ellis, *American Sphinx,* p. 249.

33. Thomas Jefferson, *Writings* (New York: Library of America, 1984), 1172.

34. Jefferson, *Writings,* p. 1231.

35. Richard K. Matthews, *If Men Were Angels: James Madison and the Heartless Empire of Reason* (Lawrence: University Press of Kansas, 1995); Ralph Ketcham, *James Madison: A Biography* (Charlottesville: University Press of Virginia, 1990).

36. Richard Morris, *Witness at the Creation* (New York: Holt, Rinehart and Winston, 1985), 96–101.

37. Gaillard Hunt, *The Life of James Madison* (New York: Russell and Russell, 1902), 325.

38. W.P. Cresson, *James Monroe* (Chapel Hill: University of North Carolina Press), 1946; Henry Ammon, *James Monroe* (Charlottesville: University Press of Virginia,

1990); Noble E. Cunningham, Jr., *The Presidency of James Monroe* (Lawrence: University Press of Kansas, 1996).

39. Harry Ammon, *James Monroe: The Quest for National Identity* (Charlottesville: University Press of Virginia, 1990); Noble E. Cunningham, Jr., *The Presidency of James Monroe* (Lawrence: University Press of Kansas, 1996).

40. *Annals of Congress*, 15C15, 1373, March 13, 1817.

41. Letter from Jefferson to John Holmes, April 22, 1820, in Paul Ford, ed., *The Works of Thomas Jefferson* (New York: G. P. Putnam's Sons, 1904), 12:158.

42. Quoted in Leonard White, *The Jeffersonians* (New York: Macmillan, 1951), 39.

43. Samuel Flagg Bemis, *John Quincy Adams and the Foundation of American Foreign Policy* (New York: Knopf, 1949); Paul C. Nagel, *John Quincy Adams: A Public Life, A Private Life* (New York: Knopf, 1998); and Mary W.M. Hargreaves, *The Presidency of John Quincy Adams* (Lawrence: University Press of Kansas, 1985).

44. Nagel, p. 296.

CHAPTER 3

1. Richard Latner, *The Presidency of Andrew Jackson: White House Politics, 1829–1837* (Athens: University of Georgia Press, 1979); Robert V. Remini, *Andrew Jackson and the Course of American Empire, 1767–1821* (New York: Harper & Row, 1984); Robert V. Remini, *Andrew Jackson and the Course of American Freedom, 1822–1832* (New York: Harper & Row, 1984); Robert V. Remini, *Andrew Jackson and the Course of American Democracy, 1833–1845* (New York: Harper & Row, 1984); Arthur M. Schlesinger, Jr., *The Age of Jackson* (Boston: Little, Brown, 1946); Leonard White, *The Jacksonians: A Study in Administrative History, 1829–1861.* (New York: Macmillan, 1954).

2. Edward S. Corwin, *The President: Office and Powers, 1787–1984.* 5th ed. (New York: New York University Press, 1984), 21.

3. Schlesinger, *The Age of Jackson*, p. 276.

4. Gary L. Rose, *The American Presidency Under Siege* (Albany: State University of New York Press, 1997), 152.

5. William N. Chambers, "Jackson," in Morton Borden, ed., *America's Ten Greatest Presidents* (Chicago: Rand McNally, 1961), 83.

6. Robert J. Spitzer, *The Presidential Veto: Touchstone of the American Presidency* (Albany: State University of New York Press, 1988), 33–39.

7. Robert Remini, "Election of 1832," in Arthur M. Schlesinger, ed., *History of American Presidential Elections 1789–1968* (New York: Chelsea House Publishers, 1971), 1:516.

8. Alexis de Tocqueville, *Democracy in America* (Garden City, New York: Doubleday, 1969), 394.

9. Edward S. Corwin, *The President*, p. 20.

10. Donald B. Cole, *Martin Van Buren and the American Political System* (Princeton, NJ: Princeton University Press, 1984); Major L. Wilson, *The Presidency of Martin Van Buren* (Lawrence: University Press of Kansas, 1984).

11. Norma Lois Peterson, *The Presidencies of William Henry Harrison and John Tyler* (Lawrence: University Press of Kansas, 1989).

12. Oliver Perry Chitwood, *John Tyler: Champion of the Old South* (New York: Appleton, 1939); Robert Morgan, *A Whig Embattled: The Presidency under John Tyler* (Lincoln: University of Nebraska Press, 1954); Norma Lois Peterson, *The Presidencies of William Henry Harrison and John Tyler* (Lawrence: University of Kansas Press, 1989); Robert Seager, II, *And Tyler Too: A Biography of John and Julia Gardiner Tyler*. (New York: Random House, 1963).

13. Paul E. Boller, Jr., *Presidential Anecdotes* (New York: Penguin, 1981), 96.

14. Paul H. Bergeron, *The Presidency of James K. Polk.* (Lawrence: University Press of Kansas, 1987); Eugene I. McCormac, *James K. Polk: A Political Biography* (Berkeley: University of California Press, 1922); Charles A. McCoy, *Polk and the Presidency* (Austin: University of Texas Press, 1960); Charles G. Sellers, *James K. Polk: Continentalist, 1843–1846* (Princeton: Princeton University Press, 1966).

15. K. Jack Bauer, *Zachary Taylor: Soldier, Planter, Statesman of the Old Southwest* (Baton Rouge: Louisiana State University Press, 1985); Elbert B. Smith, *The Presidencies of Zachary Taylor and Millard Fillmore* (Lawrence: University Press of Kansas, 1988).

16. *Millard Fillmore Papers* Microfilm Collection. Buffalo Historical Society; Robert Rayback, *Millard Fillmore: Biography of a President* (Buffalo, NY: Henry Stewart, 1959); Elbert B. Smith, *The Presidencies of Zachary Taylor and Millard Fillmore* (Lawrence: University Press of Kansas, 1988).

17. Jimmy Skaggs, *The Great Guano Rush*, (New York: St. Martin's, 1994).

18. Larry Gara, *The Presidency of Franklin Pierce* (Lawrence: University Press of Kansas, 1991); Roy Franklin Nichols, *Franklin Pierce: Young Hickory of the Granite Hills* Rev. ed.(Philadelphia: University of Pennsylvania Press, 1958).

19. Herbert Agar, *The Price of Union* (Boston: Houghton Mifflin, 1951), 357.

20. Herbert Agar, *The Price of Union* (Boston: Houghton Mifflin, 1951), 357.

21. Philip S. Klein, *President James Buchanan* (University Park: Pennsylvania State University Press, 1962); Elbert B. Smith, *The Presidency of James Buchanan* (Lawrence: University of Kansas Press, 1975).

22. J.G. Randall and Richard N. Current, *Lincoln: The President*, 2 vols. (New York: Da Capo, 1997); David Herbert Donald, *Lincoln* (New York: Touchstone, 1995); Phillip Shaw Paludan, *The Presidency of Abraham Lincoln* (Lawrence: University Press of Kansas, 1994).

23. Quoted in Randall and Current, *Lincoln the President* pp. 399–400.

24. Ibid. p. 394.

25. Ward H. Lamon, *Recollections of Abraham Lincoln* (New York: Century, 1911).

26. Abraham Lincoln, "Special Session Message," July 4, 1861, in Edward Keynes and David Adamany, eds., *Borzoi Reader in American Politics* (New York: Knopf, 1973), 539.

27. Clinton Rossiter, *Constitutional Dictatorship* (New York: Harcourt, Brace, & World, 1963).

28. Garry Wills, *Lincoln at Gettysburg: The Words that Remade America* (New York: Simon and Schuster, 1992), 145.

29. Bruce Miroff, *Icons of Democracy* (New York: Basic Books, 1993).

30. James M. McPherson, *Abraham Lincoln and the Second American Revolution* (New York: Oxford University Press, 1991), viii.

31. David Donald, *Lincoln Reconsidered* pp. 195–196.

32. Quoted in: Philip C. Dolce and George H. Skau, eds., *Power and the Presidency* (New York: Scribner's Sons, 1976), 44.

33. Clinton Rossiter, The *Supreme Court and the Commander in Chief* (Ithaca, NY: Cornell University Press, 1976), 23. For a defense of Lincoln's actions, see Mark Neely, *The Fate of Liberty* (New York: Oxford University Press, 1991).

34. Rossiter, pp. 23–25.

35. *Ex Parte Milligan*, 4 Wallace 2, 18 L.Ed., 281, 1866.

36. Rossiter pp. 34–35, 39.

37. Black, 668–670 (1863).

38. Philip C. Dolce and George H. Skau, *Power and the Presidency* (New York: Scribner's Sons, 1976), 47.

39. See: Robert V. Bruce, *Lincoln and the Tools of War* (Indianapolis: Bobbs-Merrill, 1956); John Hay, *Lincoln and the Civil War* (New York: Dodd, Mead & Co., 1939).

CHAPTER 4

1. Albert Castel, *The Presidency of Andrew Johnson* (Lawrence: Regents Press of Kansas, 1979); David Miller Dewitt, *The Impeachment and Trial of Andrew Johnson* (New York: Macmillan, 1903, 1967); Eric L. McKitrick, *Andrew Johnson and Reconstruction* (Chicago; University of Chicago Press, 1960); George Fort Milton, *The Age of Hate: Andrew Johnson and the Radicals* (1930); Hans L. Trefousse, *Andrew Johnson: A Biography* (New York: Norton, 1989).

2. See Michael Nelson. *The American Presidency* (Washington, D.C.: Congressional Quarterly) pp. 175–178.

3. Ulysses S. Grant, *Personal Memoirs,* 2 vols. (New York: Da Capo, 1885–1886); William S. McFeeley, *Grant: A Biography.* (New York: Norton, 1981); Brooks D. Simpson, *Let Us Have Peace: Ulysses S. Grant and the Politics of War and Reconstruction, 1861–1868* (Chapel Hill: University of North Carolina Press, 1991).

4. Ari Hoogenboon, *The Presidency of Rutherford B. Hayes* (Lawrence: University Press of Kansas, 1988); Charles R. Williams, *Life of Rutherford B. Hayes*, 2 vols., (New York: Scribner's, 1914).

5. Walter Bagehot, *The English Constitution* (1867; reprint, London: Fontana, 1993), 70.

6. Theodore Clarke Smith, James Abram Garfield: *Life and Letters* (New Haven, Conn.: Yale University Press, 1925).

7. Justus D. Doenecke, *The Presidency of James A. Garfield and Chester A. Arthur* (Lawrence: Regents Press of Kansas, 1981).

8. Sumner, quoted in Richard J. Ellis, ed., *Speaking to the People: The Rhetorical Presidency in Historical Perspective* (Amherst: University of Massachusetts Press, 1998), 13.

9. Richard E. Welch, Jr., *The Presidencies of Grover Cleveland* (Lawrence: Univer-

sity Press of Kansas, 1988); Grover Cleveland, *Presidential Problems* (New York: Century, 1904).

10. Homer E. Socolofsky, *The Presidency of Benjamin Harrison* (Lawrence: University Press of Kansas, 1988).

11. Woodrow Wilson, *Congressional Government* (Boston: Houghton Mifflin, 1885), 31.

12. Sidney Milkis and Michael Nelson, *The American Presidency* (Washington, D.C.: Congressional Quarterly, 1994), 195.

13. Lewis L. Gould, *The Presidency of William McKinley* (Lawrence: Regents Press of Kansas, 1980); H. Wayne Morgan, *William McKinley and His America* (Syracuse, NY: Syracuse University Press, 1963).

14. H.W. Brands, *T.R.: The Last Romantic* (New York: Basic Books, 1997); Matthew Miller, *Theodore Roosevelt: A Life* (New York: Quill, 1992); Lewis L. Gould, *The Presidency of Theodore Roosevelt* (Lawrence: University Press of Kansas, 1991).

15. Harold Evans, *The American Century* (New York: Knopf, 1998).

16. Bruce Miroff, *Icons of Democracy*, p. 161.

17. Miroff, p. 161.

18. Miroff, p. 164.

19. Tourtellot, p. 116.

20. Milkis and Nelson, *The American Presidency*, p. 209.

21. Theodore Roosevelt, *The Works of Theodore Roosevelt* (New York: Scribner's, 1926), 490.

22. Paolo E. Coletta, *The Presidency of William Howard Taft* (Lawrence: University Press of Kansas, 1988).

23. Ray Stannard Baker, *Woodrow Wilson* (London: Heinemain, 1932); Arthur Walworth, *Woodrow Wilson* (New York: Norton, 1978); Kendrick A. Clements, *The Presidency of Woodrow Wilson* (Lawrence: University Press of Kansas, 1992); August Heckscher, *Woodrow Wilson* (New York: Collier, 1991).

24. Arthur S. Link, *Wilson and the New Freedom* (Princeton, N.J.: Princeton University Press, 1956); Daniel D. Stid, *The President as Statesman* (Lawrence: University Press of Kansas, 1998).

25. 272 U.S. 52 (1926).

26. John Morton Blum, *The Progressive Presidents* (New York: Norton, 1980), 61.

CHAPTER 5

1. Eugene P. Trani and David L. Wilson, *The Presidency of Warren G. Harding* (Lawrence: University Press of Kansas, 1977); Robert K. Murray, *The Harding Era* (Minneapolis: University of Minnesota Press, 1969).

2. Claude M. Fuess, *Calvin Coolidge: The Man from Vermont* (Boston: Little, Brown, 1940); Donald R. McCoy, *Calvin Coolidge: The Quiet President* (Lawrence: University Press of Kansas, 1988).

3. David Burner, *Herbert Hoover: A Public Life* (New York: Knopf, 1979); Martin L. Fausold, *The Presidency of Herbert C Hoover* (Lawrence: University Press of Kansas, 1985); Joan Hoff-Wilson, *Herbert Hoover: Forgotten Progressive* (Boston: Little, Brown, 1975); George H. Nash, *The Life of Herbert Hoover* 2 vols. (New York:

Norton, 1983, 1988); Jordan Schwarz, *The Interregnum of Despair: Hoover, Congress, and the Depression* (Urbana: University of Illinois Press, 1970).

4. See: Fred I. Greenstein, "Nine Presidents in Search of a Modern Presidency," in Greenstein, ed., *Leadership in the Modern Presidency* (Cambridge, MA: Harvard University Press, 1988), 296–352; see also John Hart, *The Presidential Branch* (New York: Pergamon Press, 1987); Malcolm Shaw, ed., *The Modern Presidency: From Roosevelt to Reagan* (New York: Harper and Row, 1987).

5. 295 U.S. 602 (1935).

6. Edward S. Corwin, *Total War and the Constitution* (New York: Knopf, 1947) p. 91.

7. 320 US. 81 (1943).

8. 323 US. 214 (1944).

9. 323 U.S. 283 (1944).

10. Thomas E. Cronin, *The State of the Presidency* (Boston: Little, Brown, 1980).

11. Mary Stuckey, *The President as Interpreter-In-Chief* (Chaltham, NJ: Chaltham House, 1991), 35.

CHAPTER 6

1. Robert J. Donovan, *Conflict and Crisis: The President of Harry S. Truman, 1945–48.* (New York: Norton, 1977); Robert J. Donovan, *Tumultuous Years: the Presidency of Harry S. Truman, 1949–1953* (New York: Norton, 1982); Michael Lacey, ed. *The Truman Presidency* (New York: Cambridge University Press, 1989); Donald R. McCoy, *The Presidency of Harry S. Truman* (Lawrence: University Press of Kansas, 1984); David McCullough, *Truman* (New York: Simon & Schuster, 1992).

2. Stephen Ambrose, *Eisenhower the President* (New York: Simon & Schuster, 1984); Fred Greenstein, *The Hidden-Hand Presidency* (New York: Basic Books, 1982); Herbert Parmet, *Eisenhower and the American Crusades* (New York: Macmillan, 1972).

3. Fred I. Greenstein, ibid. *The Hidden-Hand Presidency* p. 113.

4. Irving Bernstein, *Promises Kept: John F. Kennedy's New Frontier* (New York: Oxford University Press, 1991); James N. Giglio, *The Presidency of John F. Kennedy* (Lawrence: University Press of Kansas, 1991); Herbert S. Parmet, *JFK: The Presidency of John F. Kennedy* (New York: Dial, 1983); Richard Reeves, *President Kennedy: Profile of Power* (New York: Simon & Schuster, 1993).

5. Thomas E. Cronin, "John F. Kennedy: President and Politician" in Paul Harper and Joann P. Krieg, eds., *John F. Kennedy: The Promise Revisited* (New York: Greenwood, 1988), 2, 17.

6. James MacGregor Burns, *The Power to Lead* (New York: Simon & Schuster, 1984), 75.

7. Irving Bernstein, *Promises Kept: John F. Kennedy's New Frontier* (New York: Oxford, 1991).

CHAPTER 7

1. Vaughn Davis Bornet, *The Presidency of Lyndon B. Johnson* (Lawrence: University Press of Kansas, 1983); Eric F. Goldman, *The Tragedy of Lyndon Johnson* (New York: Dell, 1968).

2. Richard N. Goodwin, *Remembering America: A Voice from the Sixties* (Boston: Little, Brown, 1988), 20.

3. Stephen E. Ambrose, *Nixon*, 3 vols., (New York: Simon and Schuster, 1989, 1991, 1995); Michael A. Genovese, *The Nixon Presidency: Power and Politics in Turbulent Times* (Westport, Conn.: Greenwood, 1990); Stanley Kutler, *The Wars of Watergate* (New York: Knopf, 1990); Richard M. Nixon, *RN: The Memoirs of Richard Nixon* (New York: Grosset and Dunlop, 1978); Michael A. Genovese, *The Watergate Crisis* (Westport, Conn.: Greenwood, 1999).

4. Michael A. Genovese, *The Presidency in an Age of Limits.* (Westport, CT.: Greenwood, 1993).

5. Cecil V. Crabb and Kevin V. Mulcahy, *Presidents and Foreign Policy Making* (Baton Rouge: Louisiana State University Press, 1986), 237.

6. Henry Kissinger, *White House Years* (Boston: Little, Brown, 1979). p. 57. For a more elaborate discussion of presidential policies dealing with relative decline, see Genovese, *The Presidency in an Age of Limits.*

7. Robert Osgood, et al., *Retreat from Empire?* (Baltimore: Johns Hopkins University Press, 1973).

8. While Nixon has denied that his policies were designed to face an era of relative decline, he certainly acted as if that were precisely what he and Kissinger were aiming at. Now Nixon has especially harsh words for the politicians and academics who speak and write about decline; see Richard Nixon, *Victory Without War* (New York: Simon & Schuster, 1998).

9. William W. Lammers and Michael A. Genovese, *Comparing Presidents: Leadership Styles and Domestic Policy* (Washington, D.C.: Congressional Quarterly, 2000); Richard Nathan, *The Plot that Failed: Nixon and the Administrative Presidency* (New York: Wiley, 1976).

10. William W. Lammers and Michael A. Genovese, *Comparing Presidents: Leadership Styles and Domestic Policy* (Washington, D.C.: Congressional Quarterly, 2000).

11. Report of the Committee on the Judiciary, U.S. House of Representatives, August 20, 1974.

12. John Robert Greene, *The Presidency of Gerald R. Ford* (Lawrence: University Press of Kansas, 1995); Richard A. Reeves, *A Ford, Not a Lincoln* (New York: Harcourt Brace Jovanovich, 1975).

13. See: William Lammers and Michael Genovese, *Comparing Presidents* (Washington, D.C.: CQ Press, 2000).

14. Carter, Jimmy, *Keeping Faith: Memoirs of a President* (New York: Boston) (1982); Erwin C. Hargrove, *Jimmy Carter as President: Leadership and the Politics of the Public Good* (Baton Rouge: Louisiana State University Press, 1988); Charles O. Jones, *The Trustee Presidency: Jimmy Carter and the United States Congress* (Baton Rouge: Louisiana State University Press, 1988); Burton I. Kaufman, *The Presidency of James Earl Carter, Jr.* (Lawrence: University Press of Kansas, 1993).

15. See: Robert Dallek, *Hail to the Chief* (New York: Hyperion, 1996), 195.

16. James Fallows, "The Passionless President," *Atlantic Monthly,* (1979): 33–48.

17. Jimmy Carter, *Keeping Faith: Memoirs of a President* (New York: Bantam, 1982), 27.

18. Hedrick Hertzberg, "Jimmy Carter," in Robert A. Wilson, ed., *Character Above All* (New York: Simon and Schuster, 1995), 180.

19. Lou Cannon, *President Reagan: The Role of a Lifetime* (New York: Simon & Schuster, 1991); Ronald Reagan, *An American Life* (New York: Simon and Schuster, 1990); Edmund Morris, *Dutch: A Memoir of Ronald Reagan* (New York: Random House, 1999).

20. Jane Mayer and Doyle McManus, *Landslide: The Unmaking of the President 1984–1986* (Boston: Houghton-Mifflin, 1988).

21. Sidney M. Milkis, "Franklin D. Roosevelt, Progressives and the Limits of Popular Leadership." in Richard J. Ellis, ed., *Speaking to the People: The Rhetorical Presidency in Historical Perspective* (Amherst: University of Massachusetts Press, 1998), 14.

CHAPTER 8

1. Richard Ben Cramer, *What It Takes: The Way to the White House* (New York: Random House, 1992); Michael Duffy and Dan Goodgame, *Marching in Place : The Status Quo Presidency of George Bush* (New York: Simon & Schuster, 1992).

2. Bert A. Rockman, "The Leadership Style of George Bush," in C. Campbell and B. Rockman, eds., *The Bush Presidency: First Appraisals* (Chatham, N.J.; Chatham House, 1991), 29.

3. See Michael Duffy and Dan Goodgame, *Marching in Place: The Status Quo Presidency of George Bush* (New York: Simon & Schuster, 1992).

4. George Bush and Brent Scowcroft, *A World Transformed* (New York: Knopf, 1998).

5. Quotes from Larry Berman and Bruce W. Jentleson, "Bush and the Post-Cold War World," in Campbell and Rockman, eds., *The Bush Presidency*, p. 94.

6. Comments delivered at the annual meeting, *American Political Science Association*, Chicago, IL (September 1992).

7. David Mervin. *George Bush and the Guardianship Presidency* (New York: St. Martin's, 1996).

8. In early 1992, Secretary of State Baker attempted to spell out the U.S. approach to foreign policy for a post-cold war world. In many ways, it reflected the political reality of an age of limits, but making a speech and changing institutions and behavior are two very different things. See Thomas L. Friedman, "Baker Spells Out U.S. Foreign Policy Stance," *New York Times* (April 22, 1992), p. A6.

9. Alan Tonelson, "Prudence or Inertia? The Bush Administration's Foreign Policy," *Current History* 91, no. 564 (1992): 145.

10. David Maraniss, *First in His Class* (New York: Simon & Schuster, 1995). Martin Walker, *Clinton: The President They Deserve* (London: Vintage, 1997).

11. E.J. Dionne, Jr. 1998. "High-Wire Centrism," *Washington Post* (March 6); and Will, George F. 1998. "The Politics of Contentment." *Washington Post* (January 1).

12. Thomas E. Cronin and Michael A. Genovese, "President Clinton and Character Question," *Presidential Studies Quarterly* 28, no. 4, (1998): 892–897.

13. Elizabeth Drew, *The Corruption of American Politics: What Went Wrong and Why* (Secaucus, NJ: Carol Publishing Group, 1999), 343.

14. Elizabeth Drew, *The Corruption of American Politics: What Went Wrong and Why* (Secausus, NJ: Carol Publishing Group, 1999), Chapter 9.

CHAPTER 9

1. Arthur M. Schlesinger, Jr., *The Imperial Presidency* (Boston: Houghton Mifflin, 1973), 431.

2. James David Barber, "The Nixon Brush with Tyranny," *Political Science Quarterly*, (Winter 1977–1978): 581.

3. Miroff, *Icons of Democracy*, (New York: Basic 1993) p. 81.

4. Burns, *Leadership* (New York: Harper & Row, 1978) p. 9.

5. Glen A. Phelps, *George Washington and American Constitutionalism* (Lawrence: University Press of Kansas, 1993).

6. Quoted in Larry Berman, *The New American Presidency* (Boston: Little, Brown, 1987), 339.

7. Genovese, *The Presidency in an Age of Limits*. (Westport, Conn.: Greenwood, 1993).

8. Harold Koh, *The National Security Constitution*, (New Haven, Conn.: Yale University Press, 1990), chap. 9.

9. Norman C. Thomas, Joseph A. Pika, and Richard A. Watson, *The Politics of the Presidency* (Washington, D.C.: CQ Press, 1993), 434.

10. Thomas Cronin, "Leadership and Democracy," in *Liberal Education* vol. 73 no. 2, March/April 1987, p. 36.

11. Ibid., pp. 36–37.

12. Quoted in Benjamin R. Barber, "Neither Leaders nor Followers," *Essays in Honor of James MacGregor Burns*, ed. Michael R. Beschloss and Thomas E. Cronin (Englewood Cliffs, N.J.: Prentice Hall, 1989). p. 117.

13. Quoted in Mark E. Kan, "Challenging Lockean Liberalism in America: The Case of Debs and Hillquit," *Political Theory*, no. 8 (May 1980): 214.

14. Cronin, "Leadership and Democracy," p. 36.

15. James Bryce, *The American Commonwealth* (New York: MacMillan, 1888), vol. 2, 460.

Selected Bibliography

GEORGE WASHINGTON

Brookhiser, Richard, *Founding Father: Rediscovering George Washington*. New York: Free Press, 1996.

Ferling, John E. *The First of Men: A Life of George Washington*. Knoxville: University of Tennessee Press, 1988.

———. *George Washington: Anguish and Farewell*. Boston: Little, Brown, 1969.

———. *Washington, the Indispensable Man*. Boston: Little, Brown, 1974.

Freeman, Douglas S. *George Washington: A Biography*. 7 vols. New York: Scribner's, 1948–1957.

Phelps, Glenn A. *George Washington and American Constitutionalism*. Lawrence: University Press of Kansas, 1993.

Schwartz, Barry. *George Washington: The Making of an American Symbol*. Ithaca: Cornell University Press, 1987.

Smith, Richard N. *Patriarch: George Washington and the New American Nation*. Boston: Houghton Mifflin, 1993

JOHN ADAMS

Adams, Charles F. *The Life of John Adams*. Rev. ed. 2 vols. Philadelphia: Lipincott, 1871.

Brown, Ralph A. *The Presidency of John Adams*. Lawrence: Regents Press of Kansas, 1975.

Ellis, Joseph J. *Passionate Sage: The Character and Legacy of John Adams*. New York: W.W. Norton, 1993.

Ferling, John E. *John Adams: A Life*. Knoxville: University of Tennessee Press, 1992.

Kurtz, Stephen G. *The Presidency of John Adams: The Collapse of Federalism, 1785–1800*. Philadelphia: University of Pennsylvania Press, 1957.

Smith, Page. *John Adams*. 2 vols. Garden City, NY: Doubleday, 1962.

THOMAS JEFFERSON

Brodie, Fawn M. *Thomas Jefferson: An Intimate History*. New York: W.W. Norton, 1974.

Cunningham, Noble E. *In Pursuit of Reason: The Life of Thomas Jefferson*. Baton Rouge: Louisiana State University Press, 1987.

———. *The Process of Government Under Jefferson*. Princeton, NJ: Princeton University Press, 1978.

Ellis, Joseph T. *American Sphinx: The Character of Thomas Jefferson*. Random House, 1997.

Fleming, Thomas J. *Man from Monticello: An Intimate Life of Thomas Jefferson*. New York: William Morrow and Company, 1969.

Johnstone, Robert M., Jr. *Jefferson and the Presidency, Leadership in the Young Republic*. Ithaca, NY: Cornell University Press, 1978.

Malone, Dumas. *Jefferson and the Ordeal of Liberty*. Boston: Little, Brown, 1962.

———. *Jefferson the President: First Term, 1801-1805*. Boston: Little, Brown, 1970.

———. *Jefferson the President: Second Term, 1805-1809.* Boston: Little, Brown, 1974.

———. *Thomas Jefferson as a Political Leader.* Berkeley: University of California Press, 1963.

McDonald, Forrest. *The Presidency of Thomas Jefferson.* Lawrence: Regents Press of Kansas, 1976.

Padover, Saul K. *Jefferson.* New York: Merton, 1952.

Peterson, Merrill D. *The Jefferson Image in the American Mind.* New York: Oxford University Press, 1960.

Randall, Willard S. *Thomas Jefferson: A Life.* New York: Holt, 1993.

Tucker, Robert W. *Empire of Liberty: The Statecraft of Thomas Jefferson.* New York: Oxford University Press, 1990.

JAMES MADISON

Brant, Irving. *James Madison.* 6 vols. Indianapolis: Bobbs-Merrill, 1941–1961.

Ketcham, Ralph L. *James Madison: A Biography.* New York: Macmillan, 1971.

Matthews, Richard K. *If Men Were Angels: James Madison and the Heartless Empire of Reason.* Lawrence: University Press of Kansas, 1995.

McCoy, Drew R. *The Last of the Fathers: James Madison and the Republican Legacy.* New York: Cambridge University Press, 1989.

Rakove, Jack N. *James Madison and the Creation of the American Republic.* New York: HarperCollins, 1990.

Rutland, Robert A. *The Presidency of James Madison.* Lawrence: University Press of Kansas, 1995.

JAMES MONROE

Ammon, Harry. *James Monroe: The Quest for National Identity.* New York: McGraw-Hill, 1971.

Cresson, William P. *James Monroe.* Chapel Hill: University of North Carolina Press, 1946.

Cunningham, Noble E. *The Presidency of James Monroe.* Lawrence: University Press of Kansas, 1996.

Dangerfield, George. *The Era of Good Feelings.* New York: Harcourt Brace, 1952.

JOHN QUINCY ADAMS

Bemis, Samuel F. *John Quincy Adams and the Foundations of American Foreign Policy.* New York: Knopf, 1949.

———. *John Quincy Adams and the Union.* New York: Knopf, 1956.

Hecht, Marie B. *John Quincy Adams: A Personal History of an Independent Man.* New York: Macmillan, 1972.

Nagel, Paul C. *John Quincy Adams.* New York: Knopf, 1998.

Weeks, William Earl. *John Quincy Adams and American Global Empire.* Lexington: University Press of Kentucky, 1992.

ANDREW JACKSON

Cole, Donald B. *The Presidency of Andrew Jackson.* Lawrence: University Press of Kansas, 1993.

Latner, Richard B. *The Presidency of Andrew Jackson: White House Politics, 1829–1837.* Athens: University of Georgia Press, 1979.

Remini, Robert V. *The Age of Jackson*. Columbia: University of South Carolina Press, 1972.

———. *Andrew Jackson and the Course of American Democracy, 1833–1845*. New York: Harper & Row, 1983.

———. *Andrew Jackson and the Course of American Empire, 1767–1821*. New York: Harper & Row, 1977.

———. *Andrew Jackson and the Course of American Freedom: 1822–1832*. New York: Harper and Row, 181.

Schlesinger, Arthur M., Jr. *The Age of Jackson*. Boston: Little, Brown 1945.

White, Leonard D. *The Jacksonians: A Study in Administrative History, 1829–1861*. New York: Macmillan, 1954.

MARTIN VAN BUREN

Cole, Donald B. *Martin Van Buren and the American Political System*. Princeton, NJ: Princeton University Press, 1984.

Curtis, James C. *The Fox at Bay: Martin Van Buren and the Presidency, 1837–1841*. Lexington: University of Kentucky Press, 1970.

Niven, John. *Martin Van Buren: The Romantic Age of American Politics*. New York: Oxford University Press, 1983.

Remini, Robert V. *Martin Van Buren and the Making of the Democratic Party*. New York: Columbia University Press, 1959.

Wilson, Major L. *The Presidency of Martin Van Buren*. Lawrence: University Press of Kansas, 1984.

WILLIAM HENRY HARRISON

Cleaves, Freeman. *Old Tippecanoe: William Henry Harrison and His Time*. New York: Scribner's, 1939.

Peckham, Howard H. *William Henry Harrison: Young Tippecanoe*. Indianapolis: Bobbs-Merrill, 1951.

Peterson, Norma L. *The Presidencies of William Henry Harrison & John Tyler*. Lawrence: University Press of Kansas, 1989.

JOHN TYLER

Chitwood, Oliver P. *John Tyler: Champion of the Old South*. New York: Appleton, 1939.

Young, Stanley P. *Tippecanoe and Tyler, Too!* New York: Random House, 1957.

JAMES K. POLK

Bergeron, Paul H. *The Presidency of James K. Polk*. Lawrence: University Press of Kansas, 1987.

McCormac, Eugene I. *James K. Polk, A Political Biography*. Berkeley: University of California Press, 1922.

McCoy, Charles A. *Polk and the Presidency*. Austin: University of Texas Press, 1960.

Sellers, Charles G., Jr. *James K. Polk, Continentalist: 1843–1846*. Princeton, NJ: Princeton University Press, 1966.

———. *James K. Polk, Jacksonian: 1795–1843*. Princeton, NJ: Princeton University Press, 1957.

ZACHARY TAYLOR

Hamilton, Holman. *Zachary Taylor.* 2 vols. Indianapolis: Bobbs-Merrill, 1941–1951.
Smith, Elbert B. *The Presidencies of Zachary Taylor and Millard Fillmore.* Lawrence: University Press of Kansas, 1988.

MILLARD FILLMORE

Rayback, Robert J. *Millard Fillmore: Biography of a President.* Buffalo, NY: Henry Stewart, 1959.
Smith, Elbert B. *The Presidencies of Zachary Taylor and Millard Fillmore.* Lawrence: University Press of Kansas, 1988.

FRANKLIN PIERCE

Gara, Larry. *The Presidency of Franklin Pierce.* Lawrence: University Press of Kansas, 1991.
Hoyt, Edwin P. *Franklin Pierce: The Fourteenth President of the United States.* New York: Harper & Row, 1972.

JAMES BUCHANAN

Curtis, George T. *Life of James Buchanan, Fifteenth President of the United States.* 2 vols. New York: Harper, 1883.
Klein, Philip S. *President James Buchanan: A Biography.* University Park: Pennsylvania State University Press, 1962.
Smith, Elbert B. *The Presidency of James Buchanan.* Lawrence: University Press of Kansas, 1975.

ABRAHAM LINCOLN

Cox, LaWanda C. *Lincoln and Black Freedom: A Study in Presidential Leadership.* Urbana: University of Illinois Press, 1985.
Fehrenbacher, Don E. *The Leadership of Abraham Lincoln.* New York: Wiley, 1970.
Findley, Paul A. *Lincoln, the Crucible of Congress.* New York: Crown, 1979.
Handlin, Oscar and Lilian Handlin. *Abraham Lincoln and the Union.* Boston: Little, Brown, 1980.
Herndon, William H., and J. William Weik. *Herndon's Lincoln: The True Story of a Great Life, the History and Personal Recollections of Abraham Lincoln.* 3 vols. Chicago: Belford, Clarke, 1889.
Oates, Stephen B. *Abraham Lincoln: The Man Behind the Myths.* New York: Harper & Row, 1984.
Paludan, Philip S. *The Presidency of Abraham Lincoln.* Lawrence: University Press of Kansas, 1994.
Sandburg, Carl. *Abraham Lincoln, The Prairie Years.* 2 vols. New York: Harcourt Brace, 1926.
———. *Abraham Lincoln: The War Years.* 4 vols. New York: Harcourt Brace, 1939.
Wills, Garry. *Lincoln at Gettysburg: The Words That Remade America.* New York: Simon & Schuster, 1992.

ANDREW JOHNSON

Beale, Howrd K. *The Critical Year: A Study of Andrew Johnson and the Reconstruction.* New York: Harcourt Brace, 1930.

Castel, Albert. *The Presidency of Andrew Johnson.* Lawrence: Regents Press of Kansas, 1979.

DeWitt, David M. *The Impeachment and Trial of Andrew Johnson, Seventeenth President of the United States: A History.* New York: Macmillan, 1903.

McKitrick, Eric L. *Andrew Johnson and Reconstruction.* Chicago: University of Chicago Press, 1960.

Sefton, James E. *Andrew Johnson and the Uses of Constitutional Power.* Boston: Little, Brown, 1980.

Trefousse, Hans L. *Andrew Johnson: A Biography.* New York: W.W. Norton, 1989.

ULYSSES S. GRANT

Carpenter, John A. *Ulysses S. Grant.* New York: Twayne, 1970.

Mantell, Martin E. *Johnson, Grant, and the Politics of Reconstruction.* New York: Columbia University Press, 1973.

McFeely, William S. *Grant, a Biography.* New York: W.W. Norton, 1981.

Simpson, Brooks D. *Let Us Have Peace: Ulysses S. Grant and the Politics of War and Reconstruction, 1861–1868.* Chapel Hill: University of North Carolina Press, 1991.

RUTHERFORD B. HAYES

Davison, Kenneth E. *The Presidency of Rutherford B. Hayes.* Westport, CT: Greenwood Press, 1972.

Hoogenboom, Ari A. *The Presidency of Rutherford B. Hayes.* Lawrence: University Press of Kansas, 1988.

Morgan, H. Wayne. *From Hayes to McKinley: National Party Politics, 1877–1896.* Syracuse, NY: Syracuse University Press, 1969.

JAMES A. GARFIELD

Booraem, Hendrik. *The Road to Respectability: James A. Garfield and His World, 1844–1852.* Lewisburg, PA: Bucknell University Press; Cleveland: Western Reserve Historical Society Press, 1988.

Doenecke, Justus D. *The Presidencies of James A. Garfield and Chester A. Arthur.* Lawrence: Regents Press of Kansas, 1981.

Peskin, Allan. *Garfield: A Biography.* Kent, OH: Kent State University Press, 1978.

CHESTER A. ARTHUR

Doenecke, Justus D. *The Presidencies of James A. Garfield and Chester A. Arthur.* Lawrence: Regents Press of Kansas, 1981.

Reeves, Thomas C. *Gentleman Boss: The Life of Chester Alan Arthur.* New York: Knopf, 1975.

GROVER CLEVELAND

McElroy, Robert M. *Grover Cleveland, The Man and the Statesman: An Authorized Biography.* 2 vols. New York: Harper and Row, 1923.

Merrill, Horace S. *Bourbon Leader: Grover Cleveland and the Democratic Party.* Boston: Little, Brown, 1957.

Nevins, Allan. *Grover Cleveland: A Study In Courage.* New York: Dodd, Mead, 1932.

Welch, Richard E. *The Presidency of Grover Cleveland.* Lawrence: University Press of Kansas, 1988.

BENJAMIN HARRISON

Sievers, Harry J. *Benjamin Harrison: Hoosier President: The White House and After.* New York: University Publishers, 1968.

———. *Benjamin Harrison: Hoosier Statesman from the Civil War to the White House: 1865–1888.* New York: University Publishers, 1959.

———. *Benjamin Harrison: Hoosier Warrior: 1833–1865, Through the Civil War Years.* 2d ed. New York: University Publishers, 1960.

WILLIAM MCKINLEY

Gould, Lewis L. *The Presidency of William McKinley.* Lawrence: University Press of Kansas, 1980.

Morgan, H. Wayne. *William McKinley and His America.* Syracuse, NY: Syracuse University Press, 1963.

THEODORE ROOSEVELT

Blum, John M. *The Progressive Presidents: Roosevelt, Wilson, Roosevelt, Johnson.* New York: W.W. Norton, 1980.

———. *The Republican Roosevelt.* 2d ed. Cambridge, MA: Harvard University Press, 1977.

Cooper, John M., Jr. *The Warrior and the Priest: Theodore Roosevelt and Woodrow Wilson.* Cambridge, MA: Harvard University Press, 1983.

Gould, Lewis L. *The Presidency of Theodore Roosevelt.* Rev. ed. New York: Oxford University Press, 1975.

Miller, Nathan. *Theodore Roosevelt: A Life.* New York: William Morrow and Company, 1992.

Morris, Edmund. *The Rise of Theodore Roosevelt.* New York: Coward, McCann and Geoghegan, 1979.

Mowry, George E. *The Era of Theodore Roosevelt, 1900–1912.* New York: Harper and Row, 1958.

———. *Theodore Roosevelt and the Progressive Movement.* Madison: University of Wisconsin Press, 1946.

WILLIAM HOWARD TAFT

Anderson, Judith I. *William Howard Taft: An Intimate History.* New York: W.W. Norton, 1981.

Burton, David. *The Learned Presidency: Theodore Roosevelt, William Howard Taft, Woodrow Wilson.* Rutherford, NJ: Fairleigh Dickinson University Press, 1988.

Coletta, Paolo E. *The Presidency of William Howard Taft.* Lawrence: University Press of Kansas, 1973.

Mason, Alpheus T. *William Howard Taft: Chief Justice.* New York: /Simon & Schuster, 1965.

Pringle, Henry F. *The Life and Times of William Howard Taft: A Biography.* 2 vols. New York: Farrar, Straus, 1939.

WOODROW WILSON

Baker, Ray S. *Woodrow Wilson: Life and Letters.* 8 vols. Garden City, NY: Doubleday, 1927–1939.

Blum, John M. *The Progressive Presidents: Roosevelt, Wilson, Roosevelt, Johnson.* New York: W.W. Norton, 1980.

Canfield, Leon H. *The Presidency of Woodrow Wilson: Prelude to a World in Crisis.* Rutherford, NJ: Fairleigh Dickinson University Press, 1966.

Clements, Kendrick A. *The Presidency of Woodrow Wilson.* Lawrence: University Press of Kansas, 1992.

Cooper, John M., Jr. *The Warrior and the Priest: Theodore Roosevelt and Woodrow Wilson.* Cambridge, MA: Belknap Press, 1983.

Knock, Thomas J. *To End All Wars: Woodrow Wilson and the Quest for a New World Order.* New York: Oxford University Press, 1992.

Link, Arthur S. Wilson: *Confusions and Crises: 1915–1916.* Princeton, NJ: Princeton University Press, 1964.

———. *Wilson: The Struggle for Neutrality, 1914–1915.* Princeton, NJ: Princeton University Press, 1960.

———. *Woodrow Wilson.* 5 vols. Princeton, NJ: Princeton University Press, 1947–1965.

———. *Woodrow Wilson and a Revolutionary World, 1913–1921.* Chapel Hill: University of North Carolina Press, 1982.

———. *Woodrow Wilson and the Progressive Era, 1910–1917.* New York: Harper & Row, 1954.

Walworth, Arthur C. *Woodrow Wilson.* 3d ed. New York: W.W. Norton, 1978.

WARREN G. HARDING

Downes, Randolph C. *The Rise of Warren Gamaliel Harding: 1865–1920.* Columbus: Ohio State University Press, 1970.

Murray, Robert K. *The Harding Era: Warren G. Harding and His Administration.* Minneapolis: University of Minnesota Press, 1969.

Russell, Francis. *The Shadow of Blooming Grove; Warren G. Harding in His Times.* New York: McGraw-Hill, 1968.

Sinclair, Andrew. *The Available Man: The Life Behind the Masks of Warren Gamaliel Harding.* New York: Macmillan, 1965.

Trani, Eugene P., and David L. Wilson. *The Presidency of Warren G. Harding.* Lawrence: Regents Press of Kansas, 1977.

CALVIN COOLIDGE

Fuess, Claude M. *Calvin Coolidge, The Man from Vermont.* Boston: Little, Brown, 1940.

McCoy, Donald R. *Calvin Coolidge, The Quiet President.* Lawrence: University Press of Kansas, 1988.

Murray, Robert K. *The Politics of Normalcy: Governmental Theory and Practice in the Harding Coolidge Era.* New York: W.W. Norton, 1973.

HERBERT HOOVER

Best, Gary D. *Herbert Hoover: The Postpresidential Years, 1933–1964.* 2 vols. Stanford, CA: Hoover Institution Press, 1983.
Burner, David. *Herbert Hoover: A Public Life.* New York: Knopf, 1979.
Fausold, Martin L. *The Presidency of Herbert Hoover.* Lawrence: University Press of Kansas, 1985.
Fausold, Martin L., and George Mazuzan, eds. *The Hoover Presidency: A Reappraisal.* Albany: State University of New York Press, 1974.
Hoff-Wilson, Joan. *Herbert Hoover, Forgotten Progressive.* Boston: Little, Brown, 1975.
Nash, George H. *The Life of Herbert Hoover: The Engineer, 1874–1914.* New York: W.W. Norton, 1983.
Schwarz, Jordan A. *The Interregnum of Despair: Hoover, Congress, and the Depression.* Urbana: University of Illinois Press, 1970.
Smith, Richard N. *An Uncommon Man: The Triumph of Herbert Hoover.* New York: Simon & Schuster, 1984.
Warren, Harris G. *Herbert Hoover and the Great Depression.* New York: Oxford University Press, 1990.

FRANKLIN D. ROOSEVELT

Abbott, Philip. *The Exemplary Presidency: Franklin D. Roosevelt and the American Political Tradition.* Amherst: University of Massachusetts Press, 1990.
Burns, James M. *Roosevelt: the Lion and the Fox.* New York: Harcourt Brace, 1956.
———. *Roosevelt: The Soldier of Freedom.* New York: Harcourt Brace, 1970.
Dallek, Robert. *Franklin D. Roosevelt and American Foreign Policy, 1932–1945.* New York: Oxford University Press, 1979.
Davis, Kenneth S. *FDR, Into the Storm 1937–1940: A History.* New York: Random House, 1993.
Freidel, Frank B. *Franklin D. Roosevelt.* 4 vols. Boston: Little, Brown, 1952–1973.
———. *Franklin D. Roosevelt: A Rendezvous with Destiny.* Boston: Little, Brown, 1990.
Leuchtenberg, William E. *Franklin D. Roosevelt and the New Deal, 1932–1940.* New York: Harper and Row, 1963.
Miller, Nathan. *FDR: An Intimate History.* Garden City, NY: Doubleday, 1983.
Morgan, Ted. *FDR.* New York: Simon & Schuster, 1985.
Schlesinger, Arthur M., Jr. *The Age of Roosevelt.* 3 vols. Boston: Houghton Mifflin, 1957–1960.
Tugwell, Rexford G. *FDR: The Architect of an Era.* New York: Macmillan, 1967.

HARRY S TRUMAN

Daniels, Jonathan. *The Man of Independence.* Philadelphia: Lippincott, 1950.
Donovan, Robert J. *Conflict and Crisis: Presidency of Harry S. Truman: 1945–1948.* New York: W.W. Norton, 1977.
———. *Tumultuous Years: The Presidency of Harry S. Truman, 1949–1953.* New York: W.W. Norton, 1982.
Ferrell, Robert H. *Harry S. Truman: A Life.* Columbia: University of Missouri Press, 1994.
———. *Harry S. Truman and the Modern American Presidency.* Boston: Little, Brown, 1983.

Lacey, Michael J., ed. *The Truman Presidency*. New York: Cambridge University Press, 1989.

McCoy, Donald R. *The Presidency of Harry S. Truman*. Lawrence: University Press of Kansas, 1984.

McCullough, David G. *Truman*. New York: Simon & Schuster, 1992.

DWIGHT D. EISENHOWER

Alexander, Charles C. *Holding the Line: The Eisenhhower Era, 1952–1961*. Bloomington: Indiana University Press, 1975.

Ambrose, Stephen E. *Eisenhower: President and Elder Statesman, 1952–1969*. New York: Simon & Schuster, 1984.

———. *Eisenhower: Soldier and President*. New York: Simon & Schuster, 1990.

Greenstein, Fred I. *The Hidden Hand Presidency: Eisenhower as Leader*. New York: Basic Books, 1982.

Pach, Chester J. *The Presidency of Dwight D. Eisenhower*. Lawrence: University Press of Kansas, 1991.

Parmet, Herbert S. *Eisenhower and the American Crusades*. New York: Macmillan, 1972.

JOHN F. KENNEDY

Beschloss, Michael R. *The Crisis Years: Kennedy and Khruschev, 1960–1963*. New York: Edward Burlingame Books, 1991.

Giglio, James N. *The Presidency of John F. Kennedy*. Lawrence: University Press of Kansas, 1991.

Miroff, Bruce. *Pragmatic Illusions: The Presidential Politics of John F. Kennedy*. New York: McKay, 1976.

Parmet, Herbert S. *Jack: The Struggles of John F. Kennedy*. New York: Dial, 1980.

———. *JFK: The Presidency of John F. Kennedy*. New York: Dial, 1983.

Reeves, Richard. *President Kennedy: Profile of Power*. New York: Simon & Schuster, 1993.

Schlesinger, Arthur M., Jr. *A Thousand Days: John F. Kennedy in the White House*. Boston: Houghton Mifflin, 1965.

Sorensen, Theodore C. *Kennedy*. New York: Harper and Row, 1965.

Wills, Garry. *The Kennedy Imprisonment: A Meditation on Power*. Boston: Little, Brown, 1982.

LYNDON B. JOHNSON

Bornet, Vaughn D. *Presidency of Lyndon B. Johnson*. Lawrence: University Press of Kansas, 1983.

Califano, Joseph A. *The Triumph & Tragedy of Lyndon Johnson: The White House Years*. New York: Simon & Schuster, 1991.

Caro, Robert A. *Means of Ascent*. New York: Knopf, 1990.

———. *The Years of Lyndon Johnson: The Path to Power*. New York: Knopf, 1982.

Dallek, Robert. *Lone Star Rising: Lyndon Johnson and His Times, 1908–1960*. New York: Oxford University Press, 1991.

Dugger, Ronnie. *The Politician: The Life and Times of Lyndon Johnson: The Drive for Power, from the Frontier to Master of the Senate*. New York: W.W. Norton, 1982.

Goldman, Eric F. *The Tragedy of Lyndon Johnson: A Historian's Interpretation.* New York: Knopf, 1969.

Kearns, Doris. *Lyndon Johnson and the American Dream.* New York: Harper and Row, 1976.

RICHARD M. NIXON

Ambrose, Stephen E. *Nixon.* New York: Simon & Schuster, 1987–1991.

Brodie, Fawn M. *Richard Nixon: The Shaping of His Character.* Cambridge, MA: Harvard University Press, 1983.

Evans, Rowland, Jr., and Robert D. Novak. *Nixon in the White House: The Frustration of Power.* New York: Vintage, 1971.

Genovese, Michael A. *The Nixon Presidency: Power and Politics in Turbulent Times.* New York: Greenwood Press, 1990.

Hersh, Seymour M. *The Price of Power: Kissinger in the Nixon White House.* New York: Summit Books, 1983.

Hoff-Wilson, Joan. *Nixon Reconsidered.* New York: Basic Books, 1994.

Litwak, Robert S. *Détente and the Nixon Doctrine: American Foreign Policy and the Pursuit of Stability, 1969–1976.* New York: Cambridge University Press, 1984.

Morris, Roger. *Richard Milhous Nixon: The Rise of an American Politician.* New York: Holt, 1990.

Parmet, Herbert S. *Richard Nixon and His America.* Boston: Little, Brown, 1990.

Safire, William. *Before the Fall: An Inside View of the Pre-Watergate White House.* Garden City, NY: Doubleday, 1975.

GERALD R. FORD

Cannon, James M. *Time and Chance: Gerald Ford's Appointment with History.* New York: HarperCollins, 1994.

Greene, John R. *Gerald R. Ford: A Bibliography.* New York: Greenwood Press, 1994.

———. *The Presidency of Gerald R. Ford.* Lawrence: University Press of Kansas, 1995.

Reeves, Richard. *A Ford, Not a Lincoln.* New York: Harcourt Brace Jovanovich, 1975.

TerHorst, Jerald F. *Gerald Ford and the Future of the Presidency.* New York: Third Press, 1974.

JIMMY CARTER

Campbell, Colin. *Managing the Presidency: Carter, Reagan, and the Search for Executive Harmony.* Pittsburgh: University of Pittsburgh Press, 1986.

Fink, Gary M. *Prelude to the Presidency: The Political Character and Legislative Leadership—Style of Governor Jimmy Carter.* Westport, CT: Greenwood Press, 1980.

Hargrove, Erwin C. *Jimmy Carter as President: Leadership and the Politics of the Public Good.* Baton Rouge: Louisiana State University Press, 1988.

Jones Charles O. *The Trusteeship Presidency: Jimmy Carter and the United States Congress.* Baton Rouge: Louisiana State University Press, 1988.

Kaufman, Burton Ira. *The Presidency of James Earl Carter, Jr.* Lawrence: University Press of Kansas, 1993.

Lynn, Laurence E., Jr. *The President as Policy Maker: Jimmy Carter and Welfare Reform.* Philadelphia: Temple University Press, 1981.

RONALD REAGAN

Campbell, Colin. *Managing the Presidency: Carter, Reagan, and the Search for Executive Harmony.* Pittsburgh: University of Pittsburgh Press, 1986.
Cannon, Lou. *President Reagan: The Role of a Lifetime.* New York: Simon and Schuster, 1991.
Dallek, Robert. *Ronald Reagan: The Politics of Symbolism.* Cambridge, MA: Harvard University Press, 1984.
Greenstein, Fred I. *The Reagan Presidency: An Early Assessment.* Baltimore: Johns Hopkins University Press, 1983.

GEORGE BUSH

Campbell, Colin, and Bert A. Rockman, eds. *The Bush Presidency: First Appraisals.* Chatham, NJ: Chatham House, 1991.
Duffy, Michael. *Marching in Place: The Status Quo Presidency of George Bush.* New York: Simon & Schuster, 1992.
Hill, Dilys M., and Phil Williams, eds. *The Bush Presidency: Triumphs and Adversities.* New York: St. Martin's Press, 1994.
Kolb, Charles. *White House Daze: The Unmaking of Domestic Policy in the Bush Years.* New York: Free Press, 1994.

BILL CLINTON

Drew, Elizabeth. *On the Edge: The Clinton Presidency.* New York: Simon & Schuster, 1994.
Hohenberg, John. *The Bill Clinton Story: Winning the Presidency.* Syracuse, NY: Syracuse University Press, 1994.
Maraniss, David. *First In His Class: A Biography of Bill Clinton.* New York: Simon & Schuster, 1995.
Oakley, Meredith L. *On the Make: The Rise of Bill Clinton.* Washington, DC: Regnery, 1994.
Renshon, Stanley A., ed. *The Clinton Presidency: Campaigning, Governing, and the Psychology of Leadership.* Boulder, CO: Westview Press, 1994.
Woodward, Bob. *The Agenda: Inside the Clinton White House.* New York: Simon & Schuster, 1994.

Index

Note: Page numbers in **boldface** indicate extended discussion of topic.